Identities, Borders, Orders

BORDERLiNES

For more titles in the series, see page 350.

Identities, Borders, Orders
Rethinking International Relations Theory

**MATHIAS ALBERT, DAVID JACOBSON, AND
YOSEF LAPID, EDITORS**

BORDERLINES, VOLUME 18

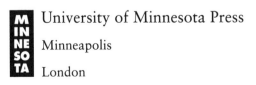

University of Minnesota Press

Minneapolis

London

An earlier version of chapter 9 originally appeared as "Dual Nationality" in *Migrants and Citizens: Demographic Change in the European State System,* by Rey Koslowski. Copyright 2000 Cornell University. Used by permission of the publisher, Cornell University Press.

Published by the University of Minnesota Press
111 Third Avenue South, Suite 290
Minneapolis, MN 55401-2520
http://www.upress.umn.edu

Printed in the United States of America on acid-free paper

Library of Congress Cataloging-in-Publication Data

Albert, Mathias.
    Identities, borders, orders : rethinking international relations
theory / Mathias Albert, David Jacobson, Yosef Lapid.
        p.   cm. — (Borderlines ; 18)
    Includes bibliographical references and index.
    ISBN 0-8166-3607-9 (HC : alk. paper) — ISBN 0-8166-3608-7 (PB :
alk. paper)
    1. International relations. 2. National state. 3. Territory
National. 4. Boundaries. 5. Geopolitics. I. Jacobson, David.
II. Lapid, Yosef, 1947–   III. Title. IV. Borderlines (Minneapolis,
Minn.) ; v. 18.
JZ1305 A425 2001
327—dc21   2001000479

12 11 10 09 08 07 06 05 04 03 02 01   10 9 8 7 6 5 4 3 2 1

Contents

Acknowledgments

This book is the result of an ongoing collaborative effort of a number of scholars with backgrounds in various disciplines and from different countries. Although undoubtedly operating against a background of North American–style International Relations, the Identities, Borders, Orders group (or Las Cruces Group, as it has become alternatively known) has always sought to actively reflect on the cross-disciplinary nature of its enterprise.

The group is not a closed community but rather a network of scholars interested in exploring the possibilities of new vistas for conceptually innovative research on the changing global order. The group's main activities have so far consisted in a number of meetings at New Mexico State University in Las Cruces, New Mexico. During the second meeting, in late November 1995, the IBO triad became the "official" thematic signpost of the group's activities. The initial drafts for most of the chapters in this volume were presented and discussed at an authors' conference near Aschaffenburg, Germany, in January 1998.

The completion of this volume would not have been possible without financial contributions from a number of sources. In this respect, we would particularly like to express our gratitude to the German-American Academic Council, the International Studies Association, the Ford Foundation, the Leonard Davis Institute for International

Relations at the Hebrew University of Jerusalem, and the Political Science Department of New Mexico State University.

In terms of intellectual input, it is impossible to list all those whom we wish to thank for providing valuable comments at the workshops and conferences at which the IBO concept was discussed. Special thanks go to Michael Kearney and Ole Wæver for their particularly extensive and regular input on these occasions. Valuable comments for revising the full manuscript were provided by Francis Beer and Michael Shapiro. Carrie Mullen efficiently guided us through the publishing process. Jesper Sigurdsson provided help beyond the call of duty in preparing the manuscript.

We have certainly profited from putting together this volume and engaging with its themes. We hope it will prove to be a rich source of intellectual stimuli for those interested in advancing conceptually innovative thought in IR as well as in other disciplines.

Mathias Albert, David Jacobson, and Yosef Lapid

Identities, Borders, Orders:
Nudging International Relations Theory in a New Direction

YOSEF LAPID

> It is incumbent upon us all, no matter what our starting point may be, to explain what our perspectives can bring to the next stage in international relations theory. (Linklater 1992, 98)

"What makes the world hang together in the international sense?" asks John Ruggie. He goes on to credit this question with guiding him on his influential and innovative journey to better international relations (IR) theory (1998, 1). To understand why this deceptively simple question could perform such a formidable role, one needs to situate it in the context of what is still the accepted mode of asking questions in International Relations. Such an exercise reveals that IR's dominant discourses have long precluded a sense that something may be seriously problematic, or genuinely puzzling, in the way in which our international world hangs together. On the contrary, converging on an assumptive framework that allows, and perhaps even requires, an a priori stipulation of preformed identities and interests, neorealism and neoliberal institutionalism have practiced their theoretical trade in a profoundly durable "world" (Ruggie 1998, 4–16; Alker 1996, xi). Resting on very different premises, Ruggie's question allowed him to effectively alert IR's mainstream positions to the fact that they may be lacking both a logic and a vocabulary for

1

transformative change. Benefiting also from an all-too-rare ability to propose theoretical modifications without needlessly upsetting established scholarly hierarchies, Ruggie eventually earned recognition as a master of "the art of nudging the course of the mainstream in some new direction" (Neumann 1997, 365).

Recent developments, however—both inside and outside the narrow confines of the IR discipline—have forced a new recognition that mobility and flux (rather than fixity and stasis) will increasingly determine the mercurial horizon against which the contemporary IR theory project needs to be reworked (Anderson 1998; Appadurai 1997; Leach 1999). Confirming Joseph Margolis's astute reading of broader trends in current social theory, we may be witnessing a major realignment between IR's newly energized "partisans of flux" and its still well-entrenched, but now increasingly beleaguered "partisans of modal invariance."[1] New opportunities may thereby surface to close the gap between a still chronically static theory and a more transparently mobile reality (Jackson and Nexon 1999). To that extent, a restless and manifestly disoriented discipline may now be ready for another round of vigorous "nudging" in some new direction.

This introductory chapter offers intellectual and conceptual resources for such an undertaking. The analytical triad formed by the concepts of identities, borders, orders (IBO) serves as our main "nudging" instrument. This triad is deliberately situated in a processual/relational/verbing approach that allows us to treat it as a set of (temporarily stabilized) processes rather than as an assembly of inert and sedimentary things. I argue that the dynamic nexus constituted by interrelated processes of bordering, ordering, and collective identity building opens a uniquely well-situated analytical window to observe issues of mobility, fluidity, and change in contemporary world politics. The argument is developed in three steps. First, I present some philosophical (processism, relationalism, verbing) and conceptual (identities, borders, orders) assets and tools that can further enhance IR's ability to engage with a subject matter increasingly "on the move." Next, I ask what can these assets do for present-day IR theory? The profile of an IBO-inspired research agenda is skeletally presented, with special emphasis on the ability to enhance compatibility between a multitude of topics otherwise separately treated. The introduction winds down with further reflections on the prerequisites of a productive IBO reorientation of the IR theoretical agenda.

THEORIZING "ON THE MOVE": ENRICHING THE IR TOOLBOX

"The methodological shift from a language of interacting variables to a language of mutually constitutive processes," says Jonathan Bach (1999, 10), "requires a somewhat different approach than traditionally found in the toolboxes of International Relations."

Concurring with this observation, in this section I introduce three philosophically enriched perspectives (processism, relationalism, and verbing) that can help further problematize IR's still dominant ontology of stability and continuity. I continue with a processual/relational recasting of identities, borders, orders as three ascending key concepts in the post–Cold War theoretical and political transition. I claim that, together, these moves can improve IR's proverbial toolbox enhancing, in particular, its ability to engage with Ruggie's fecund, and far from depleted, puzzle.

Processism, Relationalism, and Verbing

Process thinking, or "processism," is not new in Western philosophy. As noted by Nicholas Rescher, the ascendence of a powerful ontological doctrine known as the "things-with-timeless-qualities" paradigm signified a massive "revolt against process" in Western thought (Rescher 1962, 410). The rise of positivism in the social sciences, in particular, bears the heavy marks of this doctrine. As aptly noted by Robert Chia (1997), positivist epistemology—with its emphasis on empirical verification, its noncompromising pro-observational attitude, and its Humean notion of constant conjunction—is predicated on a strong ontological commitment to an already constituted and permanent reality. The axioms of this static ontology postulate that reality is made up of discrete, self-identical things; that these things and entities are primary to process; and that the state of rest, stability, and equilibrium is a natural state, with movement occurring only when things are disturbed or perturbed. This doctrine—which downgrades change and time in ontological considerations—continues to inform much social scientific theorizing today.

Fortunately, however, "We are now experiencing the slow revenge of time: the gathering, subterranean insistence on historicity" (Margolis 1999, 9). The recent revival of process philosophy is arguably part and parcel of this "revenge." As noted by Rescher, process thinking is guided by the idea "that natural existence consists in and is best understood in terms of *processes* rather than *things*—of modes of change rather than fixed stabilities. For processists, change of every sort...is the pervasive and predominant feature of the real" (Rescher 1996, 49). In Rescher's more formal words, at the level of basics, process philosophy "replaces the troublesome ontological dualism of *thing* and *activity*, with a monism of activities of different and differently organized sorts" (ibid.). That it may be "easier to explain stasis as an emergent phenomenon in a fundamentally changing universe than vice versa" (Abbott 1995, 858) is perhaps the key promise of process thinking. However, as wisely acknowledged by Andrew Abbott (himself a declared processist), it may be "nearly as difficult to account, in a processual ontology, for the plain fact that much of the social world stays the same much of the time."[2]

"Relationism" (Emirbayer 1997) is intimately connected to process thinking. Mustafa Emirbayer's point of departure is, in fact, no different from Rescher's: namely, the fundamental dilemma of "whether to conceive of the social world as consisting primarily in substances or in processes, in static 'things' or in dynamic unfolding relations" (ibid., 281). But closer examination reveals an important difference well-captured by the respective labels. Whereas processists emphasize the priority of process, relationalists emphasize "the anteriority of radical relationality." Michael Dillon and Julian Reid (1999, 9), who coined this phrase, mean by it "that nothing is without being in relation, and that everything is—in the ways that it is—in terms and in virtue of relationality." More generally in the context of the human sciences, "the notion of relatedness points to the fundamental necessity of locating and comprehending all of people's experiences (and activities) within the community (of the other)" (Prus 1998, 15).

Processual and relational thinking are, as noted, compatible and complementary. Relations "are best understood in processual terms (or as having natural histories) with respect to their emergence, intensification, dissipation, and possible reconstitution" (ibid.). Patrick Jackson (1999, 142–43) is therefore on the right track in combining these ideas for convenient consumption by the IR scholarly community under a processual/relational (or p/r) label. Great compatibility notwithstanding, processism seems anterior to, and possibly also more encompassing than, relationalism. For the concept of process cuts across and incorporates distinctions and premises informing other, more narrowly cast, philosophical and theoretical positions (Rescher 1996, 4; Prus 1998, 16; Dervin and Huesca 1997, 66).

"Verbing" shifts the focus to the discursive or rhetorical level and reflects the meteoric rise of language and linguistics to prominence in scholarly fields ranging from philosophy and psychology to physics and cultural studies. As an approach to social theorizing, verbing resonates well with David Bohm's idea of the *Rheomode,* a verb-based language appropriate to quantum reality. Bohm, a noted physicist, concluded that the grammatical style of English and other Indo-European languages (the subject-verb-object structure) promotes the division of reality into static and isolatable events and phenomena (Bohm 1980). Brenda Dervin's (1993, 51) call for an extensive and philosophically informed "verbing" of her field of specialization (communication studies) is driven by similar concerns. "How does one focus on moves," she asks, "when all one has is nouns with which to work?" (ibid.). For some time now, IR scholars—subscribing to otherwise very different perspectives—have shown a tendency to turn familiar nouns into awkward verbal forms such as "securitizing" (Wæver 1995b), "bordering" (Albert and Brock 1996), or "refugeeing" (Soguk 1999). As an approach to social theorizing, verbing alerts us to the fact that we are dealing here with the linguistic tip of a huge philosophical iceberg rather than with a bizarre and inconsequential fad.

Subscribing to processual/relational/verbing modes of thinking should allow us to do far more than just marginally improve on our ability to refer to the accelerated movement of preformed entities (actors, agents, identities, bodies, capital, information, ideas, etc.) through preformed and predemarcated spaces, places, and territories (Dillon and Reid, 9). In terms of our present interests, it should improve on our ability to theorize identities, borders, and orders "in-formation" and "in-relation." A full digestion of the theoretical, conceptual, and methodological ramifications of these ideas will most likely necessitate profound changes also in our understanding of every single component in IR's long-troubled disciplinary self-designation (the "inter," the "national," the "relational," and by extension also the "political"). In the following, I focus on the processual/relational triad constituted by interrelated processes of bordering, ordering, and collective identity building to briefly explicate this admittedly sweeping argument. The intention is to demonstrate that this dynamic and politically charged triad opens a well-situated observational window for issues of mobility, change, and transformation in contemporary world politics.

Why Identities, Borders, Orders (IBO)? The Rationale for a New Triad

Among the many intellectual and substantive reasons that may justify special interest in identities, borders, and orders (IBO), four seem particularly pertinent in our context. First, our three terms qualify, individually and together, as ascending "key concepts" (Carville et al. 1996) in current social theory and practice. This being an age allergic to any and all inequalities, it bears noting that concepts are not born equal (Gerring 1999, 357). Picking good concepts is, in fact, somewhat analogous to taking out a "conceptual loan" that must be repaid if we are to succeed in our scholarly ventures. Key concepts are, in this respect, solid picks with excellent collateral backing. For, as put by McLennan (1995, x), such concepts are "ever-interesting" and "indispensable." They are ever-interesting by virtue of their ability to reconfigure in face of changing realities. They are indispensable on the strength of their sustained relevance to many major theoretical undertakings. This is not to say, of course, that key concepts will not encounter temporary indifference. As evidenced, for instance, by "identities" in international relations theory (Lapid and Kratochwil 1996) and by "borders" in political geography (Newman in this volume), such is hardly the case. Over time, however, key concepts will be rediscovered and redeployed to close theoretical gaps invariably left by their arbitrary omission.

Alert to their enduring relevance and centrality, and taking advantage of the proprietary nature of the modern division of scientific labor, established scholarly communities have long claimed exclusive competence in the deployment of "their" key concepts. Following this logic, identity, for instance, could be claimed by psychology or anthropology, borders would "belong" to geography, and order would go to the political disciplines. This dubious practice is finally breaking down (Levine 1996, 260). The moves proposed in this volume take advantage of the fact that key concepts are now increasingly free-floating; they no longer "belong" to any single discipline. This development opens the door for new combinatory possibilities, along the lines of Dogan's (1996) concept of hybridization. Unlike conventional interdisciplinary endeavors (which typically involve whole disciplines), hybridization refers to the creative recombination and blending of disciplinary fragments, specialties, and/or key concepts. The rekindled interest in hybridization is partially driven by the current predicament of many disciplines, IR included, struggling to keep up with complex phenomena that regularly defy formal disciplinary demarcations. Cut loose from specific disciplinary homes, identities, borders, and orders have been dramatically reconfigured in vibrant cross-disciplinary discussions; they are now ripe for synthesis and new intellectual blending. Our proposed IBO project seeks a realization of this potential in IR theory.[3]

The second reason to look carefully at our three concepts is a direct elaboration of our previous point. Confirming the relationalist insight, massive bodies of cross-disciplinary literature strongly suggest that the IBO concepts are intimately related to each other; they are therefore best defined, and best discussed, *in relation* to each other. Processes of collective identity formation invariably involve complex bordering issues. Likewise, acts of bordering (i.e., the inscription, crossing, removal, transformation, multiplication and/or diversification of borders) invariably carry momentous ramifications for political ordering at all levels of analysis. Processes of identity, border, and order construction are therefore mutually self-constituting. Borders, for instance, are in many ways inseparable from the identities they help demarcate or individuate. Likewise, they are also inseparable from orders constituted to a large extent via such acts of individuation and segmentation. Thus, in any specific case, if we want to study problems associated with any one of our three concepts, we can richly benefit from also considering the other two. This is to say that identities, borders, and orders constitute a triad in a sense that is still quite foreign to many IR scholars.[4] We will return to illustrate this central point later in this chapter.

Third, to the extent that the processual/relational approach advocated in this volume renders moments of stabilization inherently problematic, the IBO triad is interesting because it identifies three key "moments" central to the stabilization of any conceivable world. The narrow and surprisingly durable modern stabilization of identities (as national states), of borders (as sharply drawn territorial lines), and of orders (as relatively stable configurations of power among sovereign states) is a striking, and historically unique, exemplar of such an arrestation. That the modern IBO configuration was so durably "nouned" in the Westphalian mold—despite the complex plurality of processes that has never ceased to animate its always problematic historical production and reproduction—is a genuinely puzzling observation. That contemporary historical and intellectual developments have finally shattered the self-evident nature of these stabilizations—rendering transparent their plural, fluid, and political nature—makes new processual/relational IBO studies urgently relevant today. For we have only a dim comprehension of what may happen to our international (and political) world once the continual "(re)verbing" of the modern IBO configuration (in theory and practice) decisively tips to the fluid side.

This takes us to our fourth and final reason for paying special attention to the IBO triad. As demonstrated by Ruggie (1998, 131), the modern IBO pattern would not have been possible without the rise of the profoundly influential notion of territoriality hammered out at Westphalia in 1648. This historically specific notion of territoriality depicts political space in terms of distinct, disjoint, and mutually exclusive formations. This notion of space has been at the heart of the assumptive "territorial trap" so ably distilled by John Agnew (1998, 49–66). But the impact of territoriality, so defined, has expanded way beyond international relations. "By the mid–twentieth century," notes Neil Brenner (1999), "each of the conceptual building blocks of modern social science—in particular the notion of state, society, economy, culture, and community—had come to presuppose this territorialization of social relations within a parcelized, fixed, and essentially timeless geographical space. The resultant territorialist epistemology has entailed the transposition of the historically unique territorial structure of the modern interstate system into a generalized model of sociospatial organization, whether within reference to political, societal, economic, or cultural processes."

Brenner's analysis suggests that in modern times Westphalian territoriality plays a formative role in explaining what makes the world hang together, not only in the international, but also in the economic, sociological, anthropological, geographic, and historical senses. To that extent, the modernist configuration of the IBO triad is stabilized by the formidable force of multiple territorializations operating across

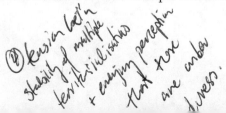

the human sciences. With reference to IBO, IR scholars have come to treat territoriality as a fixed, ahistorical parameter. Complicating matters is, however, a new generalized perception of a massive weakening of territoriality as an ever-present and ever-available stabilizing and centering force. As a result, it is now regularly assumed (in discussions of globalization, in particular) that our world is increasingly shaped by an unruly swirl of deterritorialized forces involving capital, information, and people on the move. What happens, however, to our ingrained notions of territorialized identities, borders, and orders when these become spatialized (or despatialized) in some radically new ways? The challenge of figuring out the contours of an emerging world, now problematically stabilized by a continually changing balance of territorial, semiterritorial, and nonterritorial vectors is an urgent priority, setting the stage for the research agenda profiled in the next section.

SHAPING A NEW IR RESEARCH AGENDA

Informed that a new triad is now available in their toolbox, IR theorists will be curious to find out what they can do with it to improve their performance. If so, it is prudent to start with a warning regarding the pretheoretical intent of this construct. As a heuristic tool, IBO is intended primarily to highlight interesting, substantive, and theoretical intersections without stipulating analytical primacy, causal directions, and/or preferred methodologies. Furthermore, as demonstrated by most of the chapters in this volume, substantive work guided by this triad need not always involve all three components; depending on specific interests, the analysis can gravitate toward one or more intersections. Moreover, the same phenomenon can be productively situated at different intersections. Situating nationalism, for instance, at the identities/borders (IB) nexus would highlight its boundary creation and boundary maintenance manifestations (Conversi 1995); situating it at the border/order (BO) nexus seems ideal for studying integrative and disintegrative ramifications of national self-determination, ethnic separatism, and irredentism (Fuller 1997); and, as aptly demonstrated by Rodney Hall (1999), situating it at the identity/order nexus (IO) can help link it to major systemic transformations in world politics. To that extent, our hope is that the triad will lend theoretical depth, thematic comparability, and conceptual coherence to many other such efforts. Below, I unpack the IBO triad

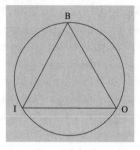

Figure 1. The IBO triad.

into its intersections (see Figure 1) to illustrate some of its possible uses for energizing and reorienting the IR research agenda.

Identities and Borders (IB): From I-to-B to B-to-I and (Partially) Back Again

The existence of an intimate relationship between identities and borders is well recognized in the humanities and in the social sciences. Routine depictions of identities and borders as "different parts of the same coin" have long served, however, to conceal the absence— rather than to confirm the presence—of genuine theoretical puzzlement with the IB nexus. As long as both identities and borders were conceived as quasi-natural givens, a flat equivalence was easily postulated between them: borders were simply a logical correlate of identities and vice versa (Eisenstadt 1998, 140; Abbott 1995, 857–60). This static view did not seek temporal accounts for either borders or identities and failed to question which came first or how they were related. At the same time, it also discouraged imaginative leaps into nontraditional combinations such as borders without identities and identities without (territorial) borders.

The new cross-disciplinary preoccupation with identities and borders has rendered such views largely untenable (Krause and Renwick 1996; Lapid and Kratochwil 1996; Spener and Staudt 1998). An additional side benefit has been the extensive rethinking and theoretical upgrading of the IB nexus in many scholarly fields, including international relations. Some of the most innovative thinking in recent IR theory—including, for instance, John Ruggie's work on principles of separability and differentiation (1998); James Rosenau's (re)discovery of the (domestic-foreign) "frontier" (1997); Andrew Linklater's inquiries into the sociological constitution of "boundedness" (1998); David Campbell's reframing of foreign policy as a boundary/subject constituting political performance (1998); Der Derian's critique of defining and uniting national identities "through the alienation of others" (1992); Shapiro and Alker's convergence on "mobile identities and shifting boundaries" (1996, xi); and Rob Walker's sustained attack on the inside/outside constitution of the IR subject matter (1993)—variously reflects, in fact, the enhanced theoretical gravity of the IB nexus.

Two quick observations can bring into sharper focus some related agenda-setting ramifications. First, as a scholarly field mandated with the theorization of (political) relations across borders (Walker 1993, 18), in an ever-more-mobile and fluid world, international relations must closely monitor continual reconfigurations occurring at the identities/borders (IB) nexus. For in both theory and practice, world-constituting distinctions—such as inside/outside, anarchy/hierarchy, domestic/foreign, self/other, here/there, and so on—materialize at this critical intersection. And to the extent that both the "inter" and the "national" are largely shaped and stabilized at this nexus, the road to a processual/relational understanding of international relations will inevitably take us through the IB intersection (see the introduction to part I of this volume).

Second, the theoretical productivity of the IB nexus is already well established. It is noteworthy that this achievement can be largely attributed to a rather simple inversion of the identity-to-borders (I-to-B) sequence that was long believed to exclusively dominate this intersection. In this understanding identities come first, then borders. Building, however, on Fredrick Barth's seminal work (1969; Verdery 1994), recent engagements with the IB nexus have tended to foreground the borders-to-identities (B-to-I) sequence. In such analysis, "Boundaries come first, then entities" (Abbott 1995, 859). Here, my agenda-setting point suggests that the pendulum may have swung too far in this direction. Although welcome at the time as an antidote to reification and essentialism, such discussions tend to lose sight of the continuing relevance of the identities-to-borders (I-to-B) dynamic. Yet, as both Roosens (1994) and Conversi (1995) point out, we cannot always reduce what is found inside boundaries (i.e., identities) to a product of boundary formation. Which dynamic comes first, in any specific case, is ultimately an empirical question. More importantly, the IB nexus is theoretically vibrant because *both* identities and borders qualify in their own right as key concepts. Borders may, and do, have many important functions that are only marginally related to identities, and there is also much more to identities than a corresponding set of borders.

That corrective action may be urgently needed at the IB nexus is clearly demonstrated, for instance, by Patrick Jackson's otherwise excellent adaptation of a processual/relational approach to international relations. Processual/relational (p/r) approaches, says Jackson (1999, 142–43), "regard their object of analysis to be unfolding processes and projects . . . which serve to draw and re-draw boundaries between entities. For a p/r approach, this 'bounding' is the essence of a social entity; in a very real sense, an entity *is* its boundaries, which serve to differentiate it from other entities both conceptually and spatio-temporally." To posit, however, that an identity "is" its boundaries unnecessarily risks a possible conflation of these two terms and voluntarily abdicates the option of harnessing the explanatory power entailed in both sequences (B-to-I and I-to-B) that continue to animate the currently vacillating IB nexus.

With respect to borders and identities, it is extremely risky to endorse a simple borders-all-the-way-down attitude. That such is the case is amply demonstrated, for instance, by map-shaking political processes such as African decolonization (Ratner 1996) and Yugoslavia's disintegration (Radan 1999). The extensive redrawing of internal and external borders was guided, in both cases, by a rigid adherence to the *uti possidetis* principle. Foregrounding exclusively the borders-to-identities sequence, this principle encouraged (in the name of simplicity and order) new state formation on the basis of preexisting colonial and/or administrative territorial demarcations. Operating with a dubious model of identity (which naively affirmed the possibility of constituting new identities within any borders), ignoring profound differences between the vastly different identity functions of internal and external borders, and failing to seriously consider many other predictable complications entailed more generally in the identity-to-borders sequence, bordering practices shaped by the *uti possidetis* principle have produced many tragic results. To that extent, the continued popularity of this principle confirms the urgent need for a serious rethinking of the IB nexus.[5]

Borders and Orders (BO): Constitutional Politics, Principles of Separability, and Bordering Practices

As we move on to the borders/orders (BO) intersection, we enter less vibrant and more problematically charted territories. The problem of order is, of course, at the very top of the post–Cold War policy agenda. And yet, as of 1998, "outstanding ideas for improving world order" were still justly included in the notorious "wanted" list (Payne 1998, 861). One reason for this sad situation is the fact that the cross-disciplinary enrichment of orders pales by comparison to its two counterparts in the triad. To their detriment, discussions of (world) order have been confined largely to international relations, where they are still stuck deep in "the Wesphalian blind alley" (Paul 1999, 217).[6] To that extent, the hope that new explorations of the BO intersection will result in much improved understandings of the core concept of order qualifies, in itself, as a top IR agenda item. With respect to the BO nexus, however, let us note first that borders (and bordering) are absolutely indispensable to any notion of linguistic or social order. Human inquiry depends on language to make sense of the world, and "language depends upon borders to construct the concepts required for cognition and communication" (Speener and Staudt 1998, 7). In Etienne Balibar's eloquent words, "what can be demarcated, defined, and determined maintains a constitutive relation with what can be thought" (1998, 216). Social order presupposes, furthermore, some underlying mental order based on fundamental distinctions between that which is included and that which is excluded (Zerubavel 1991). Add the fact that powerful cognitive and emotional needs for closure may be "at the very heart of our quest for order,"[7] and you have the ingredients for equating borders and orders as "different parts of the same coin." To that extent, the risk of collapsing the analytical distinctions between these two concepts needs, once again, explicit flagging. Borders and orders need to be allowed to vary independently of each other, allowing for two separate sequences (borders-to-orders and orders-to-borders) to co-materialize at the vital BO intersection.

Such is surely the case with respect to IR theory. The BO nexus is absolutely essential to an understanding of the dyadic conception of political order (hierarchy inside and anarchy outside) that continues to inform both theory and practice in international relations. In Waltzian terms (1979), anarchy and hierarchy are not only different, but mutually exclusive modes of political ordering. They require, in turn, a corresponding mode of territorial bordering allowing for a sharp carving up of the world into "mutually exclusive and jointly exhaustive parcels of land (Goodin 1996, 366). Westphalian ordering and Westphalian bordering hence go hand in hand, but the question of which comes first seems to be case-specific rather than transhistorically invariant. Still, it may be possible to institute some analytical clarity in this context by judiciously situating the discussion in our IBO framework. Converging on the borders-to-orders (B-to-O) and orders-to-borders (O-to-B) sequences would be key to such an undertaking. The centrality of the borders-to-orders (B-to-O) sequence becomes obvious once we apply it to recent events such as the implosion of the Soviet empire, the removal of the Iron Curtain, the reunification of Germany, the expansion of NATO, European integration, the collapse of apartheid, the multiplication of failed states, the Kosovo crisis, and so on. It is also a vital theoretical node in current debates on neomedievalism, globalization, democratization, national self-determination, multiculturalism, immigration, citizenship, societal security, and more. Individually, and together, these events and debates convey an indisputable message: acts of inscription, crossing, removal, transformation, multiplication and/or diversification of borders carry momentous ramifications for the political orders (domestic, regional, and international) in which they transpire.

The orders-to-borders (O-to-B) dynamic is equally important—and perhaps even more enigmatic—in IR theory. "We understand the order in relations among things or actions," suggest Pauline Rosenau and Harry Bredemeier, "if we can articulate the general principle or principles of which they are an instance" (1993, 335). The "national order of things" is a good and relevant illustration of this insight (Malkki 1995). Indeed, it was the onset of general confusion regarding such "ordering principles" that has most clearly violated our "deeper sense of the order of things" in the aftermath of the Cold War (Gusterson 1993, 279). In retrospect, it is clear that IR theory has entered the post–Cold War transition with an impoverished understanding of such ordering devices. Some modest advances have been registered, however. Benefiting from Ruggie's influential work, we have now a vastly improved understanding of territorial sovereignty as the master ordering principle under the Westphalian blueprint. A more preliminary understanding of nationalism as a problematic mutation of this strictly territorial principle is now also available (Hall 1999), and there are new efforts to elucidate a variety of other putative ordering principles (Kaufman 1997; Cronin and Barkin 1994; Ikenberry 1998).

The following point seems critical to a proper understanding of the orders-to-borders (O-to-B) sequence. This sequence is indispensable if we are to understand epochal—premodern-to-modern and/or modern-to-postmodern (Ruggie 1998)—transitions. For although both borders and orders are socially constructed, actors are contextually limited in their bordering practices by a variety of (single/multiple, formal/informal, territorial/nonterritorial) principles of separability and individuation. As ably noted by John Ikenberry (1998, 148), such principles are gradually hammered out in a contested process called constitutional politics. "[O]rder formation," he says, "takes the form of constitution building" (ibid.). If so, the bordering repertoire available to political agents in dynastic, territorial, or nation-based political orders, for instance, will vary considerably (Hall 1999, 29). To that extent, I posit that an elucidation of the currently emerging configuration of principles of separability and individuation—and its associated modes of bordering practices and group fragmentation—should figure as a major IR agenda item derived from the rapidly changing nature of the BO nexus (Lapid and Kratochwil 1996, 124).

Identities and Orders (IO): Exploring Epochal Change

"A world without identities," says Ted Hopf (1998, 175), "is a world of chaos, a world of pervasive and irremediable uncertainty, a world much more dangerous than anarchy." These strong words echo a theme that resonates, in various modulations, in many recent debates ranging from civilizational conflict (Huntington 1996) to societal security (Wæver 1995a). This theme posits the existence of a close relationship between identities and orders. As put by Daniel Deudney and John Ikenberry (1999, 193), "No enduring political order can exist without a substantial sense of community and shared identity." This is not to say that all IR theorists have always agreed that identity is a theoretically interesting dimension of political order, or that order (international or domestic) is a theoretically fertile context for studying contemporary issues of collective identity. Far from it. But the neglect of identity by IR's mainstream approaches is a familiar story that needs no retelling in this context. What needs emphasizing is the fact that current theoretical and empirical discussions of the "order problem" are likely to refer to the "identity problem," and vice versa (March and Olsen 1998; Barnett 1996/97, 598).

To acknowledge IO as a separate intersection is more than to merely posit a new theoretical juncture with bidirectional (I-to-O and O-to-I) traffic. It is also to call attention to the fact that the identities-to-orders and the orders-to-identities sequences need not always be mediated by an analytically dominant borders (B) factor. Borders of one kind or another will figure empirically in most IO dynamics, but occasionally we may have good reasons to mute their theoretical significance.[8] Such is the case when political actors institute new internal borders with the declared intention of *enhancing* (rather than reducing) the unity of an existing identity. "I don't want in Yugoslavia borders that will separate," declared Tito in 1945. "As I have said one hundred times, I want borders to be those that will unite our people" (Radan 1999, 141). Such is the case also where the nation-state is "developed not just as a boundary creating or maintaining device, but as a system of symbols and shared identity" (Laffan 1996, 84). And there are many other situations where the "nature" of identities—rather than their borders or interests—seem to serve as the main source of conflict or the main threat to order. Samuel Huntington's "clash of civilization" thesis has reached dubious notoriety in this category, but there are many other applicable examples.

Be that as it may, the identities/orders (IO) nexus with its two associated sequences (I-to-O and O-to-I) has been recently a site of notable creativity in IR theory.[9] Rod Hall's (1999) recently published book on national collective identity is exemplary in this respect. Departing from a valid determination that the current IR theory is still seriously limited in its engagement with national identities, Hall moves vigorously to fill in this gap at both the conceptual and the historical levels. The result is a nuanced reconstruction of fascinating mutations occurring at the IO nexus in the context of three epochal transitions.[10] The analytical effort extends well beyond demonstrating a strong historical relationship between collective identities and systemic ordering principles. Hall methodically addresses "sequencing" (I-to-O and O-to-I) dynamics at the IO nexus. "Must collective identity change within a given society, or all societies, before the system changes?" he asks. "Can the converse be true? Can the system change and thus force changes in societal collective identity upon some members of international society? Do changes in collective identity at the level of domestic society result in changes in the rules of the international system, or is the converse the case?" (1999, 47). Hall convincingly posits that the answer is "actor specific" (ibid.). The more general conclusion is that the IO nexus belongs on any IR agenda seeking to seriously engage with the elusive issue of epochal change. For whether our emerging world will hang together in an international or some other sense will be largely determined by intellectual and political practices shaped and stabilized at this critical juncture.

CONCLUDING REMARKS

So, why process analysis and why IBO? Process analysis is called for because the "idea of the 'state of rest,' of immobility, makes sense only in a world that stays still or could be taken for such; in a place with solid walls, fixed roads and signposts steady enough to have time to rust. One cannot 'stay put' in moving sands" (Bauman 1998, 78). IBO analysis, on the other hand, seems promising because identities, borders, orders signify three vital nodes of arrestation, where the "moving sands" of international relations come to be variably and temporarily stabilized. To that extent, IBO designates an ideally situated conceptual zone where the question of how (various IR) "worlds hang together" can be productively engaged (Moisi 1999). Current debates on identities, borders, orders seem increasingly polarized between advocates of modal invariance (who fail to see any transformational changes whatsoever) and advocates of flux (who see nothing but mobility and flows). In sharp contrast, the conceptual moves advocated in this chapter were designed with a viable *via media* in mind. For in IBO matters, neither invariant fixity nor radical fluidity seem possible.

For all too long, IR scholars interested in transformative change have followed a familiar strategy. First, some new unit of agency—such as multinational corporations, regions, civilizations, self-defined ethnic groups, or cities—is identified as the new "basic building block of the coming international order" (Fuller 1997, 11). Next, the old map is reconfigured to make room for this new "building block" (ibid.). Finally, the theoretical enterprise is again put on automatic flight, now more reliably guided by a presumably much improved map. The problem with this procedure is that the theoretical effort starts too late into the process. Successful inquiry still depends on having pre-given maps, with clearly inscribed actors, and with fully configured patterns of segmentation. The IBO triad will be helpful to scholars who are eager to advance beyond such static theoretical practices. It will be appreciated by theorists who are less interested in already constituted and individuated actors and more in the social production and reproduction of agency or actorhood: less in pre-given enemies or "others" and more in the production and reproduction of difference and emnification; less in an already segmented or fragmented "inter" and more in the historical production, reproduction, and transformation of boundedness and segmentation ("intering").

As a group, our contributors are such scholars. Subscribing to different approaches and driven by different research agendas, they are nonetheless in agreement with respect to three basic points. First, living in an era of momentous transformations, our scholarly task is to rethink intellectual resources and rework conceptual tools to render them more highly compatible with the fundamental problems and challenges that will confront us in the years to come. Second, meeting this challenge of innovative scholarship presupposes extensive intellectual cross-fertilization and hybridization (Biersteker 1999, 8). The IBO triad was deliberately conceived in this mold; it is a heuristic tool spacious enough to attract intellectual inputs from several disciplines, yet specific enough to foster new collaborative research. Finally, from among the many tasks to which the IBO triad can be productively harnessed, the issue of epochal change seems the most promising. For insofar as we are moving to a world shaped by a new or different IBO configuration, we may have to seriously reexamine some constitutive concepts standing at the heart of our respective scholarly enterprises.

The international and the political are two such concepts. The format and the organization of this volume reflect a shared recognition of the urgent need to seriously rethink both of these concepts. Whereas each chapter more narrowly orients itself toward one or more of the intersections entailed in the IBO triad, the organization of the volume is intended to cumulatively highlight some broader thematic ramifications related to these two core concepts. These broader themes, as well as the chapters subsumed within each of them, are presented in brief introductions prefacing each of our two sections. It is our intention to "nudge" in this manner not only the IR theory project, but also other related scholarly enterprises, in some new direction.

NOTES

I would like to thank all the participants in the Las Cruces Group on Identities, Borders, and Orders. I also thank the Ford Foundation and the Leonard Davis Institute at the Hebrew University in Jerusalem for their partial support for this project.

1. "[B]eneath the hubbub of the modernist/post-modernist dispute," says Joseph Margolis (1999, 9), "a deeper contest is looming: one between the partisans of modal invariance and the partisans of flux."

2. Abbott 1995, 858. Three clarifications seem necessary. First, despite their insistence on process and change, process philosophers in no way deny the reality of substances and nouns; they merely reconceptualize them as temporarily stabilized moments in the implicate movement of flux and transformation. Just how temporary or enduring such stabilizations will prove to be in each instance is an empirical or historical, rather than philosophical, question. Second, processism is not a unitary philosophical position, much less a clearly defined theory. Much like constructivism, it is a loose doctrinal tendency that incorporates sometimes radically different positions. And third, despite this depiction of process philosophy as a loose philosophical umbrella, it has important ramifications for empirical (i.e., first order) research as it inspires new questions and opens up new venues for inquiry. For, at minimum, "partisans of modal invariance" and "partisans of flux" will have diametrically opposed ideas on whether to treat *occurrence of change* or *the attainment of stability* as truly problematic.

3. An additional clarification becomes relevant at this point. The attentive reader may wonder about the plural configuration of our three concepts. The "s" is deliberate and denotes a principled recognition that the conceptual moves proposed in this volume are best approached in the plural form. With respect to IBO, in particular, pluralization seems necessary to counteract the effects of an intimate affiliation with long-dominant (positivist/realist/materialist) monistic interpretations. Never fully absent from the IR toolbox, our three concepts have maintained their relevance mainly in a narrow and unitary sense: a border meant a territorial line; an identity

meant a (state) nationalism; and an order meant a stable distribution of power among (Westphalian) states. The plural form reflects a realization that, in the aftermath of the Cold War, a diverse plurality of identities, borders, and orders are at once substantively important and theoretically interesting.

4. This is to say that, despite a traditional association with different disciplines, identities, borders, and orders belong to the same semantic field. And, with respect to terms located in the same semantic field, "It is impossible ... to redefine one term without redefining others, for the task of definition consists of establishing relationships with neighboring terms" (Gerring 1999, 382).

5. "Yugoslavia's secessionist wars," concludes Radan (1999, 144) "were fundamentally wars about where the border lines should be between the states that were to emerge out of the Yugoslav debris. The insistence on the application of the Badinter Principle only served to prolong and intensify the agony that was the breakup of Yugoslavia. Nevertheless, the Badinter Principle has been cited by commentators as being of relevance in relation to existing secessions such as Cyprus and Kosovo, as well as possible future secessions from the United Kingdom, South Africa and Canada."

6. See, however, Deudney and Ikenberry (1999) and March and Olsen (1998).

7. See also Fukuyama's (1999) provocative argument regarding the powerful innate human capacity for reconstituting social order.

8. Katherine Pratt Ewing (1998, 263), for instance, decides to detach "the issue of multiple narratives and identities from that of borders, so that we can assess when the negotiations of identities is experienced as border crossings and when it is not."

9. See Patrick T. Jackson's "Europe *Already* Exists, or Thoughts on the Real Role of Identity in Political Life" (paper presented at the 1999 ISA meeting in Washington, D.C.).

10. In Hall's own words, "The first is the transition from the medieval, heteronomous, feudal-theocratic order to a dynastic-sovereign (Augsburg, 1555) system, the second was the transition from the Augsburg system to the territorial-sovereign (Westphalian, 1648) system that is featured prominently in realist analysis. The third is the transition to the national-sovereign (the first post-Westphalian) system" (1999, 6).

I

Rethinking the "International": IBO Clues for Post-Westphalian Mazes

Rethinking the "International": IBO Clues for Post-Westphalian Mazes

YOSEF LAPID

This volume is premised on the idea that the road to a better theory of international relations passes through the intersections of the IBO triad. Seriously pursued, however, this road leads also to a near evaporation of the "international" as a coherent or worthwhile theoretical destination. At the beginning of the new millennium, thinking the international through IBO terms is tantamount to rethinking it. To be sure, there is still an "inter" and a "national" out there. Processes of integration and globalization have been largely matched, and perhaps exceeded, by co-occurring processes of fragmentation and disintegration. And whatever evidence there might be to support the end of the nation-state thesis, it can be easily matched by counterevidence attesting to the continued health of the national. All considered, however, it is nonetheless questionable whether our world still hangs together in the international sense. It would take considerable myopia to look at IR's declared subject matter through an IBO-sensitized lens and miss the fact that the "inter" is now thoroughly crisscrossed (and zonally yoked) by the "sub," the "trans," the "intra," and the "supra" (Ong 1999, 4). Does it make sense, one wonders, to impose a coherent "inter" pattern and logic upon such a fluid and complexly fractured landscape? What is the theoretical status and relevance of IR's constitutive "inter" in view of recent technological, sociological, and geopolitical transformations that seem to have irreversibly blurred its once crisply visible and viable territorial contours?

As to the national, it was always intended to lend historical and sociological specificity to the sovereignty-based territorial pattern of segmentation (the "inter") instituted at Westphalia in 1648. When the territorial logic that held this state-centric "inter" together started losing part of its legendary force, a more problematic national-sovereign structuring formula emerged to institute the first post-Westphalian order (Hall 1999, 6). However, in a historical and intellectual context that continued to privilege territorial over nonterritorial principles of separability and individuation, in practice, the national continued to be fully eclipsed by the sovereign part of this formula. The resulting "inter" became a problematic and explosive hybrid, whereby the national was doing most of the legitimizing work at the rhetorical level and the sovereign was doing most of the "intering" work at the territorial level. The key to the temporary defusion of this explosive mixture was a hegemonic nation-state construct, solidly held together by a mostly mythical, yet rarely politically challenged or theoretically problematized, hyphen.

In IBO terms, the nation-state construct anchored a solidly stabilized international world, with national and statist identities, borders and orders consistently reinforcing and mapping into each other. For as long as the gulf separating nations and states remained a distinction with no theoretical or political difference, both of these concepts remained equally capable of "nationalizing" the contemporary IBO configuration. Escaping theoretical attention was the fact that a world nationalized by the national (properly defined) would have been vastly different from a world nationalized via effective territorial etatization. Be that as it may, we are witnessing now, as noted by Benedict Anderson, "the impending crisis of the hyphen that for two hundred years yoked nation and state" (1996, 8–9; Cheah 1998, 22). As a result, all three components of the nation-state (the nation, the state, and the hyphen) are undergoing profound and only partially convergent transfigurations.

Emerging with clarity from all this is the realization that a world consisting of many thousands of nations, but only two hundred or so states, is profoundly "unhyphenable" (Tolz 1998). To that extent, we live in a more disarticulated, more volatile, and correspondingly less international world. We may be entering, in other words, one of those historical moments "when the basic organization of political order is up for grabs" (Ikenberry 1998, 148). In IBO terms, this means that the triad is vacillating as it mutates into a more complex and less familiar configuration. Some have misinterpreted this vacillation as an indication that we are moving into a meaningless, borderless, and orderless world. Such is not the case. As Etienne Balibar correctly notes, "Less than ever is the contemporary world a 'world without borders'" (1998, 220). The same holds true for identities and orders. As a result, it is increasingly difficult to make sense of our world with the familiar (international) IBO key. To successfully navigate currently emerging post-Westphalian labyrinths, we may need some extensively reconfigured IBO clues.

The six chapters included in this section are variations and comments on this basic theme. In different ways, they all address post-Westphalian (re)configurations of the international. Albert and Brock's opening chapter sets us vigorously on this course. As indicated by their title, Ruggie's puzzle is tacitly driving their argument. That a deeper plumbing of the historical, sociological, and normative depths of a post-Westphalian transition can be undertaken with the orienting help of the IBO construct is the implicit subtext of Albert and Brock's contribution. From among the many interesting arguments presented in this chapter, three seem particularly noteworthy. First, Westphalia is important because the modern system of states "came about by way of territorializing space." Second, the formative impact of territoriality as the organizing principle of the modern state system has been so decisive because it has penetrated into our deepest normative understandings, not only of states and sovereignty but also of society and community. And third, although it may be "premature to diagnose an all-encompassing evaporation of the Westphalian normative order," it is high time to acknowledge a fundamental shift in the balance of territorial, semiterritorial, and nonterritorial vectors that shape the intricate texture of contemporary world politics. In terms of the IBO triad, Albert and Brock's focus on territorialization (and deterritorialization) leads to a special convergence on the border/bordering element. However, insofar as their goal is to convince the reader "that there is political life beyond territoriality," their contribution spaciously includes reference to the entire analytical space constituted by our triad and covered by this volume.

The Peace of Westphalia, in 1648, designated state sovereignty as the primary constitutive principle of modern political systems in the context of a wider attempt to enhance domestic and international order and security. Since then, state sovereignty and security have evolved in a symbiotic relationship (Makinda 1998). It is with this realization in mind that the *New York Times* editors have designated March 24, 1999 (the day NATO started bombing Serbia and also the day England's high court ruled against Augusto Pinochet), "sovereignty's worst day in memory" (Rosenberg 1999, 16). The following three contributions confirm that, with respect to warfare and security, the Wesphalian order is indeed going through some very difficult and testing times. Mansbach and Wilmer depict a world in which the Westphalian state system, with respect to management of violence issues, is no longer "the only game in town." A world of increasingly destabilized identities and blurred boundaries does not easily lend itself to territorially based (Westphalian) solutions. With the concept of "moral boundaries," these authors situate themselves at the identities/borders (IB) intersection of our triad to elucidate possible responses to an emerging world in which problems of war and violence are becoming daily more unmanageable in traditional (Westphalian) terms (Tharoor 1999).

In chapter 3, Ronnie Lipschutz stays close to the theme of moral bordering. Drawing and redrawing lines that separate good and evil is essential to the constitution and legitimation of both domestic and international orders. It is also essential to "the distinction between the 'good' national Self and 'bad' foreign Others." The related ability to differentiate between "zones of moral order and immoral disorder" is, in turn, central to both constituting order and waging war in modern times. Lipschutz takes us back to Westphalia to trace the historical evolution of territorial, and later national, states into focal moral authorities. The bulk of the argument deals, however, with the emerging contradiction between narrow state-centric moralities and the rise of liberal individualism. Recent events such as the Strategic Defense Initiative and the War over Kosovo are reinterpreted as (misguided) attempts by American and other Western nation-states to recapture their moral right to reimpose the "borders of order."

Didier Bigo also situates himself at the identities/borders (IB) nexus to address the remarkable merging of internal and external security functions. Traditionally, the functions and modes of operation of security-providing institutions (such as the police and the army) were clearly differentiated along the Westphalian, inside/outside, divide. Bigo concludes that, with respect to security, the Westphalian age is coming to an end. "The frontiers between 'inside and outside' are under discussion," he says, "because we are at the limits of our political imagination." To overcome these limits, Bigo situates the IBO triad "at the heart of the discussion concerning security." More than other contributors to this volume, he also articulates his own version of a processual/relational approach and devotes considerable effort to suggesting a metaphor (the "Möbius ribbon") equal to the task. More generally, however, Bigo defines his larger project as an effort to constitute a new international political sociology.

This takes us directly to Chris Brown's opening observation regarding the absence of a convincing liberal or nonliberal account of borders in international political theory. The bulk of the chapter consists of a reflective effort to retrieve, thematize, and assess liberal and communitarian positions on borders and identities. The tacit hope is thereby to facilitate the growth of a new and more vibrant international political theory. In terms of our triad, Brown's analytical effort is noteworthy for its normative focus on identities-to-borders dynamics. Engaging the larger theme of this section, he concludes that normative theories developed over the past centuries have been addressing a (Westphalian?) world that is now fast disappearing. Be that as it may, the normative turn apparent in all the chapters included so far in this section culminates with Brown's sober indictment of the record of theorization on border-related issues in both international and political theory.

Finally, David Newman's analytical survey of traditional and new geographic literatures on boundaries deepens the intellectual foundations of the IBO project by expanding it into related spatial disciplines. Read against the background of a growing fascination with putative post-Wesphalian transitions, the chapter carries the pertinent warning that "the territorial compartmentalization of the globe has not changed as much as many commentators have recently argued"). At the same time, it also demonstrates that present-day political geographers have placed the study of territoriality and borders in an updated social theory matrix, leaving the door wide open for innovative cross-disciplinary ventures. Striking in this context is the remarkable convergence that obtains between recent efforts by political geographers to link the spatial and the social in new studies of territoriality and the identities/borders (IB) nexus, as conceptualized in our triad (Paasi 1999a). The complex nature of currently evolving relationships between territories, boundaries, and identities is well illustrated by Newman's condensed summary of the Israeli experience in the last fifty years.

1

What Keeps Westphalia Together? Normative Differentiation in the Modern System of States

MATHIAS ALBERT AND LOTHAR BROCK

MOVING BORDERS ACROSS STATES:
FROM COMPROMISING TO TRANSCENDING WESTPHALIA

The new inconclusiveness of social practice that Habermas exposed to academic debate in the early eighties is still with us. If anything, things have become even more complicated after the East-West conflict has ended. As a response, issues of "culture and identity" have been meeting with a rapidly growing interest in post–Cold War theorizing on international relations (Assmann 1993; Deudney 1996; Dyer 1993; Falk 1990; Haas 1993; Lapid and Kratochwil 1996; Said 1993; Walker 1990). "Similarly, following a period of hostile indifference to 'ideational explanations' the time for 'ideas' seems to have come around once again in International Political Economy" (Lapid 1996, 3).

This observation reflects new challenges to theory building and a slowly growing readiness to deal with the "national" in "international relations" that "figures among the most important issues awaiting theorization in the post–Cold War era" (Lapid and Kratochwil 1996, 118). Taking up new challenges does not automatically lead to new theories. Rather there is a strong temptation to reaffirm old explanations by integrating some new aspects into them (cf. ibid., 116).

As Lapid and Kratochwil demonstrate, this practice of *inclusionary control* can be found in recent efforts by some authors to treat the persistence or reappearance of nationalism in a way that confirms state-centered thinking "in its excessive dependence on capability-driven and anarchy-sustained explanations and, above all, in its neglect of the subjective underpinnings of the international system." Therefore, a primary task lies in moving from inclusionary control to theoretical reconstruction (ibid., 116 and 120).

Furthermore, referring to "new challenges" does not imply from the outset that we are confronted with developments that constitute a substantive change of Braudel's "long durée" type (but see Holm and Sørensen 1995b). It only signifies that we are not in a position yet to (fully) explain what is happening, whether new or not. Thus "new challenges" can also refer to "old" modes of social practice that reappear after a period of absence or continue without obvious reasons (cf. Katzenstein 1989).

But what is it exactly that is difficult to explain? In a neat formula, it is the interrelationship between integration and fragmentation on local and global levels (see Rosenau 1997; Brock 1994; Zürn 1995). On the one side the world seems to be moving from complex interdependence to cyberspace, from old-fashioned multinationals producing material goods that can be controlled on borders to new strategic alliances that trade not goods but expectations and information and in doing so challenge both, the power of states and the identity of nations. On the other side, as economic globalization goes on, *national* competitiveness becomes a major focus for ordering social relations, modern cosmopolitanism is losing ground to a new parochial thinking, the heterogeneous nation-state meets a militant and at times brutal tribalism, the international division of labor is superseded by ethnic monopolization, and nation building gives way to genocide. Physical boundaries are being transformed into social and electronic boundaries as new zones of exclusive lifestyles and of exclusive access to information emerge from the vestiges of modernity.

The present chapter examines how integrative and fragmentive tendencies interrelate under the new mode of differentiation that is usually subsumed under the somewhat murky concept of "globalization." Globalization seems to imply that territoriality is losing out as an organizing principle of the modern world system (Ruggie 1993;

Elkins 1995). On the other hand, fragmentive developments that are part and parcel of globalization (glocalization) could be interpreted as an affirmation of territoriality. With a view to these seemingly contradictory trends, Lapid and Kratochwil (1996, 123) call for a new account "of the diversity entailed in the changing balance of territorial, semi-territorial and nonterritorial elements that increasingly structure struggles in world politics." The present chapter is to contribute to the task of addressing these issues with the help of the analytical triad of identities, borders, orders (IBO). It will utilize various parts and segments of this triangle and pursue them to varying analytical depths. The chapter proceeds on the assumption that the *national* is to be viewed as an outcome and as a determining factor of social processes that shape territoriality while being shaped by it. This implies that nationalism, in the present chapter, figures not only as an instrument of the state (Haas 1993) but also as a force influencing its behavior, its attributes, and even its being (in the case of ethnic separatism) (Jepperson et al. 1996). In juxtaposing state and nation, Ole Wæver (1995a, 423) hypothesizes that just as there were states without nations in the pre-Westphalian system, there are going to be nations without states in the years to come. Thus, in the future as in the pre-Westphalian past, international relations for a large part would be relations without states.

Current trends seem to point in a different direction, however. Under the pressure of globalization (tightening world-market competition, migration), state and nation seem to be moving together rather than apart. In some parts of the world there is a strong drive toward a homogenization of state and nation either in the way of peaceful separation (former Czechoslovakia) or in the form of brutal fighting (former Yugoslavia, southern rim of the former Soviet Union). Are these mere transitory phenomena that will succumb to an overriding global trend toward a deterritorialization of social practice? Is the territorial state doomed while nations will prosper? Will the Westphalian system adapt to globalization or will it be overwhelmed by it? If the latter should be the case, would the outcome resemble a globalized Columbia or a universalized Switzerland?

In the present chapter *nation* refers to an ensemble of people who, sharing a common living space, are of the conviction that they form a unit with a specific *identity* (i.e., somehow distinct from other units). The term thus differs from the understanding of the nation as the entirety of citizens *(Staatsnation)*. The conviction to form a unity is not at the disposal of day-to-day experiences. In a general way it guides individuals' perceptions of social life in its political context. This does not imply that the individuals constituting a nation all have the same reading of the history, the values, the outlooks, or the symbols that are associated with the nation. Rather, each may believe in *her* or *his* nation. However, the different readings of the nation converge in the notion that they describe an essential unity of specific people, though this unity does not preclude conflict among them (Douglas 1993). In this notion of essential unity, culture and civic conscience (*civilizational* attitudes) mix. *Culture* is understood as "any interpersonally shared system of meanings, perceptions and values" (Jacquin et al. 1993, 376; Geertz 1973) that can be distinguished from other such systems. *Civic conscience* refers to the understanding that belonging to a social entity involves certain rights and duties. When focusing on shared rights and duties among the members of a social unity, we are dealing with the concept of *society*. When focusing on collective identities (and citizenship), we are dealing with the concept of *community*. Community, however, is not necessarily identical with nation. A community is formed by (feelings of) *local, folkloristic,* or *ethnic embeddedness* and *solidarity* that go beyond—as we may now say—the *cultured* conviction of belonging together as a nation (World Society Research Group 2000). The more culturally homogeneous a nation is, the more it may resemble a community. At the same time, a community at the national level is likely to resemble a society.

With these working definitions in mind, the chapter proceeds in the following way. First, we try to establish how the formation of state and nation interact and how closely nation building has been tied up with the politics of territoriality. Second, we look at how globalization affects the relationship between the territorial state and the nation. In this context we deal with the complexity of international relations under the Westphalian model, prominently presented by Stephen Krasner, or the "Copenhagen School." Departing from the observation that the "logic" of fragmentation is at least in part a function of defining the effects of internationalization (globalization) as a security qua survival problem, we will try to demonstrate that new patterns of differentiation evolve that cannot be adequately grasped in these terms.

Third, we shift attention to one of the major issues emerging from the continued unbundling of state, territory, and nation in the process of globalization, namely the transformation of the Westphalian system as a "normative order." In analyzing integrative and disintegrative tendencies in this system, we will have to take into account the fact that it may very well be the basic sociological concepts of society and community themselves that require a revision in the light of a continuing blurring, transformation, and redrawing of borders (around states, nations, etc.). "Transcending Westphalia" may then come to mean more than merely challenging the modern state by global homogenization on the one hand, and national reassertiveness on the other. Instead, new modes of differentiation and segmentation may be evolving that are more complex than dualistic concepts such as community-society, security-identity, or integration-fragmentation would suggest. Although we will not be able to pursue this in any detail, we will suggest that the historical form of Westphalia expresses and accommodates a *normative* structure of the social world. This normative structure is basically conceived in terms of Western ethics; its discursive field is demarcated by the positions of cosmopolitanism and communitarianism (see also the chapter by Brown, as well as Mansbach and Wilmer, in this volume). Showing some of the intricate relationships in this regard will allow us to explore how factual change in international relations is inextricably linked to "normative" transformation.

In this context, the boundary lines around which nations and states are formed are of special interest. The persistence and mutation, the simultaneous fading away and reproduction of boundaries (see Albert 1999a), may serve as an indicator of the increasing volatility of collective identities, of notions of equality and accountability, and of the cherished attributes of a good life in the present world. This "richness" of the ongoing change, though, should not deceive us. It is loaded with conflict and there are no grand strategies available to solve them.

THE FORMATION OF STATE AND NATION

The modern system of states came about by way of territorializing space. *Space* offers a referential system for ordering individual and collective thoughts, perceptions, and feelings (Sack 1980, 4). In this sense it corresponds closely with culture if we understand the latter as a life-sustaining medium for making sense of the world (Geertz 1973).

Territoriality is conceived here as a specific arrangement of space, a "geographical expression of social power" (Sack 1986, 5; Ruggie 1993, 151). It is a way to control people and resources by staking out a marked claim and by defending it against rivaling claims. In doing so, it links up with culture that, performing similar functions, is more and more coming to be defined territorially in modern times, thus in effect "doubling" territorial divisions. Of course, culture and territory cannot be reduced to one another. Although in a historically specific context their effects may be similar and in fact reinforce each other, they are based on different material and ideational foundations.

The territorialization of the public sphere in Europe proceeded as cultural homogenization in the wake of the wars of religion. It resulted from two converging trends in the "long sixteenth century." On the one hand, feudal property structures in general and the institution of the commons in particular got in the way of capital accumulation in the avant-garde areas of modernization. On the other hand, as the secular rulers of Europe freed themselves from the tutelage of the church, there was a need to replace the spiritual basis of power by some other medium for its practice. These needs were served by dividing up resources on the microlevel (*fencing,* introduction of private property as a public institution) and on the macrolevel by recreating political authority in such a way that it was no longer upheld by reference to a divine will but by the ability to control a certain territory and the population living on it. This ability was eventually recognized as sovereignty in its connotation as a claim of individual governments and as an ordering principle of international relations (cf. Kratochwil 1986).

From Europe, modern territoriality spread via colonialism, and was completed by decolonization and the dissolution of yet another empire, the Soviet Union and the socialist world system. In brief, modernization drove a process of global territorialization that has gained considerable momentum in recent decades and that includes by now huge parts of the open seas, the latter having been territorialized through the installation of 200-mile economic zones. Today, territorialization of the world may be regarded as almost complete.

Though territorialization served as a way to establish and exert political authority, it did not suffice to create the modern state system. Territorialization, as understood in this chapter, "flattens" space; it reduces it to two dimensions. In this respect, while facilitating political control through geographical contiguity, its cost-effectiveness decreased to the extent that traditional sources of legitimacy were lost in the transformation from the transterritorial medieval order to the territorial state. In the formative stage of the modern state system, such losses were partly offset by the provision of new public goods like intrastate peace and the facilitation of trade. However, the ongoing technological change, the accumulation of capital, and the shifting power balance between the feudal elites and the new bourgeois groups, between the countryside and the city, led to a new mode of achieving political legitimacy beyond the means offered by absolutism and mercantilism and their functional equivalents. This new mode proceeded as, and ensued from, nation building. Nation building followed different patterns. In France and Spain the state invented the nation by reconstituting the subjects of political authority as a social unit comprising all those living on the state's territory (political or civic nation as *demos*). In Germany and Italy the nation was invented to foster the merger of autonomous political units to form a central state (preexisting nation as *ethnos)*. Nation building thus worked as a two-way process: top down from state to nation and bottom up from nation to state. Paradoxically, the top-down version, by creating *demos,* unleashed the claim for democratic control, while the bottom-up version, by affirming *ethnos,* helped to enhance political authoritarianism (cf. Stichweh 1994; Schoch 1995). Both historical processes converged, however, in the understanding that *nation* refers to a uniting of the people living on a state's territory as a community of citizens with certain rights and duties but also with feelings of solidarity, vis-à-vis the state and fellow citizens. This way, territorial rule was reconstituted, through nation building, as a three-dimensional spatial arrangement of social practice.

Nation building was not a necessary consequence of territorialization; but nation building matched territorialization in a historically specific and successful way (Agnew and Corbridge 1995, 83). In this sense, the modern state system is not only the product of the

Peace of Westphalia, but also of the French Revolution (Lapid and Kratochwil 1996, 122). This observation underlines the need to avoid the "territorial trap" into which, according to Agnew and Corbridge, a good part of international relations theory has fallen by treating its object as being determined by territoriality (1995, 78). International relations have to be seen in the context of social change. On the other hand, social change remains affected by the (geographically almost complete) partition of the world into territorial states.

FROM FLATTENING SPACE TO EVAPORATING IT?

The interplay between social change and territorial politics continues in the face of globalization. The latter transforms the spatial aspects of social order. This implies first and foremost a change in the social function of borders. Borders may be defined as that part of national territory "where there is some critical reduction of the frequency of a certain type of transaction" (Deutsch 1969, 99). In this respect, borders function as bottlenecks; they constitute barriers (Nijkamp 1994). This function may be regarded as an unintended consequence of "thin" infrastructures in areas that are remote from the economic and political centers. More often than not, however, it is the result of conscious efforts, for economic, political, or social reasons, to keep border transactions under control. Economic protectionism and the control of entry into a country are the most obvious examples of the intentional use of borders as bottlenecks.

Though borders slow down transactions, as a matter of rule they do not stop them. On the contrary, the creation of the modern system of territorial states went hand in hand with a quickly growing international division of labor resulting in the formation of a world market. Today, there are some indications that the function of borders as barriers is losing in importance compared to their function as bridges. According to Lawrence Herzog (1992, 4–5), "in the last four decades, the functions of international boundaries have been redefined. ... The most obvious change has been the shift from boundaries that are heavily protected and militarized to those that are more porous, permitting cross-border social and economic interaction." Or, as Peter Nijkamp states (1994, 5), "Borders are no longer barriers to development, but also windows of opportunities." Indeed, new centers of development across borders are forming that make use of locational factors in border areas of two or more countries. Examples for this development may be found in the European Union and North America, as well as in Asia (Jordan and Khanna 1995; Albert and Brock 1996).

In the context of global sourcing, transnational economic integration, and the increasing linkages between substate entities on the global level, economic actors tend to pursue their interests "without too much consideration of the former borders of nation-states" (Nijkamp 1994, 5; cf. Ohmae 1993; Sassen 1991). Ruggie speaks of a "blurring of boundaries between domestic and international realms" (1995, 513). However, this is only one side of the picture. While international boundaries are being blurred, new domestic boundaries evolve as social cleavages resulting from neoliberal globalization are deepening even in the OECD world (Hurrell and Woods 1995). In this respect, boundaries are being moved across states (cf. the ever-more-fortified housing areas of the rich or the ethnically defined boundaries between various living quarters of immigrants and between immigrants and the "incumbent" population). These boundaries are being guarded more intensively than many of the international boundaries of today. In the wake of these developments, security is being turned into a market good without, however, losing its character as a public concern.

There is, of course, the danger of overstating the novelty of globalization and thus to exaggerate change. As is generally recognized now, economic globalization, to a certain extent, constitutes a return to the levels of internationalization that were reached in the last quarter of the nineteenth century (cf. Krasner 1994; Kapstein 1993; Halliday 1995). But this does not imply that there is nothing new under the sun. Today, as economies globalize and societies are fused and split up at the same time by transnational communities of migrants, the social construct of territorial congruency between nation, state, society, and economy crumbles. As this construct formed the very core of the modern territorial system, this system itself is being transformed.

True, multinational corporations should not be regarded as stateless bodies, given that they are still subject to legal provisions of the states within which they operate and generally have a national base. In this sense it is also true that the world economy, in theory, does not have any offshore zones. However, the "offshore" activities of large-scale economic players, in most cases, effectively invalidate attempts to put legal provisions into practice and to exert controls. More important, the national provenance of multinationally operating firms ceases to have any bearing on the power of "their" countries to tax them. Thus we may speak of a debordering of national economies that is being matched, if to a lesser degree, by a debordering of societies. Both trends foster countermoves directed at regaining the lost territorial congruency of all aspects of the public realm around which perceptions of the self could converge and that would promise a feeling of belonging together with, or grounded on, the expectation of partaking in what the commonwealth has to offer.

Globalization has caused a debate on the fate of sovereignty. Robert Keohane observes that under complex interdependence sovereignty no longer enables states to exert effective supremacy over what occurs within their territories (Keohane 1995, 177). In a similar vein, Michael Zürn (1995) argues that there is another "great transformation" going on in the context of globalization that manifests itself in a loss of effectiveness of state action in the issue areas of welfare, security as well as culture and communication. Keohane concludes that the meaning of sovereignty is changing. Based on the exercise of supremacy within a given territory, its traditional functions were "to clarify boundaries, institutionalize practices of reciprocity, limit intervention" (Keohane 1995, 185). Today, under complex interdependence, "sovereignty is less a territorially defined barrier than a bargaining resource for politics characterized by complex transnational networks" (ibid., 177). This is to say that sovereignty under globalization does not reify territorial divisions, but rather is "deterritorialized" itself by being transformed into influence over other states via international institutions.

According to Zürn, the central role of the state as an actor in social relations may be questioned: "[T]he future role of the nation-state cannot be taken as a given. Other powerful corporate actors may prefer to utilize other, possibly more effective, institutions for the regulation of world politics.... Correspondingly, people may increasingly look for other, subnational as well as supranational, institutions as the foci of legitimate political authority" (1995, 162). In the same vein, Ferguson and Mansbach (1996a) suggest as a model the public sphere as a continuum of polities from the substate to the global level, not in order to put them all in one basket (as polities), but to challenge state-centered thinking by confronting it with the richness of institution building in human history. As a result of economic globalization and global communication, territorial boundaries as representations of sovereignty "are not so much being altered as ignored or transcended" (Ferguson and Mansbach 1996c, 42–43).

The assumption that there is political life beyond territoriality continues to meet with harsh opposition in IR theory from a Westphalian perspective. On the other hand, there are interesting attempts to accommodate the arguments. Thus Stephen Krasner takes a close look at the claim "that sovereignty is now being altered because the principles of Westphalia are being transgressed" (1995, 115). However, Krasner concedes that territorial states cannot be regarded as "ontological givens." They rather constitute historically specific forms of political order. Krasner even goes so far as to state that other forms of political order are not confined to pre-Westphalian times. On the contrary, they are part and parcel of international relations since Westphalia. Among the examples cited are the British Commonwealth and the European Union, Antarctica as well as the newly established maritime Exclusive Economic Zones. Likewise, Krasner maintains that the claim of states to autonomy has frequently not been successful. He concludes, "The assertion that the contemporary system represents a basic transformation because sovereignty seems to be so much at risk is not well-founded: it ignores the fact that violations of the principles of territoriality and autonomy have been an enduring characteristic of the international system both before and after the Peace of Westphalia" (ibid., 123). The strategic advice following from this conclusion is to keep "violating" Westphalia, to the extent that this is pareto-improving and helps the strong states control the weak, and to stick to the basic Westphalian model for the regulation of relations among the strong states. In other words, Krasner wants to foster *a new understanding of the lack of novelty* in international relations.

Krasner's "think piece" is valuable in that it impressively demonstrates the complexities of political order and interstate relations in spite of global territorialization and of the codification of sovereignty and self-determination (autonomy) through international law. It demonstrates the shortcoming of neorealism, neoliberalism, and "international society approaches" to adjust their system of reference against which change and continuity are being measured (ibid.,

121–22). However, it also offers an example of "inclusionary control." The latter is achieved by summarizing all the different phenomena (so aptly described by Krasner) that do not fit the Westphalian model as *violations* of the model that serve to uphold the model. Arguing that such violations have occurred all along, present developments that do not fit the model are being neutralized as a conceptual challenge by defining them as a mere variation of what has been going on before. On this level of abstraction Krasner is, of course, right. But choosing this level of abstraction functions as a blinker that helps to give a rather one-sided account of history since 1648, if not of all history. Krasner's argument is determined by the *purpose* to demonstrate that there is nothing new under the sun. The way Krasner uses his empirical illustrations of violations of the Westphalian model does not address the question to what extent violations are changing quantitatively and qualitatively. No doubt, there were bondholders' committees that regulated financial activities in Balkan states in the nineteenth century (ibid., 116), but does that prove that the way the debt crisis of the 1980s was handled had nothing new to offer? As defined by Krasner, every major peace treaty since 1648 may indeed have violated the Westphalian model. On this account they may all be similar. But on all other accounts they may not be (cf. Lapid and Kratochwil 1996, 116).

The paradox, irony, or beauty of Krasner's approach is that the way he goes about demonstrating the lack of change helps to pin down change and even to understand better when and how it would transcend Westphalia. Krasner writes that the European Union could either just become a larger state or revert to a conventional international agreement.

> The third alternative, however, would be a political arrangement in which different authority structures governed different functional areas. Foreign trade and monetary policy might be determined at the Union level. Environmental issues might be decided by regional entities that crossed existing territorial boundaries. Social policy might be set by the national state. Such a structure would be different from the Westphalian state in which authority is coterminous with territory. (Krasner 1995, 134)

In short, Krasner, by claiming that every new development may be interpreted as evidence of the continuity of old patterns, arrives at a point at which he offers us the tools to distinguish the new from the old. The new, in this case, would be a process that would not only curtail sovereignty and autonomy, but would actually lead to the construction of new principles of political order superseding or transcending (instead of just violating temporarily) the Westphalian model. This way the Krasner text may be read as offering support for the view that there is life not only in violation of, but actually beyond, the Westphalian model, i.e., beyond an order based on the principles of territoriality and autonomy.

Nonetheless, taking the process of European integration as an example may also serve to illustrate that far-reaching predictions about the fate of the nation-state may be premature. It seems as if the viability of any change toward an innovative model of organizing rule in the context of the EU—such as the model envisaged by Krasner—depends on the compatibility of this model with the way that the individual nations conceive their identities. Thus, Ole Wæver (1995a) uses the concept of "societal security" to show that the way that Europe is constructed has to fit into the narrative structures of how the French, German, and other European nations construct themselves; otherwise, any such construction would be prone to be perceived as a threat to the identities constructed by these narrative structures.

Wæver's reasoning, just as Krasner's, alerts us to the need to keep our expectations of change in bounds. With a view to the interrelationship between state building and nation building described above, change cannot be expected to form a linear process, in much the same sense that Rosenau referred to "turbulence" in world politics. This turbulence is not confined to the zones centered around the equator, rather it has been spreading to large parts of the former Soviet empire and is affecting life in the OECD world, too. While globalization optimists like Giddens or Beck emphasize the chances that globalization offers, there is ample reason to question the possibility of moving from the Westphalian to a post-Westphalian system in a gradual fashion. We rather expect increasing tensions within the system arising out of the need to fulfill socially integrative functions that the state cannot fulfill any longer. For instance, the way Mansbach or Ferguson constructs a continuum of polities, the way Zürn conceives of change as a process of optimizing governance, the way Keohane redefines sovereignty as a bargaining chip, all these efforts to accommodate the new in an affirmative way neglect the contradictions inherent in the process of change, i.e., the stubbornness of the old, which is not rooted in mere nostalgia but in the need to be able to make sense of what is going on and at the same time to make a living out of it. After space was flattened by territoriality, it had to be thickened by nation building in order to make territoriality serve its purpose as a realm of rule and the common good. Today, political space is thinning out again and it seems there is no ready-made mode at hand to thicken it once again.

However, we argue that a change of the Westphalian system not only is more complicated but also goes deeper than even the analyses mentioned would be prepared to acknowledge. Of course, there may be no European society or European community (in the sense of a felt solidarity among its members), and the existence and reassertiveness of separate nations and nation-states may prevent such a European community/society to build an identity of its own. But making this observation and drawing the accompanying conclusion rests on the usage of basic categories of social analysis that are themselves part of the Westphalian framework, yet rarely thematized as such. Thus, it is not only the way that community and society are expressed in the Westphalian order, as nation-states, that is changing nowadays, but the very meanings of "community" and "society" are being recast.

TRANSCENDING WESTPHALIA:
WESTPHALIA AS A NORMATIVE WORLD ORDER

The idea that the territorial state also provides the boundaries of a society, which in turn is upheld as a normative order by a comprehensive community that has taken the form of a nation, is not peculiar to theories of international relations. It rather forms a basic proposition still operative in sociological theory as well, at least insofar as it can be traced back to the theories of classical sociology, especially the theories of Weber and Durkheim (cf. Albert 1999c). One of the most prominent expressions that this conception leaves in modern social theory can be found in Parsons's concept of a societal community:

> A society must constitute a societal *community* that has an adequate level of integration or solidarity and a distinctive membership status. This does not preclude relations of control or symbiosis with popu-

lation elements only partly integrated into the societal community, such as Jews in the Diaspora, but there must be a core of more fully integrated members. (Parsons 1969, 19)

It is exactly this conception of society as a system that is made up by a core group—its members conceived as citizens—that is challenged during globalization. Nowadays, a significant part of most countries' populations is made up of people who partake in the social, political, and economic life of these countries to a substantial degree, yet are not officially members of the societies in question. When diasporic and other transnational communities do not wither away but rather seem to flourish in a kind of new global nomadism, it seems doubtful that communal and societal bonds, in order to support a stable social structure, would have to take the form of a societal community—a form in which both community and society are congruent with the territorial borders of the nation-state.

As Ferguson and Mansbach have pointed out in their study on *Polities* (1996a), authority has been and—as can be seen by comparing the EU to its member states—continues to be organized in various, sometimes radically diverging, ways. It is only a small step to extend this insight and see that the way a normative order is produced in relation to the organization of political authority—and hence the way that communal and societal elements combine—is highly variable over space and time. Thus, although under the Westphalian mode all states are of the same form in being sovereign, states rarely share the same concept of statehood, i.e., of the legitimatory basis for their sovereignty: while statehood rests on people's sovereignty in Switzerland, it rests on parliamentary sovereignty in the UK, on constitutional sovereignty in Germany, etc. (cf. Abromeit 1995).

The fact that society and community, as well as their expression in the nation-state, are not of a fixed character can clearly be seen in the case of the radically different paths that nation building took in Europe. Nations were invented to strengthen states as well as to create states (see above). In the first case the emphasis was on citizenship (*demos*), in the second case on ethnic cohesion (*ethnos*). Of course, even a superficial glimpse at these two different models of the nation-state reveals their character as ideals unrealized in practice. They provide points of reference in order to characterize the various "really" existing blendings of civic and affectual cohesion in individual nation-states. However, as Max Weber (1980) has observed, these blendings are not static. A civic association based on the rationality of shared interests of members with the ensuing creation of abstract yet binding rules, norms, and institutions forms a society. An association of felt togetherness, an association of individuals based on affectual bonds, forms a community. The point is that the two do not simply mingle as such; there is rather an interrelationship between the processes of society formation *(Vergesellschaftung)* and community formation *(Vergemeinschaftung)* (cf. World Society Research Group 2000) under this perspective. The concepts of community and society are by no means outdated today; it rather seems necessary to remind oneself of their basically processual character (*Vergemeinschaftung* and *Vergesellschaftung*) and to utilize this notion in order to analyze *possible* forms of statehood that would transcend the Westphalian model. Put differently, the question is not one of which different forms of society and community formations do exist—forms that then always can be interpreted as deviations from the Westphalian model. Rather, the question is why and how it is that the Westphalian model has proved so successful in asserting a basic congruence of society and community. Uncovering the mode of normative cohesion that is embodied in the Westphalian model can then serve as a means to look into the way in which the modes of interaction between community and society formation change. Thus, there may develop forms of togetherness that do not simply supersede, but rather structurally modify and in the end transcend the Westphalian order (without, of course, being able to judge that to be better or worse). In the following, we would like to argue that the way the Westphalian state has been able to serve as a dominant model of normative cohesion can best be analyzed by pointing to the functions of the boundary in this regard: the main argument is that the territorial boundary as the most distinct formal construction circumscribing the Westphalian state also provides a pragmatic solution to normative paradoxes that are difficult to reconcile in modern thinking and practice (of cosmopolitanism and communitarianism as two normative approaches to world society).

The main issue we are dealing with is the bifurcation of a normative world order that develops with the modern system of states. This normative world order relies on territorial boundaries to negotiate its intrinsic paradoxes and, in this respect, is intimately linked to the Westphalian order of the international system. In formal terms, there is an increasing discrepancy between communal solidarity that is based on and solely related to interaction among individuals on the one hand, and forms of solidarity that are based on rules of abstract reciprocity on the other.

This pattern is not confined to the evolution and differentiation of societies *within* modern nation-states. Since the very idea of a territorial society is one of *outcomes* rather than processes (cf. Luhmann 1997), it is possible to recast the nature of a bifurcated normative world order. The basic problem was—and remains—that during the course of modernization of society, a model of normative cohesion based on the concrete solidarity of *individuals* could no longer be applied to complex social *systems*. The problem was aggravated by the fact that modernization did not even leave the old normative orders in place but—via Enlightenment thinking—challenged them in their very substance by questioning their abstract and mythically removed sources of legitimacy (God, nature, etc.). This development inscribed the fundamental tension into the modern normative world order: the tension between Kantian universalism on the one hand, and the de facto normative integration of the Westphalian order via the nexus of orders, borders, and identities on the other. Though ethical norms are about universality, this universality is never achievable universally.[2] If this is the case, why then not confine this universality to state boundaries and create a particularistic universe inside territorial markers? The Westphalian solution to the tension between the universal validity and the practical applicability of ethical norms was solved by introducing an exclusive layer of social control that effectively limits the normative order by containing it inside national societies. Thus understood, the Westphalian order, not as historic datum, but as a normative form, provides the solution that keeps the social continuum together for quite a while. The sociological fact and normative fiction of a continued unity of the social world in modernity is provided by the installation of territorial boundaries. This international society of states seems increasingly to have outlived its role in this regard. Its parts still inherit the idea of an exclusive sovereignty as the basis for an international order and the very mythical structure of an unquestionable origin of the legitimacy and validity of norms—it thus rests on exactly those foundations that modern thinking sought to abolish.

Viewed in such a way, territoral boundaries are means to process differences and paradoxes that cannot be reconciled for the time being. The Westphalian solution was to clearly distinguish between different nations, states, and societies. This, however, formed only part of the solution. Another part consisted in the assertion of a territorial congruence of nation, state, and society. Given the different evolutionary trajectories of these concepts, it may appear as if the Westphalian solution to the problems of a modern normative world order also includes arresting these very trajectories. Today, however, it becomes more and more impossible to overlook that different trajectories have started to take off in different directions. It would be entirely premature to diagnose an all-encompassing evaporation of the Westphalian normative world order. This order is *not* superseded by an entirely new order as much as the territorial state is *not* superseded by entirely new forms of governance; the same applies to the concepts of political community, nation, etc. These concepts are being transformed into continuing processes of ordering, etatization, *Vergemeinschaftung,* etc. In the course of this development, they do not lose their specific boundaries, but it becomes obvious that these boundaries do not necessarily overlap along territorial or other lines: debordering takes place. And this opens up new spaces in which new forms of normative cohesion, new forms to organize solidarity, can and do emerge (cf. Albert 1999b). This does not refer to a (re)emergence of a framework with which one may hope to cover the entire social world, rather the differences and paradoxes in a normative world order are reshuffled.

Some of these reshufflings become visible already, though as yet more in relation to the question of what "nation" and "national identity" may mean in the future than in relation to the concepts of state or society. However, if we look at national identity as a permanent function of communal and societal discourses, this may serve as an example of how alternatives come up that may also be applied to a transformation of the state. Thus understood, globalization would not constitute a threat to national identity as such but to specific formulations or narratives of this identity. It can be looked at as a new condition under which the old stories about the meaning of belonging to a nation have to be retold differently. And although these retellings await being tied up to a new, comprehensive narrative (if this should be possible at all), some of the new story's ingredients are well known already. First, there is the redefinition of state activities from a demand- to a supply-side-oriented policy. This creates, as mentioned above, incentives for substate entities to develop stronger transnational links, a process that may be accompanied by a new emphasis on subsidiarity. At the same time, national equity schemes are being threatened. While the state stresses national competitiveness, intercommunal solidarity is being weakened as the central state tries to get rid of some of the externalities of its policies by dumping them on the lower level. Second, the deepening of intranational social cleavages under the pressure of structural adjustment is being dramatized by migration, which deepens social cleavages by overlaying them with ethnic dividing lines. Third, local cultures are being leveled by global patterns of communication, consumption, housing, and entertainment, whereas new cultural differences are being constructed through migration and the evolving claim to multiculturalism. As a normative concept, multiculturalism is self-contradictory in that it encourages various social groups to claim a cultural identity, and then asks the population at large to play down the resulting cultural differences in order to keep the society viable. Having to deal with this contradiction creates additional social stress. Fourth, migrant groups form transnational communities that, by establishing cross-territorial links, question the function of territoriality for national identity. At the same time, transnational issue coalitions are gaining in importance as modes of political participation.

Migration without integration and transnational accumulation without national redistribution make international cooperation more difficult and at the same time more urgent. A possible solution may evolve around the idea of debordering the state itself by increased transstate networking. However, just as the fragmenting effects of globalization provoke the question of which values and preferences the *national* stands for, globalization also calls for a dialogue on what the *international* implies as a normative concept. This dialogue will have to be carried out on the national as well as on the international and the world-society levels. Dealing with the national and national identity should be geared toward fostering such a dialogue, not to steer away from it.

CONCLUSION

The preceding observations reveal that the discourses on identity proceed in the context of grave changes in a material as well as a normative world order. This leads McSweeney (1996, 91) to conclude that "the political concepts of interests and legitimacy suggest themselves as being more fruitful analytical tools for understanding and interpreting recent or past events in Europe than identity and societal security." But this only leads us back to the question of why, if identity claims are nothing but political instruments that are being forged by manipulation, this manipulation has been and remains so successful. So we are not in a position to discard identity issues in favor of the analysis of interests and the achievement of legitimacy. The above reflection suggests that the former cannot be understood without studying the latter.

This implies that new cultural representations and constructions of identities are not simply counterbalancing territoriality. They partly remain patched into the territorial representations of modernity. In the same vein, it would be insufficient to view the *normative* as a mere counterforce to the *material*. Rather, the relationship between both is necessarily open-ended. So we are really talking of a changing balance between different elements of present international relations and not of the replacement of one set of elements (for example, the Westphalian order) by another (for example, post-Westphalian order). Under globalization, borders partly continue to serve, or are being reconstructed as battle grounds, while partly also functioning as a medium for conflict resolution and partly as new frontiers for the adaptation of states, societies, and communities to globalization without which the latter could not go on.

Up to now, economic globalization, the revolution in communication and transportation, the proliferation of international organizations, transnational issue coalitions, and transnational communities, as well as the formation of globally homogeneous entertainment patterns continue to blend with localism, regional closure, separatism, and other disruptive spatial practices (Harvey 1989). Thus we may talk of *parochial globalization*. That is a far cry from the cosmopolitan ideals of the Enlightenment, but it may also be as far as we can get. What for some may appear as a new fragmentation between units, in terms of a normative world order, may in fact be a continuing differentiation between interrelated processes of (national and transnational) identity formation, (territorial and nonterritorial) bordering, and (statebound as well as nonstate) ordering. Thus there is ample room for disagreement concerning the quality of the demise or the speed of the transformation of the old order, but, in our understanding, there is nothing inherent in this development that would legitimize analysts to draw far-reaching conclusions about the level of conflict or stability in newly emerging orders. True, we cannot be sure about the direction change will take in the future. But this implies nothing less than that despite systemic differentiation there might be room for politics that make a difference.

NOTES

1. For regulation theory this partition remains a precondition for upholding the capitalist world system.

2. However, see Apel (1988) and Habermas (1992) for attempts to deal with these issues within a universalist theory of ethics.

2

War, Violence, and the Westphalian State System as a Moral Community

RICHARD W. MANSBACH AND FRANKE WILMER

Much of global politics has been constructed on claims that people's dominant political identity is that of citizen/national and that sovereign boundaries demarcate a familiar (and often related) "us" from an alien and other "them." In such a world of billiard ball states, security or the regulation of violence—the raison d'être for the state and its monopoly on the legitimate use of force—consisted of protecting "us" and "our" property and interests against threats generated externally by "them." During the twentieth century, the acceleration of state interdependence, and with it the increasing interpenetration of peoples' identities and interests, has both rendered state boundaries more contestable and the state less effective as a provider of security. These changes are restructuring security institutions as well as their normative foundations. In this chapter, we examine the propositions that (a) the forms of violence the state has aimed to regulate as well as the way in which "problematic violence" has been constructed are changing dramatically, and, in consequence, (b) the management of violence by the state system is being eroded.

The state itself was constituted internally as a moral community—a community of individuals bound by reciprocal moral obligation (civility)—while at the same time, in relations with one another, states formed a kind of international moral community, reflected in the

51

concept of international law as the law among "civilized" nations.[1] This chapter examines how such claims were spread and enforced by the state's superior capacity to wage war while suppressing other identities and other bases for politicizing moral boundaries (such as religion), and how in recent decades war has eroded those same claims, thereby bringing an end to the European era of global politics.

The Westphalian state—as a particular form of social organization—benefited from the changing technology and economics of warfare, while legitimating, limiting, and regulating collective violence, both in interstate relations as well as within its boundaries. In a historical context, the Westphalian system declared illegitimate the unregulated violence of the Thirty Years' War. The Westphalian order was both the agent and structure through which norms delimiting legitimate and illegitimate violence internally and externally were constructed and acted on for several hundred years. City-states, fiefdoms, tribes, confederations, and empires also counted the regulation of violence among their functions, but none did so as effectively or for so long as the state.

The stability of boundaries constituting a moral community depended on an ordered and orderly state system capable of acting decisively in response to problems of violence. As that system decays, claims regarding what is a "good" or "just" war proliferate. The traumas of Bosnia, Rwanda, and Kosovo reveal a growing gap between norms and state-system efforts to manage the actual and threatened violence considered most problematic in the late twentieth century, including terrorism, proliferation of weapons of mass destruction, the violation of human rights within the state, ethnic or communal conflict, and genocide.

The relationship between identity and borders underlies both the process of norm articulation and the kinds of violence identified as problematic for international relations because the construction of moral boundaries presumes normative agreement among actors, expressed as politically relevant identities. Thus, nationalism became entangled with citizenship, and "civilized nations" equated with Western societies. The articulation and application of norms pertaining to violence follow from actors' agreement about how to distinguish "bad" from "good" violence, as well as their willingness to submit to what Hans Kelsen (1945) called the *Grundnorm* (basic norm), a norm of reciprocity or moral equality. Submission to a norm of reciprocity creates a status of moral equality among actors and represents an articulation of identity based on sameness. This, in turn, provides the basis for political community with regulatory authority. The authority to regulate the means of coercion derives from intersubjective agreement about actors' understanding of what constitutes "good" and "bad" violence.

The capacity of Westphalian states to regulate violence is being undermined by the proliferation of new or reformulated identities that do not allow for the intersubjective agreement necessary to constitute a stable moral community. The destabilization of identities obfuscates the boundaries on which moral community relies for consensus and legitimacy, and it is this issue that we now address.

IDENTITIES AND THE FORMATION OF MORAL COMMUNITIES

Until recently, theorizing about identity assumed ascribed characteristics and the "objective" existence of identity categories. Within the past decade, however, interrogation of the identity-conflict relationship has moved theorists to take into account a social constructionist perspective (Nagel 1996). Determining whether objective categories of identity exist or not is less important than understanding the relationship between the processes of identity construction (and maintenance) and political legitimation by presuming that some degree of normative agreement flows from common identity. Struggles over identity therefore have the potential to destabilize both the state and state system.

Any category of difference presumes a category (or in Gramscian terms, a hegemonic identity) of sameness against which difference is measured. Race, ethnicity, and even gender are identity categories that are significant not because of something intrinsic but because of the significance attached to their difference in contrast with a privileged identity. Theorizing about identity, therefore, reveals the cognitive underpinning of "us" and "them" as bases for political action and, we will argue, for legal regulation. Theorizing about identities is further complicated by the fact that identities demarcate psychological rather than territorial space and can be overlapping and intersecting, as well as exclusive (Burton 1984). While attention has been paid to the construction of "otherness" and the consequences of exclusivity for "others," there has been less interest in exploring the significance of "sameness" as a construction with moral consequences (Wilmer 1993). The significance attached to socially constructed sameness provides the foundation for moral boundaries that encompass communities of obligation based on reciprocity and fairness.[2]

First, an explanation of "moral community." We use the term much as do those who focus on moral exclusion (Opotow 1990). It does not connote agreement about a particular moral or ethical code, but rather the belief among members that they are obligated to treat one another on the basis of reciprocity of obligation. Legal philosophers argue about reciprocity as a basis for legal obligation, and we agree with those who see it as an antecedent to legal obligations in a liberal society (Luhmann 1972). Moral communities may be formal (legal), informal (normative), or both. An informal moral community, such as a kinship group, is a "community of caring" whose members feel an obligation to care for one another's well-being and view harm that comes to any member as harming all members. The rhetoric of kinship is often evoked as an imaginary of citizenship in order to legitimate the state as a moral community in matters of common defense. Whether the solidarity that forms the basis for moral community is constructed in terms of class, ethnicity, gender, nationhood, citizenship, kinship, or as the family or community of civilized states, all forms of reciprocal obligation share the presumed or socially constructed bond of sameness as their basis. For this reason, moral communities also function to exclude "others" from obligations of reciprocity and fairness.

By demarcating inclusion on the basis of sameness and exclusion on the basis of difference, moral communities designate boundaries of inside and outside according to which justice is distributed. This applies both to the distribution of justice internationally and internally within a community. One widely accepted internal boundary is illustrated by the allocation of rights and responsibilities on the basis of age—the full range of rights and responsibilities of citizenship do not attach to members of a society until they reach an age of majority or moral competence. Individuals are presumed to mature from childhood into adulthood as morally competent members of a society, at which time they are expected to understand the ethical implications of the rights and responsibilities of citizenship. The adult as morally competent/child as morally incompetent relationship was reproduced both internationally as well as in settler-indigenous relations in the normative construction of colonialism and the "civilizing mission" or "white man's burden," where non-Western peoples were placed under the colonial tutelage of European imperialists (Wilmer 1993; Doty 1996). Similarly, the marginalization of women in patriarchal societies is predicated on the assumption of women's moral inferiority to men, reflected again in language that characterizes women in relation to men as children to adults.

By legitimating systems of obligations and duties attaching to community membership, moral communities justify the monopolization and use of coercion by agents of the community against members who violate the rules attaching to membership. Through the structure of law, the community articulates obligations and consequences for violating them. So long as one fulfills the obligations of citizenship, order is maintained and individuals are (in theory) secured against official use of coercion against them. Violation of obligations may trigger the legitimate use of coercion in the name of law and order, and moral exclusion provides justification for the punishment of those who break the law. Community membership obligates us to refrain from using violence arbitrarily, but if an individual violates that obligation she or he becomes an acceptable target for exclusion. In this way, moral communities are the basis for legitimating (good) violence as a mechanism of enforcement against (bad) violence.[3]

The concept of moral boundaries makes it possible to interrogate the intersection between individual cognition and social order, or the agent-structure connection. How does the individual perception that she or he is a member of a moral community lead to the legitimation of structures in which individuals as agents construct and maintain boundaries within which norms of obligation and consequences for violating them are articulated? How does this process apply to the problem of regulating violence through (a) obligations to refrain from violence among those within a moral community, (b) the designation of certain categories of people as falling outside the boundaries of the community of obligation, (c) the legitimation of violence on behalf of the community as a sanction against internal violations? Finally, how is the regulation of violence affected by the shifting of moral boundaries? For instance, within a state society, eliminating laws that legitimate exclusionary practices affecting women and "minorities" reconfigures the moral boundaries within which justice-as-reciprocity is distributed. In "international relations," the community of "civilized nations" in the seventeenth through nineteenth centuries referred exclusively to European and then European and settler states. However, in the twentieth century, following decolonization, the term is used to include all states (the more so when fashioned to resemble Western-style states and norms) and to single out states charged with violating the terms of international civil order—for example, Germany, Japan, or Iraq for aggression against other states, and Germany, Japan, Yugoslavia (Serbia), and Rwanda for crimes against humanity.

Boundaries between communities of sameness and otherness become problematic when they legitimate political, economic, or social hierarchies and produce relationships of inclusion/exclusion, dominance/submission, and privilege/marginalization. The construction of sameness and otherness determines the distribution of political power, authority, and rights and, in cases of conflict, who is inside and who is outside the boundaries of civic obligation. A state-centric model of global politics emphasizes borders conceived of as vertical barriers separating people living in one territorial location from people living in other locations, entailing what Agnew and Corbridge call "the territorial trap" (Agnew and Corbridge 1995). However, horizontal boundaries are equally, if not more, significant than vertical ones. Stratification based on class, race, nonstate communality, and gender, for example, reflect some of the multiple identities that produce horizontal borders. Ultimately, the way in which boundaries between "us" and "them" are defined and drawn is profoundly related to the way in which violence is legitimated.

In feudal Europe, the overlap among identity-based boundaries and, therefore, political communities meant the absence of a clear identity hierarchy to determine "us" from "them." Without that hierarchy, it was difficult to distinguish legitimate and socially sanctioned violence from illegitimate violence, that is, between war and crime. The legitimacy of emerging European states rested in part on their capacity to manage violence by demarcating the boundaries of legitimate/illegitimate violence and their ability to provide subjects/citizens with security, internal or external, where security is defined as the management of threats to civic order. Indeed, the state provided a territorial basis to fix and enforce boundaries of identity so that the distinction between inside and outside became defensible.

colour

"European," as a geopolitical and cultural identity, emerged as the basis for another level of moral community—the community of "civilized nations," in the language of seventeenth-century international law. Just as violence by European Christianity against Islam (and other non-Christians) was regarded as legitimate in the Middle Ages, so the violence used by Europeans against indigenous "pagans" in the New World and, later, in Asia and Africa was seen as part of a mission to spread "civilization" around the world. Violence "to civilize barbarians" was legitimate, and as imperialism spread, violence by Europeans against non-Western peoples, though debated by international lawyers and theologians such as Bartolemé de las Casas and Juan Ginés Sepúlveda, generally fell beyond the scope of regulation through international norms, being reserved as a matter of domestic jurisdiction.[4] International legal discourse reflected one kind of moral boundary including (European) "civilized nations" and the regulation of violence in their relations through the laws of war (both in terms of the "just war" doctrine as well as the actual conduct of warfare). The same boundary excluded non-European peoples from any such protection.[5]

As the state became the preeminent form of political organization, Europeans were developing technologies that would enable them to engage in unprecedented levels of collective violence (Cohen, Brown, and Organski 1981). Specialized bureaucracies enabled Europe's states to mobilize large populations for interstate war while at the same time pacifying the intrastate arena. Prior to the emergence of the Westphalian state, both in medieval Europe as well as "the chaotic and roving warfare of the so-called wars of religion" (Palmer 1986, 94), it was almost impossible to distinguish clearly between internal and external wars. The porosity of sovereign frontiers in recent decades similarly makes it difficult to distinguish between interstate and civil war, for example, in the Great Lakes region of Africa. Instead of collisions between uniformed armies of states moving across state boundaries, these wars have a "bewildering number of combatants, all with slightly different agendas participating in a group of interconnected wars set in motion by the long-standing enmity between members of the Hutu and Tutsi ethnic groups" (McKinley 1996). In these wars, like the Thirty Years' War, political, social, economic, and religious motives are hopelessly entangled. Like seventeenth-century mercenaries, armed bands in Liberia and Sierra Leone and the Serbian paramilitaries in Kosovo "robbed the countryside on their own behalf" and "collected loot and held prisoners for ransom" (Van Creveld 1991, 50–51). In such wars, there is little distinction between soldiers and civilians. More and more civilians become war's victims, accounting for increasing proportions of war fatalities from 5 percent in World War I and 50 percent in World War II to 95 percent in the 1980s Lebanese Civil War (Barnaby 1988, 98–99).

VIOLENCE, WAR, AND THE WESTPHALIAN STATE

Definitions of the Westphalian state often rely on its monopoly of force. Legal positivists like Austin associate sovereignty with the capacity to command, backed by the threat of force (Murphy and Coleman 1984, 22–23). For political theorists, Hobbes's Leviathan was crucial for keeping peace among subjects. It was the turbulent nature of seventeenth-century English politics that inspired Hobbes's metaphor of the uncivilized state of nature as a "war of all against all," just as civil war in France had inspired Bodin to develop the idea of sovereignty a century earlier. "France in Bodin's time," declares J. L. Brierly, "had been rent by faction and civil war, and . . . the cause of her miseries was the lack of a government strong enough to curb the subversive influences of feudal rivalries and religious intolerance" (1963, 8). By proclaiming the state the final arbiter of legitimate violence, sovereignty was itself constructed as a response to the perception of anarchic violence. Therefore, one might argue that the proliferation of violence in recent years signals a failure of sovereignty, at least as currently constructed.

War in medieval Europe resembled banditry or "private" warfare (in contrast to warfare between Europeans and outsiders), with members of the military caste of knights raiding one another's lands and creating general insecurity throughout Europe. As Adda Bozeman observes, there emerged a "localization of the concepts of war and peace" that "helped to reduce the total incidence of fighting that had disturbed the Western European world" (1960, 272). Centralization of authority and the demarcation between crime and war accompanied growing recognition of a distinction between inside and outside the state and the burgeoning state capacity relative to other political forms to mobilize resources and, therefore, to wage war.

Centralized authority in Europe was accompanied by the displacement of local identities by emerging national identities, evidenced in the spread of national languages, cultural practices, and bounded histories. National identities provided the basis for legitimacy and, therefore, loyalty to the new states, some of which were experiencing civil wars among nobles and religious factions with competing claims to authority. Thus, it was through violence that the state was founded, and critical to its establishment was acquiring a monopoly over legitimate coercion (Cohen, Brown, and Organski 1981).

An equally important consequence of the centralization of authority within states was their growing capacity to channel, limit, and, on occasion, routinize violence among themselves. By the eighteenth century transborder violence in Europe was largely under control, but state regulation of violence outside of Europe was not asserted until the following century. Janice Thomson argues persuasively that the Westphalian states' monopoly over transborder violence is a relatively recent development: "[L]ittle more than a century ago, the state did not monopolize the exercise of coercion beyond its borders. This new state form . . . reflected a redrawing of authority claims such that authority over the use of violence was moved from the nonstate, economic, and international domains and placed in the state, political, and domestic realms of authority" (1994, 11). This slow process was accompanied by the strengthening of state institutions in the nineteenth century. In fact, Thomson argues, states were "reluctant to exert authority and control over nonstate violence" (ibid., 143). They did so because it was necessary in order to overcome some very specific problems "involving fundamental issues of authority" that arose in the course of Europe's outward colonial expansion.

State building entailed the appropriation of inhabitants' loyalties, especially in England and France, and, consequently, identities, so that local forms of identity and community were supplanted by the expansion of top-down socialization processes and new "civic cultures." By the late eighteenth and early nineteenth centuries, popular revolutionary movements began to employ rhetoric that naturalized the merging of nation and state. Identities tied to territorialized states and citizenship within them gradually took precedence over, and in many cases erased, local and nonterritorialized identities delineated by religious and ethnic affiliation. The articulation of moral boundaries was therefore occurring across two dimensions: within the state as civil society in which internal violence was regulated by the state, and across states in relations among European sovereigns as they articulated norms through laws of war as a feature of the "law of civilized nations," which was, as de Vattel declared, "the law of sovereigns" (de Vattel 1970, 100). As the product of interstate agreements, it is hardly surprising that international law legitimated state monopoly on coercion as it codified customary limits on interstate war.[6]

GOOD VIOLENCE AND BAD VIOLENCE

The solution to unregulated violence sweeping across Europe during the Thirty Years' War was to restrict war making to conflicts among states and to "civilize" war with elaborate rules and mechanisms that defined "acceptable" behavior by soldiers and armies toward one another and toward civilians. "Princes were supposed to wage war," argues Van Creveld, "in such a way as to minimize the harm done both to their own soldiers, who deserved humane treatment if they happened to be captured or wounded, and to the civilian population" (1991, 37). In this way, war was rationalized as a means of preventing the "savagery" that characterized the religious strife of previous centuries. In addition to norms regulating war in Europe, limitations were also imposed by straitened taxing powers, weaponry, and logistics. In this way, the Westphalian state during its dynastic period succeeded in constraining violence at home and abroad.

The evolution of norms such as balance of power, as well as those aimed at "civilizing" war in the Geneva and Hague conventions, aimed to shield states, their rulers, and their agents from the consequences of unrestrained violence. Balance-of-power rhetoric rests on the presumption that the emergence of community among sovereign (and civilized) states creates a system of reciprocated obligation. The Prussian civil servant Friedrich von Gentz spoke of balance of power as "that constitution subsisting among neighboring states more or less connected with one another" (1970, 281). Rousseau saw the balance as the result of Europeans' "identity of religion, of moral standard, of international law" (in Forsyth, Keens-Soper, Savigear 1970, 133). As Thomson concludes, "Institutions like neutrality and the balance of power constrained states to behave in particular ways toward other states but they also empowered them to expand their authority and control over even such powerful actors as the mercantile companies" (1994, 150).

In effect, the Westphalian state struck a bargain with its subjects. On the one hand, subjects would provide the state with the material and human resources necessary to fight wars. On the other, the state would demand little of its citizens in wartime and protect them from the ravages of war. Thus, rulers preferred strategies "which in wartime interfered as little as possible with civilian life" (Palmer 1986, 92). If civilians took up arms, as they did in Spain against Napoleon, they were viewed as criminals, or worse, as rebels, and could expect no mercy. Interstate norms limiting war and creating mutual obligations among states contrasted dramatically with the absence of limitations on violence between the surrogates of states and substate or nonstate individuals or groups. Identities such as "Catholic" or "European" counted for more than common citizenship, and such identities produced boundaries among people that had little to do with the frontiers of states. The treatment of religious dissidents such as France's Albigensians, indigenous tribal peoples such as North America's Indians and New Zealand's Maoris, or substate "rebels" such as the Scottish clans that came out for Charles Stuart in 1745, were accorded few of the rights that soldiers in national armies accorded one another. Since indigenous peoples, as Van Creveld observes, "did not know the state and its sharply-drawn division between government, army, and people," they "were automatically declared to be bandits."[7]

Thus, the Spanish conquistadors mercilessly exploited the Indians in the New World, looking upon them as uncivilized wards of Christian Spain and depicting them as little better than beasts. Only when missionaries like the Dominican Francisco de Vitoria, backed by the monarchy, declared that the indigenous people of the Americas had rights did their situation improve.[8] By the Laws of Burgos (1512) and the New Laws (1542), relations between Spain and the Indians were codified in a relationship marked by the moral superiority of Europeans and the moral inferiority of indigenous peoples.

Ironically, though the twentieth century opened with the Hague conferences of 1899 and 1906 where delegates celebrated a "century of peace," believing war to have become both rare and "civilized," as the century progressed the actual conduct of war was marked by more and more indiscriminate violence. World Wars I and II saw the growing involvement and victimization of civilians in war as resistance fighters, war industrial workers, prisoners in concentration camps, and casualties in urban bombings. Despite efforts to maintain the fictitious distinction between combatants and noncombatants, technology and ideology conspired to erase it. The bargain originally struck by the Westphalian state with its citizens had begun to unravel.

VIOLENCE AND THE EROSION OF STATE AUTHORITY

If the growth of state authority, linked to its monopoly on coercion and identity and consequent deepening of loyalty to the state, was aimed at achieving the limitation and rationalization of war, so the erosion of state authority and the proliferation of other identities and legitimating ideologies has been accompanied by an erosion of restraints on violence and its decoupling from political purpose. As early as the French Revolution, the state's claim to monopolize violence at home and abroad and the distinction between inside and outside enshrined in sovereignty were challenged. Wedded to state sovereignty, nationalism reinforced the vertical boundaries among peoples, reduced the flexibility of governing elites in foreign affairs, and, by giving the state the only legitimate license to kill on behalf of its nationals, intensified and broadened the scale of warfare.

To understand the link between declining state authority, the revival of old identities, and the proliferation of new ones requires a more critical consideration of how power becomes authority. The link is through identity, and identity as sameness provides basis for moral community, which in turn legitimates the regulation of behavior by members of the community. The Westphalian state was a product of social and political forces arising from the particular experience of European society. It was the state's ability to make claims on homogenizing national identities in the sixteenth and seventeenth centuries that legitimized the state's claim to monopolize coercion, initially the sovereign's paternalistic claim to the loyalty of his children-subjects.

Problematic international violence today can be thought of as falling into five categories: (a) violence by the state, (b) violence between or among states, (c) violence among nonstate actors, (d) antistate violence, and (e) anarchistic and nihilistic violence against the state system as a whole. By taking into account the strength of norm-creating boundaries, we can understand how and why some of these forms of violence are more and some less regulated under present conceptions of authority.

We begin with an emerging moral community among European states, a community among sovereign equals subscribing to the norm of reciprocity. Violence by the state within the state is relatively un-regulated, with the exceptions noted below. It is (and the analogy with a construction of the private/public distinction should be noted) a matter of "domestic jurisdiction." The "moral community of [Euro-pean] states" agreed on the norm of nonintervention in one an-other's internal affairs. This reflects the assumption that states con-stituted boundaries of moral community internally, where citizens "contracted" as equals to construct legally binding rules of behavior on the basis of an internal norm of reciprocity. The regulation of in-terstate violence, however, has been the main subject of founding documents for both the League of Nations and the United Nations, as well as both customary and positive laws of warfare and the Kellogg-Briand Pact. "Civilization" served as the ideological basis for a pan-European or Western identity at the core of an emerging "world order" and succeeded in articulating international norms regulating interstate violence, while violence among nonstate actors and antistate violence remained within the domestic sphere of juris-diction. In regulating violence by states, a distinction was made be-tween aggression and self-defense. Today, there are three bases on which a state may legitimately use force externally: as an act of self-defense, as an act of collective self-defense, or as a participant in an enforcement action. In all three cases, the use of force is still restrained by a requirement to comply with the rules of warfare.

Following the Holocaust, progress was made toward expanding the regulation of violence beyond norms pertaining to noncombat-ants and prisoners of war during a war to the general protection of individuals against state abuses through "universal" human rights. For the first time, the regulation of violence was extended into the shielded realm of state domestic jurisdiction, a condition further un-derscored by NATO's claim of legitimacy in the 1999 intervention against Yugoslavia on behalf of Kosovar Albanians. In addition to designating acts of aggression as the "crime" of war, individual state agents could be held accountable for "crimes against humanity." State monopoly over coercion was thus limited both by an obligation to refrain from aggression against other states as well as from using force to harm civilians.

Because of the state-centric nature of the present system, the regulation of violence among nonstate actors as well as antistate violence by nonstate actors remains in something of a normative gray area. Antistate violence in the form of civil war is an area in which normative agreement has long been elusive in international law (Arend and Beck 1994). No progress could be made during the Cold War since U.S.-Soviet competition often took the form of one superpower or the other "assisting" the state in securing itself against insurrection or providing support for antistate actors or "freedom fighters." Recent research suggests that the main arena for antistate war has shifted from the Global North to the Global South (Kane 1995). There is an area, however, in which normative agreement regarding antistate and anti(state)system violence seem to converge—terrorism. Like piracy, terrorism viewed from the perspective of the state constitutes a threat to the security of all states. Unlike piracy, terrorism is primarily a political strategy used to strike at both individual states as well as the state system. The IRA, for example, practices antistate terrorism, while most anti-U.S. terrorism protests the dominance of the U.S. and Western states in the state system. The proliferation of weapons of mass destruction also represents a kind of antisystem violence or threat, aimed, like some forms of terrorism, at challenging the systemic status quo.

More recently, the erosion of state authority has accelerated changes in the nature of political violence. James Rosenau argues that though we are confronted by "global changes that may amount to a world crisis of authority" (1984, 236), we remain wedded to a "static conception of authority structures, both within and between societies" (ibid., 251). In his view, this breakdown of authority is one of several factors that have fundamentally altered global politics. "Indeed, for those who see the crisis of authority as deep-seated and enduring, it no longer seems compelling to refer to the world as a State system" (ibid., 263–64).

Nowhere is Rosenau's conclusion more apt than in the vast majority of non-European states today, particularly postcolonial states. In these "late" states, the consolidation of identity and the assertion of centralized authority did not precede the construction of durable political boundaries. With artificial boundaries originally imposed by external masters, these states are increasingly characterized by internal and transnational warfare among factions making competing claims to rule based on incompatible identities and challenging existing borders. The problem of ethnic conflict is really a problem of shifting identity boundaries in a system created by Europeans to reinforce territorial claims. In many of these states, ruling elites are viewed as representing and perpetuating the privileges of a tribal, family, or regional faction rather than as surrogates for a unifying national identity. Under these conditions, elite claims to monopolize coercive force are unpersuasive, and the distinction between the official armed forces of the state and other armed groups breaks down.

The erosion of state authority heralds the emergence of new authority structures and the growing importance of other forms of governance besides that of Rosenau's sovereignty-bound actors. Global politics, as in earlier epochs, involves an extensive cast of sovereignty-free actors—"multinational corporations, ethnic groups, bureaucratic agencies, political parties, subnational governments, transnational societies, international organizations, and a host of other types of collectivities" (Rosenau 1990, 36). No longer is the Westphalian state system the only game in town.

IF SO, THEN WHAT?

As states are enfeebled and the distinction between inside and outside erodes, what are the options for developing more effective strategies for managing global violence? We suggest three possibilities, all of which assume a truncated state in which citizens share loyalties among a variety of political collectivities and the borders of which provide only one of potentially many boundaries between "us" and "them." The first entails a restructured state, most likely along the lines of neoclassical liberalism; the second is restructuring the global system and providing a greater role for nonstate and interstate institutions; and the last, escalating chaos through the incapacity of the system to manage problematic violence in areas falling beyond the scope of state authority as presently constructed. In reality, the world may feature elements of some or all of these, with different regions reflecting more of one or the other. The first two require adjusting the boundaries of moral community within and among states, which will entail rethinking state sovereignty and including non-Western perspectives in the construction of world order.

With the first possibility, the link between state and identity is weakened, and the state assumes a utilitarian role, a kind of institutionalized referee impartially enforcing the rules of the game. The state defines jurisdictional boundaries that are significant mainly for trying to manage economic markets and that assure equality of opportunity for citizens. Evidence for this possibility can be seen in the growing emphasis in Western political life on regarding politics mainly in terms of allocating resources according to consensual values. One might conceive this tendency less as a change in the state than as a movement from state to market sovereignty or the hegemony of "transnational liberalism" (Agnew and Corbridge 1995, 164–207).

What it "means" to be American or Canadian or Chinese is less important than that individuals are entitled to more or less equal life chances, which the state is bound to establish and protect, coupled with majoritarian democracy and minority rights. In this model, Westphalian states will evolve as did America's states: they were once powerful expressions of identity, but interstate economic integration and mobility relegated them to the role of managing the distribution of local resources. Under such conditions, the Westphalian state would have the limited role of managing access to economic and educational resources within an environment of equal opportunity and would distribute public goods according to the rules of majoritarian democracy while protecting the right of dissent. Since allocating resources presumes agreement over values, this version of the limited state requires an informed citizenry with access to multiple channels of political discourse and a pluralistic constellation of mediating associations.

For neoliberals, war is a waste of resources that disrupts the market; theirs is still the world of Norman Angell. Where the threat of violence remains high—as in America's urban centers—the causes can be traced to the failure of societies to satisfy the requirements of the liberal model.[9] In the case of America's race relations, minorities do not think the state provides equal life chances, and the case points to the failure of the liberal model to take account of how identity, however artificial, can legitimize raw power. However much liberals may wish that all citizens had the same motivations and incentives, identity makes this improbable. As a result, liberalism cannot cope effectively either with the integrating forces of globalism or the fragmenting impact of subnational and transnational identities. Recognizing this, Michael Sandel deplores the disappearance of civic virtue in defining citizenship:

> The growing aspiration for the public expression of communal identities reflects a yearning for political arrangements that can situate people in a world increasingly governed by vast and distant forces. For a time the nation-state promised to answer this yearning, to provide the link between identity and self-rule.... The nation-state laid claim to the allegiance of its citizens on the ground that its exercise of sovereignty expressed their collective identity. In the contemporary world, however, this claim is losing its force. (Sandel 1996, 74)

Even without the threat of civil violence, the problem of external violence remains. The prospect that a liberal state could manage external violence lies in the improbable Kantian hope that all states could be restructured along liberal lines. In sum, the liberal solution makes the dubious assumption that individuals will abandon other identities in favor of republican citizenship. The model also makes the unlikely assumption that a liberal state can or will accommodate identity groups who have irreconcilable differences regarding the values that underlie resource allocation.

A second possibility is one in which intergovernmental organizations like the United Nations, along with regional regimes or even former colonial powers, assume an active interventionist role in restoring peace, promoting reconciliation in postconflict environments, and reconstructing state institutions.[10] Here, the state in which such intervention takes place is also restructured, but the impetus for restructuring arises from the norms and institutions of interstate and transnational collaboration. United Nations involvement in Somalia, Bosnia, and especially Cambodia, in cooperation with humanitarian groups, illustrates what is meant here, as to some extent does IMF conditionality. The second model is a variation on the first, with intervention legitimated by international norms compelling states to construct majoritarian institutions, protect minority rights, and take responsibility for establishing rules of distributional fairness.[11] It assumes that norms that already exist for the management of external violence in the form of *jus in bello* (law during war), *jus ad bella* (legal reasons for going to war), and *jus contra belum* (laws against war) are still in force.

Because sovereignty precludes legal interference in domestic politics, the norms regarding international responses to civil wars are less developed than those pertaining to interstate war, offering little more than guidelines for the variety of repertoires available to the international community. Norms regarding the right of a state to request assistance from other states to secure itself against attack or to pursue collective self-defense (and therefore the legitimate use of force with the assistance of third parties) have left civil wars a gray area of international law. This was apparent in the early stages of conflict in the former Yugoslavia. Equally unclear is the issue of humanitarian intervention, as reflected in the Kosovo conundrum. There remains a need to articulate consistent norms that lead to the development of guidelines in determining appropriate actions for outsiders in civil wars.

More serious than the absence of institutional authority and enforcement capacity in realizing this model is the absence of political will among states to allow non-Westphalian institutions to act authoritatively to manage the use of force during interstate, transstate, or intrastate war. Neither human-rights norms nor the laws of war have been subjects of enforcement, with the exception of the Nuremberg and Tokyo tribunals after World War II and, some half century later, the ineffective efforts to bring war criminals to justice in Bosnia and Rwanda. All legal regulation relies on the existence of sufficient political will to enforce norms and support institutional development to this end.

A variant of the second model involves providing a greater role for nongovernmental organizations in efforts to manage violence. Already a variety of NGOs like Doctors without Borders provide humanitarian relief for civilian victims of civil violence. A proposal to make the UN Trusteeship Council a forum for indigenous peoples would permit representatives of such peoples to discuss their status and seek redress for their grievances against states without violence (Nerfin 1991). Such proposals aim to increase NGO participation as a way to reduce conflict and its consequences. Another way to involve NGOs is utilizing strategies of conflict management and resolution being developed in academic settings (Birkhoff, Mitchell, and Schirch 1995).

A third possibility is an extended period of almost unimaginable chaos that would raise public anxiety and encourage authoritarian "solutions" of the sort imposed in Uruguay and Argentina in the 1970s. As states are forced to share authority with or surrender it to other collectivities, what will the world look like? Kaplan describes "the last map" in apocalyptic terms:

> Imagine cartography in three dimensions, as if in a hologram. In this hologram would be the overlapping sediments of group and other identities atop the merely two-dimensional color markings of city-states and the remaining nations, themselves confused in places by shadowy tentacles, hovering overhead, indicating the power of drug cartels, mafias, and private security agencies. Instead of borders, there would be moving "centers" of power, as in the Middle Ages. . . . Henceforward the map of the world will never be static. This future map, in a sense, will be an ever-mutating representation of chaos. (1994, 75)

These models do not exhaust possible futures, and they are not mutually exclusive. Indeed, there is evidence of all three in contemporary global politics. Thus, it is time to look with fresh eyes at the social changes that underlie contemporary global violence and the piecemeal efforts to manage it. It makes little sense to continue debating whether sovereignty is eroding, as if this were a discoverable truth, but instead to acknowledge that Westphalian states are less and less able to accomplish the most basic task for which they were designed—conflict management. This shifts the discussion from a theoretical plane to a practical one, thereby linking the abstract question of "what is happening to the state?" to the study of institutions to cope with new forms of violence.

CONCLUSION

This chapter has examined how changes in warfare accompanied the evolution of the Westphalian state. We have seen how the state was a partial answer to the unlimited war that raged across Europe during the seventeenth century and how the capacity of Europe's states to organize violence allowed Europeans to conquer non-European political forms. We have also seen how the state system demarcated a moral community of "civilized" Europeans from "uncivilized" others, and how the identity of "citizen" produced the "sovereign" borders *between* Europe's states. The European era of global politics, then, was an order based on states. That order is vanishing, partly as a result of changing identities and the alternative boundaries they expose. We do not yet know what the new global order will look like, but we reviewed three possibilities, all premised on a world of multiple and overlapping identities and loyalties and a complex network of overlapping borders.

The erosion of state authority and the revival or intensification of identities that compete with state citizenship are at least partly responsible for the increasing frequency of warfare that bears little resemblance to the Clausewitzian ideal. Overwhelmed by virulent ethnic and tribal jealousies and violent memories, as well as poverty and environmental disaster, the fabric of many states is unraveling. As Van Creveld declares, "Once the legal monopoly of armed force, long claimed by the state, is wrested out of its hands, existing distinctions between war and crime will break" (1991, 204). Unfortunately, analyses of warfare continue to focus separately on interstate war and civil violence, failing to recognize that in many instances they have merged. Unlike past wars, violence today is subject to few limitations, may be initiated by nonstate groups, fails to distinguish between soldiers and citizens, lacks clear political objectives, merges with crime, and may be organized in nonterritorial ways.

It was in response to such war that Hugo Grotius wrote in 1625, "Throughout the Christian world I observed a lack of restraint in relation to war, such as even barbarous races should be ashamed of; I observed that men rush to arms for slight causes, or no cause at all, and that when arms have once been taken up there is no longer any respect for law, divine or human; it is as if... frenzy had openly been let loose for the committing of all crimes" (1957, 21). His description could fit today's wars from Sierra Leone to Kosovo. Who, then, will be the next Grotius?

NOTES

1. Internally, the state-as-society was of course hierarchically structured according to a complex system of cross-cutting identities and cleavages, such as ethnic identity, class, gender, and religion, so that in actuality reciprocity applied among those similarly situated within the hierarchy.

2. Karl Deutsch et al. (1957) called this a "pluralistic security community." In such a community, widespread communication expands common tastes, memories, and perceptions. Elites empathize with one another.

3. "Good" violence may serve the interests of dominant actors, and "bad" violence may harm their interests, but when these are translated into normative terms, and particularly when norms are codified as regulation or law, they are constructed qualitatively.

4. Although the Westphalian state is our topic here, boundaries between inside and outside have existed in other cultural-historical contexts.

5. The debate among lawyers and theologians eventually came to rest on the notion that a war conducted to Christianize a pagan people was "just" (Anaya 1996).

6. The 1933 Montevideo conference, as well as the Buenos Aires (1936) and Lima (1938) conferences laid out the rights and duties of states, including the states' right to exist and defend themselves against internal or external foes.

7. Van Creveld 1991, 41. In many respects, the state regarded women as it did indigenous peoples, characterizing both as children or wards whose domination was necessary to their moral development. The state maintained patriarchy as an authoritative structure for both the public and private social orders. Thus, it is not surprising that violence against women and children was not a subject of institutional regulation until recently.

8. Vitoria argued that under natural law the Indians were free people who had owned land before the Spaniards arrived. See von Glahn (1996, 25–26).

9. Racial conflict arguably reflects the problem that certain identities generate fundamentally different values regarding resource allocation that majoritarian rule cannot resolve.

10. Since the distinction between domestic and international politics has broken down, Article 2, paragraph 7 of the UN Charter is increasingly ignored, most recently in NATO's bombing of Kosovo. In the case of failed states, William Pfaff advances the controversial idea of "disinterested neocolonialism." See Pfaff (1995, 2–6).

11. To some extent these are the aims of the two International Covenants on Civil and Political Rights and Economic, Social, and Cultural Rights.

3

(B)orders and (Dis)orders: The Role of Moral Authority in Global Politics

RONNIE D. LIPSCHUTZ

The War over Kosovo is history! The Allies won! The Kosovars re-venged! Serbia punished! Justice served! Peace in our time! Right? Perhaps. In this chapter, I propose that standard arguments about geopolitical stability, human rights violations, and "rogue" states provide an insufficient explanation for NATO's decision to launch the Fifth Balkan War. Rather, the rationale is to be found, as Foucault might have put it, in a Western (and especially American) drive to impose its morality on nonbelievers through "discipline and punish(ment)." By bombing the remnants of Yugoslavia into submission, the NATO allies redrew the boundaries of market morality, bringing Kosovo in and leaving Serbia out. This specific episode is not an aberration, either. Indeed, it is in the very nature of the state to seek maintenance and restoration of the borders of order, both internal and external. Without a specific *moralpolitik* as a guide to keep out the dangerous world, chaos (it is thought) will surely follow. Such tendencies to disorder must be disciplined, and it is through disciplinary deterrence that this is accomplished.

I begin this chapter with a discussion of one longstanding yet so far ill-fated effort to protect the West from immoral Others, the Strategic Defense Initiative. I then turn to a brief review of antecedents to the nation-state prior to 1648, with a specific focus on the ways in which states, as constituted following the Thirty Years' War, functioned as absolutist moral authorities, and the way in which the subsequent emergence of nationalism—the civil religion of the state—constituted a new source of moral authority. Following this, I examine the emerging contradiction between the moralities of nationalism and the rise of liberal individualism, and the way in which, more recently, the United States has attempted to impose its global moral authority through what I call "disciplinary deterrence." Finally, I address the collapse of state-centered moral authority in the New World Order of global liberalization and Western efforts to maintain the borders of moral order through the War over Kosovo.

SHIELDS UP, SCOTTY!

On March 3, 1983, President Ronald Reagan appeared on U.S. national television to announce a new program designed to protect the United States against the threat of a first-strike attack by Soviet nuclear-tipped intercontinental ballistic missiles. The Strategic Defense Initiative (SDI), or "Star Wars" as it was almost immediately tagged by its detractors, was proffered as a means of overcoming the moral dilemma inherent in Mutually Assured Destruction (MAD): the holding hostage of a people to potential nuclear annihilation as a means of preventing the Soviet Union from even contemplating such an attack. MAD had already created political madness throughout American and European politics, manifested most clearly in the Nuclear Freeze movement, the Catholic bishops' statement on nuclear weapons, and massive protests against emplacement of medium-range "Euromissiles" throughout Western Europe (Meyer 1990; Wirls 1992). Reagan, seizing on citizens' fears of nuclear holocaust, offered SDI as an alternative means of protecting and preserving them, thereby attempting to render the arguments of freezeniks, bishops, and others ineffective and impotent.

Most critics of SDI, however, chose to contest it not on moral grounds but rather on technological ones, claiming it to be quite impossible with then-current capabilities. This critique, they hoped, would blast to bits what they saw as a dangerous and destabilizing attempt to gain a viable first-strike capability against the USSR. But in the technological criticism lay an insoluble dilemma: inasmuch as one could never prove conclusively that an effective shield could never be built, how could one justify not going ahead with the project (as we now see in American debates over ballistic missile defense)? Ultimately, the defense sectors of the United States and its allies managed to absorb tens of billions of dollars in a largely fruitless attempt to develop the required technologies. Failure has not deterred various parties from continuing to argue that a strategic defense system against a few rogue missiles is both feasible and desirable (Rowny 1997) or the U.S. Congress and Clinton administration from pressing ahead with yet another antiballistic missile program.

What was largely ignored in the fracas over SDI was its essentially moral function, intended to provide an impenetrable shield not so much against nuclear missiles, rogues, or accidental wars as against notions of detente, disarmament, and the Devil. In offering the vision of a zone liberated from nuclear nightmares, Ronald Reagan was also promising to build a barrier that would redraw the wavering lines between the Free World and its unfree doppelgänger, between democracy and totalitarianism, between the "City on the Hill" and the "Evil Empire," between the saved and the damned. Indeed, SDI was a moral statement, but, more than that, it was also a reimagining and reinforcing of the borders between nations, between authorized and forbidden identities, between permitted order and feared disorder.

1989 and all that destroyed utterly and finally this imagined borderline, and globalization opened the American people up to all sorts of pernicious, malevolent, and immoral forces, beliefs, and disorderly tendencies; it is no wonder that, subsequently, the domestic politics of morality have become so pronounced in the United States and full of inconsistencies—such as "get the government off of our backs but into the bedrooms of teenage mothers"—in the effort to restore the bulwarks against the Outside. But paradoxically, I would argue that the fundamental causal explanations for such apparently contradictory stands are to be found not in domestic politics, in the culture wars between Republicans and Democrats, as is conventionally thought, but in the very nature of the contemporary nation-state itself and its place in the so-called international system. Far from being amoral, as is so often claimed by realists, state behavior, as encoded in the language and practices of world politics, nationalism, state-centricity, and anarchy, exemplifies a bounded morality in the extreme, with each unit representing a self-contained, exclusionary "moralstaat," imposing on its inhabitants a well-defined and orderly identity.

How can this be? After all, in international relations theory the conventional perspective on the nation-state is largely a functionalist one. The state serves to protect itself and its citizens against external enemies and to defend the sanctity of contracts and property rights from internal ones. Morality, as George Kennan (1985/86) and others have never tired of telling us, should play no role in realpolitik, for to allow it to enter into foreign policy considerations is to risk both safety and credibility. But can the state stand simply for the protection of material things and nothing else? After all, the essential constitutive element of the nation-state—its individual nation—stands for and demands the eternal continuity of its specific ontological purposes and values. Conversely, the disappearance of these purposes and values, whether in war or peace, represents a mortal disruption of the nation's contained identity as well as the authority and legitimacy of its state and mission. But circumstances have changed, I argue: with democratization and globalization, identities have spilled increasingly across borders, and national discipline has come under both internal and external threat. In response to this dilemma, the borders of morality are being drawn ever wider even as states become weaker and, in some instances, smaller; in global politics, the morality of market civilization is replacing the morality of the state. To explain this phenomenon, we must return to the days of yesteryear, before the West was One.

WHAT WAS WESTPHALIA?

For most international relations (IR) scholars and the bulk of IR theory, the defining moment of contemporary world politics was 1648, when the Treaty of Westphalia brought an end to the Thirty Years' War and imagined the nation-state into existence; as David Campbell (1992, 47) critically observes, accounts of this history "offer nothing less than an edifying tale of modernization in which we witness the overcoming of chaos and the establishment of order through the rise of sovereign states." There is good reason to believe that the signers of Westphalia, as well as its predecessor Augsburg, had nothing of this sort in mind at the time; it is only through the contingent and contextual lenses of subsequent centuries that such an orderly meaning was imposed on those events and treaties.

Nevertheless, this teleological story offers us two central signifiers: anarchy and sovereignty. Through anarchy, we are told, the princes who put their names to the document agreed that the Roman Catholic Church would no longer stand as a universal authority over them. Through sovereignty, each prince would come to constitute the highest authority within the borders of each state and, enjoined from interfering in the affairs of any other, would have no authority anywhere else. This state of affairs, with its apparent distinction between an internal order imposed by each prince and external disorder as regarded by each prince, was subsequently reified through realist interpretations of the writings of Hobbes, Rousseau, and others (Walker 1993).

The princes, however, were probably not very obsessed about the inside/outside distinction (certainly not to the degree we are today); we might say that they were more concerned with family matters. Indeed, the map of sixteenth- and seventeenth-century Europe shows that relations between polities were clearly more intrafamilial than interstate. More than this, relations within domestic orders—often based in noncontiguous lands scattered about the continent—had as much to do with which branch and member of a family would rule as the specific religion of each branch or individual (a point best illustrated by the intrafamilial wars among British royalty and nobility) (Bendix 1978).

Hence, while Westphalia did not put an end to such intrafamily squabbles, it did for the most part do away with the remaining vestiges of feudal authority, replacing that (dis)order with a clear hierarchy that placed prince or king above duke and lord, and invoking the moral authority of God, whether Protestant or Catholic, to bless and legitimate the new arrangement throughout Europe. Westphalia, in other words, was a social contract for European society, not for European states. To be sure, it lacked many of the elements of domestic orders, including a sovereign, but it substituted moral principles for a ruler. Those principles were frequently violated (although probably more often observed than not), but they nonetheless formed the basis for a continent-wide society with which its rulers identified (Mayall 1990, especially chapter 2).

It is important to recognize here the significance of this social contract and its implications for the modern myth of 1648. Inasmuch as the practices that followed the treaty were centered on conflicts and alliances among families and their myriad branches and not among well-defined, territorially distinct units, international relations as we understand them today were not a result of Westphalia. There were, of course, no nation-states as such and the practical basis for identity among those who had a stake in power and authority—if such a thing even existed—was certainly not the realm of the sovereign but rather the sovereign him- or herself.

Not altogether accidentally, contemporary mainstream IR theorists have been little concerned with the domestic implications of anarchy and sovereignty and have, rather, addressed the functional significance of these practices for relations among states. Hence, anarchy is said to imply self-help or self-protection, while sovereignty is said to imply self-interest or, in its modern mode, accumulation (Inayatullah 1996). I will not belabor these two points, inasmuch as they are the staple of every IR text published over the past one hundred years. I would point out, however, that as practices both concepts presuppose modes of transnational regulation rather than the complete absence of rules and norms so often associated with them (Buzan 1991). More than this, both can be regarded as expressions of a state-centric morality that presumes a legitimate order within and an illegitimate disorder without.

The first point is best seen in Kenneth Waltz's well-known (and flawed) invocation of the market as a structurally anarchic parallel to international politics (Waltz 1979). In invoking the headless market, Waltz draws on Adam Smith's famous "invisible hand" to explain outcomes without concluding that the "invisible foot" of international politics will produce anything like the orderly outcome posited by Smith. The error committed by Waltz is to regard markets and international politics as self-regulating, driven by no more than self-interest or power (Smith believed that religion would temper passions and hunger).

As social institutions, markets are subject to both implicit and explicit regulations. The market is, first of all, governed by the command "Thou shalt not kill." Other rules follow. Walter Russell Mead makes this point nicely in relation to airports and air travel, "Cutthroat competition between airlines coexists with common adherence to traffic and safety regulations without which airport operations would not be possible" (1995/96, 13). So it is between states: the two principles of anarchy and sovereignty are both constitutive of the international system and regulative of it, and they constitute moral boundaries for the state that preserve the fiction of international (dis)order and domestic order (Brown 1992, chapter 5).

It is also clear, on reflection, that sovereignty and anarchy have moral and, in consequence, legal implications for domestic as well as international politics. As Hobbes put it, "[T]he multitude so united in one person, is called a *Commonwealth,* in Latin *Civitas.* This is the generation of that great *Leviathan,* or rather, to speak more reverently, of that mortal god, to which we owe under the immortal God, our peace and defense" (1962, 132).

By establishing borders between states and permitting rulers to be sovereign within them, princes were granted the right to establish within their jurisdictions autonomous systems of law with both functional and moral content. These systems enjoined certain activities in order to prevent consequences that would be disruptive of the order of the state—that is, order as the way things should be according to the particular prince's vision. Or, as Hobbes argued, "But when a covenant is made, then to break it is unjust: and the definition of *Injustice,* is no other than the not performance of covenant" (1962, 113). Violation of the covenant is, therefore, not simply the breaking of the law; it is a repudiation of the underlying moral code of the society.

Hobbes argued that coercive power, entrusted to Leviathan, was necessary to ensure "performance of covenant" and the safety and security of each man who subscribed to that covenant. But even though the seventeenth century was quite violent, overt coercion was still relatively uncommon. Rather, it was the possibility of discipline and ostracism by the state (and the other subscribers to the covenant) as a result of a violation of order, and not repeated day-to-day punishment, that kept subjects from violating the prince's laws or the social contract. Most, if not all, of the legal systems of the time acknowledged, moreover, the hegemony of Christianity—later manifested in the divine right of kings—even if they disagreed on how the religion was to be practiced. Hence, although princes opposed a universal morality or empire that could impose sanctions on them against their wills, they sought to foster such an order within their own jurisdictions, based on their right to do so under God.

The fact that war and interstate violence among princes did not cease after Westphalia does not, however, mean that morality was absent between them or that combatants were motivated by merely functional needs. As I suggested above, the moral basis of a political entity—its ontology—provides a justificaium for its existence as well as an implication that other entities are morally illegitimate if they reject the ontology of the first. John Ruggie (1989, 28) has argued that Westphalia defined who had the right to act as a power, thereby including within its purview the numerous small and weak German territories, but the treaty further acknowledged both a moral entitlement to existence for these units and the right of each prince to impose his specific morality on his subjects within the borders of his rule (however physically disaggregated that might have been).

Westphalia did not, however, command that each prince recognize the morality or legitimacy of others or their rule. So while war and interstate violence were proscribed for specifically religious reasons (i.e., conversion), they nonetheless remained moral as well as material events. To be conquered was punishment for immoral domestic beliefs and practices; to conquer was reward for moral domestic beliefs and practices.[1] By agreement, therefore, although Westphalia commanded domestic morality and international amorality (the latter a rule rather than a condition), this did not prevent princes from trying to extend the boundaries of their domestic morality to engulf the domains of other, "immoral" princes.

The original Westphalian system lasted only about 150 years, if that long. Although the royal sovereign was invested with authority via a mysterious God, Enlightenment efforts to introduce rationalism into rule succeeded all too well, especially in Western Europe. Whereas some of the early empirical scientists, such as Newton, saw their work as illuminating the workings of a universe created by God, others took a more physicalist view. Gradually, religious morality was undermined by scientific experimentation and explanation, and philosophers and theorists subsequently sought to justify political order by reference to nature (which some still equated with God, albeit a distant one). From this tendency there emerged what came to be called "nationalism."

FROM CORPUS CHRISTI TO CORPUS POLITICUM

The first true nation-states, it is generally agreed, were Britain and France. In Britain, the nation emerged out of the civil war of the seventeenth century as Parliament fought with the king over the right

of rule and the power of the purse. The Puritan revolution represented an effort to impose on the state a moral order without external temporal sources or referents. Hence, the Puritans presented
Rome and its adherents (including, putatively, the sovereign) as the
mortal enemies of Cromwell's Commonwealth and England. This
effort to purify the body politic of religious heresy could not succeed,
however, so long as heretics could be neither expelled nor extermi-
nated (a problem resonant even today). The Restoration, which put
Charles II on the British throne, was as much a recognition of the
intractability of the moral exclusion of a portion of the body politic
itself as a reaction against the harshness of the Commonwealth itself. The emergence of the British nation during the following century—and the renewal of war with France during the 1700s—redrew the moral boundaries of society at the edges of the state, and
established individual loyalty to king and country as a value above
all others.

In France, the Revolution launched a process whereby the source
of state legitimacy was transferred from the discredited sovereign to
the people. The French nation did not, however, attempt to establish
a new moral order; that was left to the varied and successive leader-
ships in the two centuries that followed. But the French Revolution
did mark a major change in the ontology of the domestic moral
order. Whereas the princely state derived authority from God, the
nation-state derived its authority from a "natural" entity called the
"nation." Enlightened rationalism sought explanations for the workings of the universe in science, and even Hobbes looked here to explain politics and provide a model for the Commonwealth. What
could be more logical than to invoke nature to explain the origins of
the nation? And if such explanations were to be found in nature,
did this not mean that the nation was both good and right? By the
end of the nineteenth century, even though the very concept of nation was less than a century old, nations had been transmogrified
into constructs whose origins were lost in the dim mists of antiquity,
but whose continuity was vindicated by distorted theories of survival of the fittest.

This new age of moral imperialism was rooted in Darwin's ideas
about natural selection but extended from individual organisms as
members of species to states (Darwin himself had no truck with
these ideas). As Simon Dalby puts it, "[S]tates were conceptualized

in terms of organic entities with quasi-biological functioning" (1990, 35). According to some interpretations of Darwinism, states could be seen as "natural" organisms that passed through specific stages of life (ibid.); hence, younger, more energetic states would succeed older, geriatric ones on the world stage. Britons and Americans had a somewhat different perspective, seeing progress tied to mastery of the physical world through science and technological innovation. But nature was still heavily determining (ibid.).

Because national evolution was popularly seen in teleological terms, national success brought the world closer to its ultimate purpose. States must therefore continually seek advantage in order not to succumb prematurely to the vicissitudes of nature. Nations competed, moreover, to see whose history was more ancient and which ones had survived greater travails and for longer periods of time as a means of establishing greater legitimacy and authority (a process that continues, even today, in places such as Kosovo, South Asia, and Israel/Palestine). This, in turn, gave them the moral right to occupy particular spaces and delegitimated the rights of all others to remain in those spaces.

Inherent in such national organicism was also a notion of purity, not only of origins but also of motives. Long-term survival could not be attributed simply to chance; it had, as well, to be a matter of maintaining a cultural distinctiveness between the nation and its members and Others who were not of the nation. Maintenance of this distinction through culture was not enough to maintain purity; there also had to be dangers to the nation associated with difference. These dangers, as often imagined into being as being real in any objective sense, made concrete those borders separating one state from another.[2] Peoples living in the borderlands between nations were forced to choose one side or the other; those on the wrong side of the border were, often as not, made to migrate across them, as Greeks and Turks were forced to move after World War I and various groups have, more recently, been made to move across the Balkan Peninsula. Once again, a form of moral order was invoked and the borders between moral spaces maintained.

The apotheosis of this politics of danger took place during World War II in those areas of Europe that fell under Nazi rule, when the ambiguities posed by Jews, Gypsies, and gays were erased from the map. Ethnic cleansing thus served (and serves) a double purpose from the perspective of a nation. Whereas forced transfer leaves alive aggrieved populations who might try to return (as, for example in the case of Palestinians), genocide does not. Not only does it remove contenders for title to property, it also eliminates all witnesses to the heinous acts of the "moral community." At times, as in some Bosnian towns and cities and in the disappearance of many Arab villages within Israel after 1948, all physical traces are eliminated, too. Left in these purified spaces are, for the most part, those who are of the nation and will testify to the evil intentions of the Others who have so conveniently been eliminated from the scene.

DOMINATRIX TO THE WORLD

Reification of individual goodness and morality, and the drawing of lines around the self, have not resulted in unalloyed uplift; indeed, the dissolution of the old containment has led to social rather than interstate disruption. During the past two decades, right-wing attacks against immigrants and liberals, violence against the U.S. federal government, opposition to the new world order (whatever that might be), and support for family values and tradition in the United States have, therefore, emerged in an effort to reimpose a nationalistic moral frame on what some believe is becoming a socially anarchic society (Lipschutz 1998). The Kulturkampf in America is precisely parallel to the recent transformation of state practice from military-based to discipline-based behavior, especially where American and European foreign policies are concerned.

A closer investigation suggests that the two are of a piece as, for example, in the convergence of a draconian welfare policy with an increasingly vocal movement against immigrants, whatever their legal status. Welfare is deemed to sap the moral vitality of the poor, to foster promiscuity and illegitimacy, and, more generally, to be a form of theft from righteous citizens. The 1997 film *Independence Day,* in which a disciplinary environmental sensibility *(Recycle!)* was set against "aliens stealing our resources," nicely illustrates how domestic and foreign policies have come together around the extension of morality from the private (domestic) to the public (international) sphere (and further into interstellar space; Lipschutz 1999c).

To restore its moral authority, consequently, the nation-state must redraw the borders between good and evil, mastering disorder through imposition of new (b)orders. The United States—both government and conservative social elites—are attempting to restore order at home and abroad in two ways. First, the official foreign policy of "democratization and enlargement" represents an attempt to expand the boundaries of the "good world." Those who follow democracy and free markets subscribe to a moral order that makes the world safe for goodness and peace (but see the critique of this idea in Mansfield and Snyder 1995). Second, a policy of disciplinary deterrence is being directed against so-called rogue states (now called "states of concern" by the U.S. government), terrorists, and others of the "bad bloc," who are said to threaten the "good world" with destruction even though they possess only a fraction of the authority, influence, and military firepower of the latter.[3]

Ordinary deterrence, whether conventional or nuclear, is aimed against any state with the physical military capabilities to threaten or attack. Disciplinary deterrence is different. It is an act of (supra)national morality, not of national interests, of drawing lines in sand, not in blood. Disciplinary deterrence is, to be sure, warfare by other means, but it is violence inflicted through demonstration, through publicity, through punishment on those who do not follow the rules. It has the trappings of an effort to correct wayward parties, that is, those who fall out of line and violate the principles of a world moral order whose form and rules are not always so clear. It is a practice fully of the media age, relying on rapid and widespread communication and the receipt of the message by those who might think of resistance, but who are warned to think twice and induced to back down. Ideally, then, disciplinary deterrence becomes a form of self-regulation, an institutionalized practice that limits behavior simply through awareness of it.

The paradox in disciplinary deterrence is, however, that there is no there there. It is conducted against imagined enemies, with imaginary capabilities, and the worst of imagined intentions (Lipschutz 1995, 12; Lipschutz 1999b). Where these enemies might choose to issue a challenge, or why they would do so, is not at all evident. But that these enemies represent the worst of all possible moral actors is hardly questioned.

Consider the fate of that "mother of all bad guys," Iraq. Ever since it was defeated by the UN coalition in 1991, Iraq has existed in a state of limited sovereignty, as a zone that the United States holds in semilegal bondage and domination. The creation of no-fly

zones in Iraq's northern and southern regions, the constant surveillance of the country by satellites and spy planes, the regular inspec-
tions of its industrial facilities by UN representatives, and the repeated conditions on the restoration of even limited trade privileges
have all reduced Iraq to a region over which the United States exercises a suzerainty that extends even to domestic affairs. But Iraq
also serves a disciplinary function, illustrating to other rogues and
adventurers their fate should they violate the moral code of the new
global schoolmaster.

Thus the explanation of the odd events of September 1996 (as
well as the near showdowns in late 1997 and early 1998) when
fighting took place in the Kurdish region in the north, while the
United States loosed cruise missiles on Iraqi radar stations in the
south. This can best be understood not as retaliation for the Iraqi
"invasion" of the Kurdish zone but, rather, as an injury inflicted by
the international equivalent of a high-school vice principal bent on
corporal punishment of a recalcitrant student. It was intended not
so much to hurt Saddam Hussein or Iraq as to issue a warning to
others who might think of stepping out of line. "We can do this
with impunity," the White House might have been saying. "We hold
the rod. You can run, but you cannot hide." The demonstration
was more important than the effect (although it led then–Republican
presidential candidate Bob Dole to complain—insightfully, in my
view—that the president was wasting $2 million cruise missiles to
no good purpose).

Disciplinary deterrence as a moral exercise is not, however, limited to those outside of the country; it has been extended into the
domestic arena, as well. For most of the Cold War, the threat of
communist subversion and the fear of being identified in an FBI file
as a Pinko Comsymp were sufficient to keep U.S. citizens from straying too far from the Free World straight and narrow. Red baiting
continued long after the Red scares of the 1950s—one can even
find it today, in the excoriation of so-called liberals (*San Francisco
Chronicle* 1997) and Marxist academics—although the language of
discipline and exclusion has become somewhat more genteel with
the passage of time. Still, since the collapse of the Soviet Union, it
has been difficult for political and social elites to discipline an unruly polity; that things can get out of hand without strong guidance
from above is the message of the riots in South Central Los Angeles,

shootouts and confrontations between authorities and right-wing militias, and the constant and continuing search for those threats— chemical, biological, infrastructural, interstellar—that must surely be here among us (Lipschutz 1999b).

Consequently, warnings routinely issued from on high that "the world is a dangerous place" serve to replace the disciplining threat of communism with new ones (Kugler 1995). Such warnings are, however, unduly vague. We are told that weapons of mass destruction— nuclear, biological, chemical—could turn up in a truck or suitcase. Therefore, we must rely on and trust the authorities to prevent such eventualities, even though the damage done by one or several such devices would never approach the destructive potential that still rests in the arsenals of nuclear weapons states. Unnamed terrorists—usually Muslim—are discussed and dissed, but some of the most deadly actors turn out to be the "boy or girl next door" (Kifner 1995). The Clinton administration further sows paranoia and suspicion by seeking "a special computer tracking system to flag, or 'profile,' [airline] passengers and identify those with suspicious travel patterns or criminal histories" (Broeder 1996). And, in a move reminiscent of its infiltration of leftist groups in the 1960s and 1970s, the FBI has established "counter terrorism task forces" in a dozen major U.S. cities. These, according to a draft memorandum, are "dedicated full time to the investigation of acts of domestic and international terrorism and the gathering of intelligence and [sic] international terrorism" (Rosenfeld 1997). Clearly, disorder knows no borders.

IT'S ECONOMICS, STUPID!

The nation-state possessed by the siren song of its own moral efficacy is not yet an artifact of history; as illustrated by the War over Kosovo, the acts of purification required by extreme nationalism are not as willingly accepted in today's world as they once might have been. When they take place, however, interventions are explained by an old statist morality—the balance of power—or a newer humanistic one—defense of human rights. But these hardly tell the whole story. A new phenomenon—the morality of markets—has emerged to challenge these old ones. Stephen Gill argues that, as the nation-state and nationalism lose the suasion they once commanded, authority has shifted increasingly to the market and its disciplines. He points out that, more and more, access to credit is a prerequisite for citizenship in contemporary liberal democracy:

> [T]he substantive conception of citizenship involves not only a political-legal conception, but also an economic idea. Full citizenship requires not only a claim of political rights and obligations, but access to and participation in a system of production and consumption. (1995, 22)

This, argues Gill, acts to discipline and socialize consumers, beginning in adolescence. Failure to meet the terms of economic citizenship—a good credit record—means social marginalization. The threat of such exclusion keeps consumers in line. The result, he says, is the replacement of "traditional forms of discipline associated with the family and the school with market discipline" (ibid., 26; see also Drainville 1995; Lipschutz 1999a). In this way, the workers of the world of the future are bound into the new global economy.

Gill largely ignores the moral content of such forms of discipline, but there is more religion to the market than meets the eye. Those who don't adhere to the standards of the credit givers (and takers!) are cast out of the blessed innermost circle of the global economy. Whether state or individual, losing creditworthiness is tantamount to being cast into the realm of impoverished Others. To be readmitted into the inner circle requires a strict regimen of self-discipline, denial, and reconstitution of one's self-conception (especially with respect to those Other slackers). But even those with good credit ratings are subjects of this disciplinary regime. Inundated daily by offers of credit cards at enticing introductory interest rates and impossibly high credit limits (up to $100,000!), the "saved" are kept to the straight and narrow by fear of being cast into the lower circles of economic hell should they violate the inscribed codes of the credit-rating agencies. The proper response to such offers is, of course, "Get thee from me, Satan!" although not everyone has the moral character to rise above such temptations.

Nonetheless, we see here the true genius of the globalizing morality of the market system. The Catholic Church's moral authority was akin to now-discredited regulation from above—the same rules for everybody, the same punishment for everybody, with damnation conferred by the community (and salvation available for the contrite).

By contrast, market-based morality relies on self-regulation keyed to an individual self-discipline that limits the maximum credit load that one can bear—different strokes for different folks and damnation an individual responsibility. As we know from experience, self-regulation is a weak reed on which to base a social system. Moreover, the desire to consume to the limit of one's individual credit limit does carry with it a larger consequence, a domestic social anarchy that arises from self-interest as the sole moral standard to which each individual consumer hews.

The logic of the War over Kosovo is explicable, as well, by reference to market morality. Prior to and during the war, the United States and its NATO allies offered three explanations for the bombing campaign: First, violence against Albanian Kosovars constituted aggression by Milosevic and Serbia that, as experience had taught, could not be allowed to continue, lest other Hitler-like dictators take heart from the example and act in a similar fashion. Second, violence against Albanian Kosovars by Milosevic and Serbia might, some argued, spill over into both Albania and Macedonia, draw in neighboring countries, and spark a general Balkan War. Third, violence against Albanian Kosovars constituted a clear violation of their human rights by Milosevic and Serbia, to which the international community must respond in order to prevent future occurrences of the same elsewhere in Europe. Laying waste to Yugoslavia was intended to forestall all three eventualities. Yet, given the 1990s' history of ethnic cleansing in the Balkans and elsewhere, why was this time different from all other times?

The difference, I would argue, has to do with the global economy and, in particular, its trans-Atlantic component. During the Cold War, Tito's Yugoslavia occupied a peculiar strategic and economic position vis-à-vis NATO and Western Europe. First, although communist, after 1948 Yugoslavia was seen as a strategic ally against the Soviet Union in the event of war. Second, although socialist, it became highly dependent on Western markets and finance to maintain its economy. Both helped make Yugoslavia relatively prosperous. This dependence came at a price, however: during the Reagan recession of the early 1980s, the country fell into a deep economic slump from which it never really recovered. In addition, with the end of the Cold War Yugoslavia's strategic importance vanished. There was no longer any reason for the West to underwrite a poorly functioning nonmarket system, especially when other countries closer to the European Union were thought to be more important.

None of this would have mattered had Yugoslavia gone the way of the rest of Eastern and Central Europe or if Slobodan Milosevic and his minions had not sought to maintain the federation by force. Serbia would have become poorer—albeit not as poor as it is now—and the Balkans would occupy the same, hazy realm as Romania and Bulgaria. But the Third and Fourth Balkan Wars put fear into the hearts of the European Union's elites, and the possibility of a fifth war in Kosovo was truly terrifying. Repeated Serbian violence posed a threat to an ever-wealthier North American–European core and its project of market globalization, whose morale and cohesion might splinter under a failure to act. To permit such violence to proceed in close proximity to the European heartland without a disciplining response could put the European integration program at risk, result in the collapse of NATO, and lead to American withdrawal from Europe. Under those circumstances, trade wars and other economic disputes would no longer be buffered by the Atlantic security relationship and the Asian economic "flu" might spread. In other words, although it is unlikely that Serbian violence would have spread beyond the borders of the former Yugoslavia to constitute a military threat to Europe, NATO's disciplinary move was nonetheless required in order to maintain borders, identities, and order between the market morality of the New World Economic Order and the state-centric morality of the old geopolitical world.

CONCLUSION

In this chapter, I have argued that the instantiation of morality plays a central role in the emerging global politics of the twenty-first century. Historically, the imposition of borders, orders, and identities by sovereigns and their successors was intended to make manifest the distinction between the "good" national Self and "bad" foreign Others. War was not only an act of conquest, it was also a mark of moral rectitude (at least according to the terms of one's own nationalism). Today, with the growing permeability of borders, the proliferation of identities, and the diminishing risks of major war, discipline effected through both deterrence and markets has become the means of differentiating between zones of moral order and immoral disorder. In this light, the wars of the 1990s can be seen not in terms of the acting out of the traditional security dilemma but, rather, as low-cost programs meant to discipline, through example, those who might seek to transgress the borders of order (Lipschutz 2000a). The NATO occupation of Kosovo, with no room for the Russians, smacks more of franchising than pacification. It will be an interesting comparative exercise to see how Kosovars and the five countries' troops do "business" during the years to come.

NOTES

Different versions of this chapter appear in Lipschutz, *After Authority* (2000a, chapter 7) and as Lipschutz, "The State as Moral Authority in an Evolving Global Political Economy" (2000b).

1. The notion of "just war," which represented an effort to impose morality on the conduct of war, does not contradict this argument, I think. Civilians were the subjects of the prince and his morality, not the source of that morality.

2. Thereby creating an inversion of Benedict Anderson's (1991) "imagined communities," which we might call "unimaginable communities."

3. Yassir Arafat's defection from the "bad bloc" to the "good bloc" demonstrates how membership in both has more to do with morality than power. Recent events within Israel/Palestine demonstrate the lability of such change.

4

The Möbius Ribbon of Internal and External Security(ies)

DIDIER BIGO

For some time now, a number of those studying conflicts, strategy, international relations, or the police and the evolution of crime have made the same observation: internal and external security (traditionally two separate domains that were essentially the concern of different institutions, police and army), now appear to be converging regarding border, order, and the possible threats to identity, linked to (im)migration.

The IBO triangle seems to be at the heart of the discussion concerning security. Security is not only a state affair, it is a boundary function. But this observation of a growing interpenetration between internal and external security emerges more as a result of developments "in the field" rather than from a cross-fertilization in the literature. So one has a lot of approximate statements without an accurate theorization of the relationships between the discourses of the academics and of the practices of the professional actors of security. This IR theory as a cognitive region is too disconnected from political sociology of police, migration, crime, and military forces. This chapter tries to fill this gap.

THE MERGING OF INTERNAL AND EXTERNAL SECURITY: ACTORS AND ACADEMIC DISCOURSES

People, journalists, and politicians continuously evoke the emergence of new threats (mafia, terrorism, organized crime, human trafficking, border smuggling, and often illegal immigration, as well as massive flow of refugees). They speak of threats that would transgress national identities. They create links between economic and social crises in Western societies with unemployment, difficulties of the welfare state, rise of petty crime, and the international situation: globalization, end of bipolarity, and the movement of people across borders. They ask for new solutions, like global security, with old frameworks like McCarthyism in mind and demand exclusionary controls, especially toward newcomers. They are afraid of what they call "new" challenges to sovereignty, identity, and borders. They want to explain the merging between internal and external security through the entanglement of migration, crime, and war. War is less and less interstate conflict and more and more intrastate conflict, less politically motivated, and in this vision war creates criminals of war. Crime is less local and more organized, politicized, and beyond the border. Organized crime is a new form of warfare. Across state borders, migration imports criminal activities and even a fifth column for the next civilization war between the West and the rest.

This vision of the world creates a kind of functionalist vision of security where security is explained through the evolution of insecurity (threats, risks, dangers, fears, and so on) and never by the role of the security agencies. A lot of discourses (political, bureaucratic, media, or academic ones) considers as "evidence" that the agencies of security only answer to objective problems of the social world. They pertain to an empiricist vision. They don't analyze the interaction of the four worlds of crime, police, war, and army. They refuse to consider that police do not only answer to the crime or migration problem but are an active actor of the social construction of crime as a problem in the way they select through the social world what is a problem of security and what is not a problem, what is fatality, what is opportunity of change, what is a political, social, or security problem. That is not to say that the visions of the security agencies are only products of their imagination, false perceptions, or language problems, that they have no correspondence with facts, but that the facts are constructed (or not) as problems by these specific actors: crime by the professionals of internal security, war by the professionals of external security, and migration by the politicians looking for some scapegoat.

If a part of the academic community is perhaps more aware now of this social construction of the threat by the agencies of security, it is because the agencies themselves are in trouble; the evidence of crime they have constituted for years is in a process of degradation. Police are afraid of the globalization of networks of criminals and cannot continue with the traditional discourse about sovereignty; military people are afraid of legitimacy questions, after the loss of the Soviet enemy and as they try to find new tasks after the end of bipolarity and the end of all their beliefs concerning the stability of the world.

So the merging between internal and external security is not only a question posed by the academics, it is a question posed by the police and military forces as well as the politicians and often the journalists. Uncertainty is at the core of the fears (imaginary or not) and of the practices of surveillance and coercion.

Rightly or wrongly, they have fears because they believe that the dividing line, which has long been porous, between the forces in charge of security within the territory (i.e., police forces) and those responsible for defending the territory itself (i.e., military people), is now becoming more and more uncertain, that the border of the state is at the symbolic level, a powerful boundary, less than before. The distinction between the spheres of police and army is apparently being challenged by, it is said, the existence of transversal threats, by the end of bipolar relations, by the existence of transnational phenomena, and by globalization. New threats oblige global security. By projecting their violence onto domestic territory and finding their opening in the internal vulnerability of Western societies, the armed conflicts of the Third World supposedly create new conditions for the expression of violence. Drug traffickers are believed to be destabilizing the world economy and the rules of capitalism while undermining the internal foundations of social order through the young. Global mafia and systemic crime are more dangerous than the Soviet enemy because they have already infiltrated Western societies like a fifth column. The strategies against them cannot be to seal the state borders but to create new social and electronic boundaries, targeting specific peoples while a majority continue to live in freedom. And, although the street-corner criminal and the foreign enemy used to belong to two separate worlds and continue to be seen as different, the idea that police officers, customs officers, gendarmes, intelligence agencies, and the army all share the same enemies is gaining more and more support.

A common list of threats (terrorists and the countries that support them, organized crime and drug trafficking, corruption and mafiosi, the risk of urban riots of an ethnic nature and their implications for international politics with the immigration countries, and so forth) is being drawn up in different arenas of the Western world: NATO, OSCE, G8, EU, Schengen, and in each national state with the mediation of interministerial structures concerning defense, foreign affairs, justice, interior, and social ministries. Insecurity is seen as growing so much that security needs to be extended beyond traditional limits, at the risk of endangering liberties.

Academics try to deal with this question of the limits of security, but they disagree on the nature of the formulation of the question. For the empiricists the question is clear: Do the agencies underestimate or overestimate the threats? What is the correlation between the reality of the events and their visions, their rhetorics, and their capacities to manage the dangers? Some consider that it is only with a fusion of all the institutions of security that the global threat can be handled, and they accuse everybody who doubts this of being naive or an ally of the criminals. Others consider that these threats are less new than the agencies say and also less dangerous. The competition for budget and the lack of other missions could explain the discourses about global mafia. It is a kind of realism where the bureaucratic struggles explain the real stakes and the disproportion between the claims, the discourses, and the social practices. For the constructivists the question is slightly different. Even if they often agree with the idea of the disproportion between the claims and the practices, they consider that the question is not the correlation between facts and discourses, dangers and threats, or under- or overestimation. They analyze the performative role of the language in the construction of the threat and how the political, bureaucratic, and media games construct (or not) a problem or a threat. They discuss how social changes are shaped into a securitarian framework, coming mainly from the professionals of security. They discuss the "truth program" constituted by the interests of all the agents of security and how this truth becomes the reality for everybody.

But even if the disagreements are strong between these epistemological and philosophical positions, sometimes, when they come
back to public policies, it is not so clear that empiricists and some
constructivists are really that different. They often ask the same question: whose role is it to follow and anticipate these phenomena—
police officers who project their powers over the border or soldiers
who keep society under surveillance, security agencies or "social
movements," professionals or civil society? And often it is a roman-
tic pluralism that is behind a postmodern label, when the answer to
the question is everybody who can securitize needs to securitize. In
this case, the maximization of security becomes the horizon of the
discussion. To avoid this position, which could have negative impacts on ethics, it is necessary to think about the boundaries of security. So one needs to trace a new *topology* of security, new graphs
and charts of the relationships between the different forms of security and insecurity.

The question of security is not reducible to national security and
even less to the traditional questions of defense. Security is not only
the security of the state, the need for the collective survival of an entity vis-à-vis the possible aggressions coming from entities of comparable nature. It is not evolved only with the preparation for war
or of dissuasion. It always includes questions of civil safety, of acci-
dents, of the environment, and it always mobilizes more agencies of
security than just the soldiers. It includes questions of economic security, not only the questions of infrastructure, necessary to the pro-
longation of the effort of war, but also the questions of economic intelligence and struggle inside the private sectors. Security still includes
questions of social security, the maintenance of mechanisms of redistribution and solidarity, and it is related to policies concerning resources and the relations between the public and private spheres in
society.

Security exists beyond defense in the different domains of the
economy, the political, ecological, and societal sectors. So security is
enlarged in a way that Barry Buzan and Ole Wæver have tried to
conceptualize with the notion of societal security. But one will see
here that it is impossible to oppose, as two different faces, national
and state security on the one hand, and societal and identity security
on the other hand. This analysis of the social practices denies this

Janus-like or "bifocal" vision of security and fails to understand the nondiscursive practices of the agencies of security. This approach has not really understood the merging of internal and external security. So instead of this category of societal security, I will try to trace this new topology of security through the metaphor of the Möbius ribbon. This metaphor gives sense to the merging of the inside and the outside as well as putting effective limits on the process of securization. It could be that what is at stake is not only the question of the physical border of the state but of the boundaries of our understanding of the world. The frontiers between "inside and outside" are under discussion because we are at the limits of our political imagination.

METHODOLOGY IN INTERNATIONAL POLITICAL SOCIOLOGY

Starting from a critical reflection of the traditional postulates of the international relations on sovereignty, citizenship, and borders, this article connects the work of the sociologists and the political scientists who worked on the practices of control of flows of people in Europe and the work of the Las Cruces Group about the analytical triangle concerning the relations between identity, border, and order. It begins with the same assumptions concerning the episteme of the research. It tries to deconstruct the essentialisms and the forms of dualisms that structure the contemporary political thought. This triangle calls into question the dualism of state/society, the border between internal order/external anarchy, the opposition of friend/enemy, and the us/them distinction. All these dualisms are common not only in mainstream theory but also in postmodern visions through the distinctions between state and societal security or through security versus insecurity and the us/them cleavage. It tries to destroy the "naturalness" of the Schmittian vision of the world of politics as a "world of war" through a clear distinction between two camps, and tries to restore the place of the third party, of the people who do not have the chance to speak, the right to be indifferent to the war of politics, the right to play with the indetermination of the identity. It tries to break the discursive practices of traditional IR and political science theories that define the official state border as the border on which the other boundaries are fixed, including linguistic, social and political identities, public and private limits, relations of domination and obedience, and forms of exploitation and solidarity. By conceiving of a plurality of boundaries and by introducing the discussion on its limits and transgressions, it opens on other spaces of thought, other dimensions, and other topologies. In this sense these approaches to security as a Möbius ribbon is rooted on the Swiftian intuitions theorized by Rob Walker in his book *Inside Outside* (1993), concerning the multiplicity of possible spaces.

This article chooses a dynamic approach and a relational philosophy, already described by Paul Veyne and Michel Foucault or Pierre Bourdieu in another register in their different works. Using the term "field of security" engages us in *a specific perspective we can label as structuralist constructivism.* By "structuralism" Bourdieu (1986) means (and I follow him on that point) that there are, in the social world itself and not merely in symbolic systems—language, myth— objective structures that are independent of the consciousness and agents' desires and are capable of guiding or constraining their practices or their representations. By "constructivism," he means that "there is a social genesis, on the one hand, of the patterns of perceptions, thoughts and action which are constitutive of what I call the *habitus,* and on the other hand of social structures, and in particular of what I call *fields* and groups, especially of what are usually called social classes." The combination of structuralism and constructivism can be summed up: "on the one hand, the objective structures which the sociologist constructs in the objectivist moment by setting aside the subjective representations of the agents, are the basis of subjective representations and they constitute the structural constraints which influence interactions; but, on the other hand, these representations also have to be remembered if one wants to account above all for the daily individual and collective struggles which aim at transforming or preserving these structures. This means that the two moments, objectivist and subjectivist, stand in a *dialectical relation* and that, even if for instance the subjectivist moment seems very close, when it is taken separately, to interactionist or ethnomethodological analyses, it is separated from them by a radical difference: the points of view are apprehended as such and related to the positions in the structure of the corresponding agents" (Bourdieu 1986). This vision of constructivism could be quite far from Derrida, Barthes, early Foucault, Shapiro, and Dillon and is more or less connected with Berger and Luckman, Giddens, Beck, Bourdieu, and late Foucault or, in international relations, Heisler, Lapid, Wendt, and Katzenstein. It informs the project to constitute an international political sociology as a way to understand the international dimension as a "normal" social fact.

Validating a hypothesis, such as a field of security professionals at a transnational level, nearly always depends on each individual's perception of methodology and epistemology. In social sciences *validation can never be definitive* as there are always objections raised to the procedures for producing and verifying truth. Clearly there can be no validation based on a naive epistemology where evidence collected in the field represents reality or on a behaviorist program with preconceived hypotheses that are then tested afterwards. This does not mean that we should resort solely to discourses and intertextuality. Naming is important, but language is one part of reality, not all reality. A lot of American work inspired by Foucault appears to make this confusion, with a kind of neophilosophizing postmodern approach to international relations. In our view, field studies are valuable, even though there is no objectivity of experience, as there are nevertheless traces, archives, and we can reconstruct the process of construction of the agent. Field studies enable us to plot the variety of practices and emerging configurations of the agents' systems of dispositions in relation to their trajectories and positions. They allow us to distance ourselves from the academic (and philosophical) illusion of the primacy of discourse, obliging us to reflect further on the technologies of power and resistance. They are central in analyzing heterogeneity, systems of dispersion, and all practices (including discursive ones) without reconstructing categories of natural objects too hastily (the police through the ages, the army, or immigrants). It is the only way to move from a conceptualization of being and of substance to a conceptualization of belonging and of becoming. Veyne and Rescher philosophies are "process philosophies." The study of singularity, systems of dispersion, and the relationship between practices and discursive practices are certainly more familiar to historians than to sociologists and philosophers, but this approach, which highlights reflection on transversal devices, is of certain sociological interest. These field studies should not be seen as the reflection of the agent's history, but as work that is oriented according to the *intrigue* of the history of these agents.

Analyses of security, especially in IR theory, are far too inattentive to the social practices of security professionals. In many cases they are the product of secondary rationalizations that reduce security or identity to natural objects. They are discussed as if they were things or concepts rather than as part of a relationship of power-knowledge. A lot of academics try to define security or identity by reifying their objectifications as natural objects. As Paul Veyne puts it, "we take the place a projectile is going to land of its own accord for its intentional target. We apply a philosophy of the object as end or cause rather than a philosophy of relationships which approaches the problem not from both ends, but from the middle, from practice or discourse."[1] If one translates this to security issues, it is important to question the traditional phrase about the end of bipolarity, the new threats, or the migratory problem. The history of security and its various forms is explained as an anthropological need, as a legitimate demand on behalf of citizens, or as a speech act that varies with time; rather, the (nondiscursive and discursive) practices of securitization/ insecuritization and the configuration of the balance of social forces that enables the imposition of these practices should be analyzed.

This neglect of practices, of what security agents are doing, stems from an inversion that suggests that what is done determines the doing, when in fact the opposite is true. Thus we should not reflect on the right definition of security and the diverse forms that it takes according to the "sectors," but on the securitization/insecuritization practices that run across the internal sphere as much as the external sphere. We should also remember that the practices are interspersed with empty spaces, that they are very few, and that the space is filled with objectifications that update the virtualities left in the gaps. If the neighboring practices change, if the limits are moved, then the practice will update the new virtualities, and it will no longer be the same. The only solution is to think of the limits of security at a theoretical level. Security, even enlarged, does not connect all the social practices. Empty spaces are always there because the practices are rare.

Analyzing security is in this way a practice itself. It is a discursive practice connected with power and knowledge. And analyzing security could not continue to be guided by the illusion that "concepts" are the "real things," the structure of the social life. It is important not to cite everybody writing on security in IR to show how skillful we are in the academic field but to analyze the practices of coercion, protection, pacification, static guard, control, surveillance, information gathering and sorting, information management, grid-like security cover, calming, dissuasion, locking up, turning back, and removal from the territory that are deployed by security agents (private or public, police, military police, or army). One should analyze how each agency has its own repertoire of action, its own know-how, and its own technology. Practices are heterogeneous and dispersed, and a response to political rationality. As François Ewald points out, either that rationality is examined from the point of view "of the practices that it orders or forbids, of the way in which it problematizes its objects; in which case it is *programme* rationality, or it is examined as *diagramme* rationality by looking at the practices and trying to identify, *based on the practices,* what the plan for their set up, what the ideal of their adapted function, may have been."[2]

And one of my main hypotheses, following Ewald, is that the diagram rationality of the Möbius ribbon of security, of the merging of internal and external security, is not the program rationality of the prevention of terrorism, drugs, crime, or even the fear of a flood of immigrants coming to settle in Europe. It is a particular diagram of "moral panic," of "identity securitization," driven by technology of surveillance and the passage from a territorial state to a population state (Foucault 1989) where the transformation of the modalities of governmentality combines territory and ethnic, coercion and pro-activity, technological sophistication, and the old disciplines of the body, where immigration becomes a problem, a challenge for European societies because scenes from everyday life are politicized, because day-to-day living is securitized, and not because there is a threat to the survival of society and its identity.

The diagram rationality shows that securitization does not affect survival but rather intolerance toward differences, that social and historical changes are perceived as a threat or, in other words, that a structural phenomenon is transformed into an adversary. Through this "magic" operation, everything is turned into an object of insecurity—the way someone looks at you, his different cooking habits, his songs—and this rejection of all difference transforms these practices into a symptom of the undermining of a homogeneous societal identity as fantasized by the groups that declare its existence.

With this problematic in mind, we carried out interviews among the high ranks of control agencies (national police, gendarmes, customs, police and military intelligence, and armed forces) in France[3] and more briefly in the United Kingdom, Germany, Italy, Greece, and the United States. Through the interviews I have tried to describe some of the intersection points of internal and external security, and to analyze the logics of enlargement of internal security matters beyond the borders and of restructuration of external security. And these interviews have enabled us, I think, to put certain debates among scholars of international studies back into context and to emphasize and clarify the stakes involved in security, democracy, Europeanization, and contemporary forms of power.

POLICE FORCES OUTSIDE AND MILITARY FORCES INSIDE: THE CHANGING ROLES OF THE SECURITY AGENCIES

Traditionally tasks were shared out by distinguishing between those that were proper to the interior of the country, which fell to the police force and related intelligence services, and those from abroad, which fell to the armed forces and secret services. Thus the physical state frontier was also a symbolic frontier and an administrative demarcation. Internal was set against external, sovereign power against international anarchy, law against balance of power, and each agency positioned itself within a precise framework in a relationship with a different population. The physical borders of the state determined where the power of the state applied and stopped. The territorial logic was primordial for the understanding of the everyday rules of governance. It was what guided the social practices of surveillance and the control of people and resources. Now a challenge appears to this conception of the Westphalian state where the borders are the limits of the application of power with a strong differentiation between the use of force inside and outside. Bertrand Badie as well as John Ruggie have spoken of the "end of the territory," explaining that this is the end of the clear limits of sovereignty and law enforcement. Globalization or transnationalization destroys the rules of social and distributive justice. The frontiers of states are not frontiers of solidarity between the people. Some people abroad feel more proximate through political-religious solidarities than they do with people living near them in the same territory. So the question of the role of police and military force is not simply a question of a technical realignment or a process of adjustment on the merges of rules that themselves remain the same, but rather a challenge to the very rules that hitherto had shared out activities and missions on the basis of a distinction between inside and outside.

The distinctiveness of the use of force inside (the territory) and outside (abroad), which was created with the emergence of the national state and drives toward the differentiation between army and police forces, even though the army plays a role inside and police have networks outside, is now put in question. The Westphalian age is closing, and some people have noticed the comeback of a situation not so different from the time of religious wars, when the government had not yet claimed to have the monopoly of the use of force on a specific territory and had not yet proceeded to attempt cultural homogenization inside. The differentiation between security inside and outside state borders, linked with the primacy and exclusive usage of the notion of security for the outside, is contemporaneous with the effective capacity of the central power of the government to completely connect all the mechanisms of discipline throughout society, which began seriously in the nineteenth century.

Police and military social spaces have only been distinct since the sixteenth century, and they have only been institutionalized separately since the nineteenth century. Before that, during the preceding three hundred years, governments claimed to have control of their own territory, which was accepted by the other states as a regulatory principle even if conquest of territory by war was always a possibility. The state police wanted to be society's police around the mid–nineteenth century, not before. Providing intelligence had become just one of the police tasks whose functions also included providing emergency aid, crime control, and ensuring public order (peace). The enlargement of police tasks was a slow process in which democracy, self-restraint, and the power of the police concerning private life were interpenetrated. Too often the origins of this process are forgotten, and people confuse the claim to power and the capacity of the power to enforce what was claimed. "The *successful* monopolisation of the legitimate means of movement by states and the state system had to await the creation of elaborate bureaucracies and technologies that only gradually came into existence, a trend that intensified dramatically toward the end of the nineteenth century" (Torpey 1998). The massive transformations of the construction of the parliamentary state and its legitimation were followed by the progressive *demilitarization of the police* and the differentiation between the two universes.

This demarcation was all the more marked, as there were no institutions to cover the interface between these two social universes. It was more important in Anglo-American countries than in the Latin ones where there was a tradition of police officers with military status. But now uncertainty about missions and the limits between police and military spheres, in particular, undermines those organizations or agencies like the gendarmerie or border police (such as the bundesgrenzschutz in Germany), which are at the interface between these two social universes. Either they see it as an attack on their professional identity and fear for their future (in the case of customs officers and certain intelligence agencies), or, in the case of police with military status (gendarmerie, bundesgrenzschutz, carabinieri, and the guardia civil), they see these transformations of violence as an opportunity for them to come into their own, between those agencies that specialize in maintaining public order and those that specialize in combat and dissuasion. These intermediate agencies highlight the interpenetration of internal and external, the transversal aspect of these "new" threats and their own particular know-how in dealing with them. They no longer see themselves as being on the fringes of the two traditional spheres, as unappreciated intermediaries in both social universes, but rather as central to the one sole universe that is currently developing: the field of security. This is because their broad range of activities allows them to be present where police officers fear to go (reestablishing order in times of crisis) and where soldiers do not want or know how to intervene (not killing but controlling the foe).

So, in order to analyze the interpenetration and interlacing of security, one needs to trace how, over the past twenty years and through a long process of changes, we have moved from a notion of the police force that was highly marked by the idea of sovereignty to a vision of them, in terms of internal security, as police beyond the borders, and one needs to look at how matters of defense have been restructured since the end of bipolar relations and why military people are now surveilling the internal territory and immigrants.

From National Police Forces to Internal European Security

The most noticeable transformation in the police universe has arisen from the increasing depth given to security. This is not simply the collective security of the state, it increasingly refers to everyone's individual security. The contemporary state is not only expected to ensure the institutional survival of the collectivity but also the personal survival of every member that composes that collectivity. The state wants to take charge of individual security and widen the notion of public order, even if it means encroaching on the private sphere. It is seeking to implement a program that it has long claimed as its right on the basis of contract theory, but which it has never come close to carrying out. Control and surveillance technologies as well as new findings in social sciences reinforce this desire to securitize as much as possible and lead to a reliance upon private companies to carry out the surveillance program. This changes the relationship between private and public and leads to the politicization of individual security issues under the heading "insecurity feeling."

The change in the state's attitude toward individual security should not be exaggerated. It is not new and needs to be viewed in its long-term context. It has been a slow metamorphosis, gradually taking the citizens' viewpoint into consideration. It is the product of several centuries of democratization and the establishing of state control. State handling of so-called societal security and of the definition of national (or local) identity is more of a constant than a novelty. In this respect, the police role (and/or discourse on their role) has evolved and become more complex. With the advent of parliament, the state, or more precisely the governing bodies, learned to take care of its populations and learned not to treat them as an enemy, even in times of revolt. This deep-set, structural tendency leading to the handling of individual security, to taking care of individuals through all state channels—social security, civil security, road safety, and so on—stems from the development of what François Ewald calls an insurance society that minimizes individual risk taking. The police force tends to be likened to a public service despite the resistance put up by Regalian visions.

Police matters have been politicized as internal security in the sense that what was a police affair of little media interest is now a stake in political contests, and is all the more prized as it seems to be a determining factor for undecided voters, particularly at local levels (Mayer Perrineau 1995). Of course, this politicization has at different times been through cycles of both secrecy and being pushed into the public spotlight. There is nothing radically new in that. But as far as this research is concerned, it was the 1980s and particularly the 1990s that saw this public debate on police issues regarding the emergence of discourse on urban insecurity and the city on the one hand, and migration flows of salaried workers on the other.

From then on security was no longer conceived of as protection behind borders. And although a number of texts maintain the vision of a barrier border, of a "fortified castle," a fortress, individual security is no longer related to a territory. The conceptions of frontiers are changing. Democratization and Europeanization have changed the traditional security vision of the frontier for a more open frontier where economy has priority. But some people demand the reinforcement of the barrier role of the state borders against migrants in the name of nationalism, and the debate, at the public policy level, is not yet finished. The political spectacle is full of arguments for or against border controls even if everybody knows that it is impossible to seal the borders in Europe. Security has come to depend on security networks, agreements between countries and security agencies, and even on private insurance systems and companies. As to the current situation in France, internal security is now linked to the emergence (or not) of a feeling of European citizenship that transcends national frontiers and reactions from the different social groups with regard to the practical consequences of European citizenship in national life. Internal security could be said to have experienced a *double (dual) widening process*. It extends *beyond the national territory* and is directly linked to European and international issues. There is no instance in which it is autonomous and independent of collaboration by security agencies (police, customs, gendarmerie, and so on) on an international scale. On the contrary, its existence almost wholly depends upon such collaboration.

The state is actively seeking to take charge of individual security and enlarge the notion of public order and to control the population, even outside its own territory. Concern is expressed by the state with regard to religious conversion (Islam for fear of radical proselytism and sects for health reasons). The semi-integrated foreigner, even when he has citizenship, is suspected of disrespecting the host society's norms and of upsetting the notion of the public sphere. Control and surveillance technologies and new knowledge in social sciences reinforce this push toward maximizing security, to implement a body politic, to have a "life" policy where the production of life is more important for the government than the right to deliver death. A similar type of concern is expressed in declaring that too many people voluntarily use drugs and endanger their lives. This wider scope includes undertaking activities such as surveillance of illegal immigration, surveillance of cultural, religious, and social influences from the country of origin on the migrants and even on their offspring, surveillance and maintaining order in so-called problem districts, and control of transborder flows. Maintaining and restoring order without opening fire, even in situations involving hostile foreign populations, are also linked to these first activities: they require almost identical know-how, but in different contexts. The link does not concern the identity of the minority versus the majority but cross-border activities and transboundary problems (including the transgressing of boundaries of identity with mixed marriage). The result is a blurring of the line between what belongs to internal security and what belongs to external security or defense.

The Universe of Military Practices

Although war and the state, war making and state making, have been closely linked throughout the history of European state formation, and although the army has defended collective security from aggression from other groups or communities (enabling the distinction to be drawn between combatants and noncombatants, between the front and behind the front), and although behavior was long determined by the protective function of borders, the role of war is now being questioned and *the end of the military order* predicted.

War is not necessarily an eternal mode of conflict. It does not have a glorious future ahead of it. It is becoming a less frequent form of conflict, or at least it is if we accept the traditional definition of war as conflict between states. War was radically modified by the advent of aviation and the transformation of the strategic arena. It was further shaken by nuclear dissuasion and the possibility of annihilating the adversary's hostile force even before any combat takes place. The purpose of war is no longer necessarily the expansion of national borders, and power is no longer calculated according to the same norms. The world has closed borders, few adjustments are tolerated by the international community and its institutions, and frontiers can be multiplied through internal fragmentation but not through conquest, and that was perhaps the only lesson of the Gulf War. The implicit hierarchy between individual and state security, and the sacrifice of the former to the latter, is steadily becoming less acceptable.

This change in the role of war has affected strategic discourse. The "end of war" has been facilitated by a change in the perception of guerrillas and a sudden reevaluation of certain dimensions that had been neglected during the Cold War (such as guerrilla financing through drug trafficking and smuggling and the use of humanitarian aid by transnational groups). It has been much easier to make a link between guerrillas, terrorism, and organized crime when the ideological aspect of the conflict is played down. After that, the army no longer considers its missions solely in terms of interstate conflict or the clash of two opposing blocks; political pressure has forced it to take on new tasks: antiguerrilla strategy, cracking down on terrorism, international policing operations renamed peacekeeping, protecting nationals, and humanitarian operations. The techniques used in these operations transformed them into international police peacekeeping operations and not armed conflicts. All these operations are not only linked with internal security issues, but they are often connected to them. The use of force is limited, the visibility of the enemy is complicated, and the enemy could be within.

Military practices resemble those of other internal security agencies: First, they rely on information technology, in which they even have a tactical advantage over other agencies because of the superiority of the equipment they use and the advances they have made in theoretical studies of low-intensity conflict (LIC). Second, they have an interest at stake where internal security tasks require huge deployment of manpower in order to protect installations, particularly in the light of personnel cutbacks, as these justify the upkeep of a large force. Identification, information gathering, and tracking become more important than the accumulation of equipment for the combat phase, which brings military and police work closer together and places the concept of information at the heart of any security system. Not directly the result of the end of bipolarity, this trend is related to transformations linked to new technologies and new forms of control and surveillance. The problem posed by the enemy is less the balance of power equilibrium than a problem of identification; it is not their fighting strength but their visibility that poses a problem. So the police and military professions have drawn even closer as the latter has gone through some significant changes.

Since the end of bipolarity, external security, far from expanding, seems to be in full retraction or at least in a process of redeployment. Entire sectors of activity are being rethought. Arms and research programs are being canceled. In some countries the format of the armed forces are being altered. In France they are being made professional, despite the long tradition of a citizen's army. Although not all these budget decisions have been dictated by the transformation in the strategic environment, the end of bipolarity does nevertheless appear to be one of the strongest justifications for these changes. Military people are now interested in internal security matters. They have a specific doctrine, they want specific materials, and they ask for new training forces and new budgets.

Some hawks of LIC have developed an analytical framework that seeks to delegitimize political actions by criminalizing them, from the revolution in Iran to the fall of the Berlin Wall. There has been much talk of narcoguerrillas and of the criminalization of clandestine organizations. Crime, borders, immigration, threats to national identity, and fifth column ideology have become inextricably intermingled and reworked into a matrix that is almost entirely a product of the defense research that forged the actors' habitus and that in extreme cases can lead to McCarthyism. The strategization of the "threats" to internal security is justified as the fight against the enemy within. The potential capacities of terrorist activities and their effectiveness against democracies have largely been overestimated, as this enables a link to be made between "exotic" conflicts and national territory. In the same manner a link has been established between terrorism, drugs, organized crime, and immigration through the terms "gray zone" and "urban savages." Apart from considering Islamism as subversive terrorism, all countries refer to a gray zone, to global mafia organization, and to mutations of criminality. The recent debates on the threat from the South and the clash of civilizations have shown exactly how these shifts in positions have come about and why. This strategization has some practical consequences. It more or less redefines the tasks allotted to the different services. Transnational crime, drug mafias, religious integrism, and even illegal immigrants became new enemies more or less tied to the theme of Islamism.

Michael Klare (Klare and Kornbluh 1988) has dismantled this discourse and analyzed this type of motivation and the rise to power of the think tanks that were interested in low-intensity conflicts. But by the mid-1990s a sort of global configuration of converging representations had emerged that *joined* internal and external security, integrating the former into the latter. Military circles were helped by the police before proposing their solutions and "reconverting" their technical and strategic knowledge, reinforcing the movement already engaged toward technologization, the information war, and pro-active strategies. Internal security was made a priority, for the habits of the Cold War continued to imply the Russians as the enemy, and everything that happened in the South was seen as a form of criminalization of politics. Western secret services "rediscovered" corrupt practices with the hidden financing of leaders. Politics were preached and secularized in order to show more clearly that the political models of countries in the South were not "real" politics but "criminalo-political entities" or "groups of religious fanatics."

The Italian minister for defense points to Islamism as the threat replacing the threat of communism and suggests using the army in immigration control. He also includes the army in the war on drugs in Sicily. In Germany, Helmut Kohl regards the PKK as an exclusively terrorist party and a threat to national security. In France, the 1995 bombing relaunched the surveillance of all immigrant associations and the tightening of legislation not just on terrorism but on immigration and political asylum, too. The Vigipirate plan was set in motion, with the armed forces taking part in a second phase that no politician would really dare to shelve more than two years later. Intelligence services that had focused on counterespionage have found new missions in the infiltration of mafia networks and economic intelligence but still use the same procedures.

We may, however, consider that the postbipolar period has served as a catalyst for this discourse and not as a product. The disappearance of the Soviet threat has had the same effect in the field of security that the withdrawal of the gold exchange standard had to the international monetary system, and we are now engaged in a theory of floating exchange rates with regard to the threats. Many military people, a majority within the armed forces, have chosen to evoke the risk of a return to former times for lack of any other more credible threat, or believed that they could reconcile armed forces and rights through humanitarian intervention or the protection of the environment. Clearly they would rather not intervene in operations other than wars, and they continue to support the traditional division between police tasks and military tasks. On the other hand, some high-ranking military people believe that the disappearance of a huge visible opponent whose strength could easily be measured has opened up a variety of fears that, in some cases, transform their perception of social changes into the maneuvers of invisible enemies that have little power but are numerous and may well be interconnected.

The armed forces no longer know what their duties are. The rules of engaging in combat have been modified. As politicians see it, war is indeed an external projection, but this justification alone requires the global legitimacy of the army. The armed forces are returning to the national territory and emphasizing their protective role. They are thus returning to the interior at a time when war beyond national borders has become a rare occurrence.

Internal and External Security Interpenetration

Soldiers and their secret services have, of course, long been rubbing shoulders with internal security. Indeed, defense implies national territory security and the fight against internal subversion. Furthermore, in times of war soldiers may take over control of peacetime police services. However, there are far more crisis situations than there are outright wars, in which case we need to ask: who does what? The Vigipirate plan against terrorist activities in France is one example of the ambiguous relationship between the Ministries of Defense and Interior. Those soldiers that were brought in for the second phase of the plan to support the police are still in place one and one-half years after their initial deployment. The 1998 Football World Cup in France and the continuation at a low level of the civil war in Algeria purportedly indicate that the presence of the military forces will be upheld. Can we leave them indefinitely for years in our streets in the name of antiterrorism and then justify their deployment in the name of the prevention of petty crimes?

There are many other examples of the de-differentiation between matters of internal and external security. For example, the intelligence and counterespionage services (MI5, DGSE, CIA) have only about one-third of their number working on espionage; as well as international terrorism, they are dealing with economic intelligence and hence the laundering of drug money. Thus they enter into competition with the drug squads of Europol and Interpol. On the other hand, Europol wants to deal with "nuclear crime" and follows the transfer of fissile material from one country to another, but in so doing it is poaching on counterespionage and the army's hunting ground of nuclear proliferation.

This interpenetration of internal and external security is in no sense a reflection of an increase of threats in the contemporary epoch—it is a *lowering of the level of acceptability of the other*; it is an attempt at insecuritization of daily life by the security professionals and an increase in strength of police potential for action. In this regard, one observes a double movement. In terms of rhetoric, from Soviet aggression to the uncivil attitudes of children, one may imagine the same program of security, the same coercive solutions, and a militarization of the societal. Moreover, justifying (via the fight against terrorism, organized crime, and the mafia) that the dangers are increasing, that energetic solutions must be imposed, that the military can and must take part in this, what one is seeing in practice is in fact a policiarization of the military. The internal solutions are exported more toward the external than the converse, despite the discourses claiming the contrary. It was the military who in Bosnia carried out the operations of international police officers and asked the gendarmes how to maintain order without "degenerating into war," and the urban hot spots have now become the training ground for international crises; the means have been put into operation in the interior like in the exterior, being conceived of as proactive police techniques at the European level.

The practices of coercion are still present, but they have been devalued. Technology for nonlethal weapons and maintenance of public order, combined with the valuing of surveillance and prevention, put the "right to kill" into question, even for the army. Management of territories is disappearing in favor of management of people. Networking affects security professionals as much as it does professionals in crime and political violence. Information, rapidity of connections, and light-handed coercion but almost permanent surveillance of the enemy: the modes of the fight are changing. The trend toward information control is prevailing over means of force. Are the virtual, the potential, and the fluid outstepping the actual, the real, and the solid? Does information play a more important role than might? Is knowledge overtaking traditional power?

Using the theme of immigration, we have tried to show how there is an analogy with the dynamic of fluids, with pressure differentials, and the metaphor of flows that lead to images of invasion, submersion, the collapse of the dike. The depersonalization of those concerned and of their microdecisions in favor of a dehumanized vision in terms of flows that have to be stopped or channeled may explain to some extent the types of public policy with regard to immigrants in Europe and the discourse on Europe as a sieve or Europe the fortress. This rationality crosses the whole of society and can be found in the most basic representation of immigrants. Nevertheless, it originates in the practices of security professionals, and we can certainly evoke the field that these security professionals constitute, one of whose aims is to "manage and control life through concrete organizations such as schools, hospitals, the police, and the army" (Foucault 1994, 3: 857).

To sum up, in this merging of the inside and the outside in security practices, one can distinguish three levels of understanding. The first, the most obvious, is that state borders are challenged by freedom of movement of goods, ideas, and people. Internal and external security are embedded in the figure of the "enemy within," of the outsider inside, which is increasingly labeled with the catchword "immigrant," who is, depending on the context and the political interests, a foreigner or a national citizen representing a minority. The outsiders are insiders. The lines of who needs to be controlled are blurred.

The second is specific to the world of Western democracies where norms of human rights and cosmopolitanism could compete with "closed nationalism" and the rise of institutional racism. In this specific area, the networks of domination are less and less correlated with the national political power boundaries. The change of significance of national borders as barriers and the creation of a distinction at the European level between internal and external borders have made trouble for the routines of the agencies of security, especially at a moment where the European borders are always in a process of redefinition and enlargement and where the external of today is the internal of tomorrow. The discussion about European citizenship blurs the line of national citizenship and creates an additional tension on the limits of citizenship. The collective identity is redefined through a general process that no one in Europe is really managing. The borders affect the limits of the identity and the conception of order.

The third deals with the personal limits of the feeling of "what is a secure community." Security is less and less about only national security. Three major changes affect security: the evolution of surveillance technology, the privatization through commercial activities, and the individualization of "securitiness." So the identity of what is security is in a process of externalization of the inside and internalization of the outside. The "fear to have fear" creates a specific move where every social change is seen as a new threat. The insecurity continuum connects fear of crime, unemployment, foreigners, drug trafficking, terrorism, and war. It connects fear of the individual with fear of the collective survival. It connects fear of crime and fear of war as well as fear of the future. In this context the security agencies and their agents are under "stress." Their traditional guidelines and beliefs concerning their tasks, their missions, and even their meaning of life have more or less disappeared. The boundaries of the security tasks are not fixed through a clear belief of what security is (and what it is not). They don't know where the inside ends and where the outside begins. They don't know where security is beginning and where insecurity is finishing. As in a Möbius ribbon, the internal and the external are intimately connected.

In conclusion, the theme of this article is not a simple metaphor but an analogy that can be carried out in order to understand this new topology of security. The traditional design of security traces a precise border that locks up identities in specific forms. By making the official territorial border the border of the identities, by using the border as a barrier distinguishing the inside from the outside, the citizens from the foreigners, by using the border as the criterion of delimitation of attributions of the soldiers and diplomats on the one hand, of the police officers and social services on the other hand, the official system known as the Westphalian system has created a toric or a cylindrical topology of security.

The topology of the torus closes space. The state Leviathan merges with society and is protected outside as well as inside through a strategy of maximum security. It does not admit anything that might compromise security, and this is its value par excellence. The identity is that of the subject. The order reigns by "saturation." It can become deadly. Just like certain forms of totalitarianism, absolutism uses this kind of securitization that finds its foundation in the theories of Bodin and, more or less, of Hobbes. Apocalyptic discourses on the end of bipolarity reactivate these fearful diagrams of thought, which arise from the anguish about generalized destruction (annihilation of populations by wars of religion or fears of atomic threats or destruction by internal subversion).

Cylindrical topology opens the sealed shell of the torus. It allows a difference inside, a thinkable space of freedom opposed to security, a space of economic liberalism, intellectualism, a political quest in search of autonomy from the state. Locke, Rousseau, Benjamin Constant, and later institutional liberalism is used by lawyers to create such an internal opening. But according to them this must be counterbalanced by the necessary national homogenization and the determination of a clear and precise line between the citizen and the Other, the foreigner, the enemy. Security becomes interstate security. Dangers come from the outside, not from the inside. The neighbors in this universe of representations are, if not friends or close friends, at least potential close relations, equal persons. They are not seen as potential, virtual traitors, the enemy within to pursue and exclude. The inside is free and sure. It is the place of the contract. The outside is subject to the reign of anarchy, violence, and aggression. From Morgentau to Hedley Bull through Raymond Aron and Kenneth Waltz, and in spite of the differences between them, it is this vision of security that will be carried out by the different liberal governments. In spite of its incapacity to encompass the sociohistorical processes of construction of the state, this cylindrical model benefits from an extreme simplicity of representation in the alignment between inside, internal, contract, police force, monopoly of violence, and citizenship and outside, external, organized violence, army, anarchy, and foreigner. All is resolved on the borderline of the state, a line as thin as possible, a no-man's-land, a paper line, a line of sovereignty.

The transnationalization, globalization of the contemporary world calls into question these two models for understanding the practices and the manifestations of security. The forms of security are no longer directional. Notwithstanding the "truth program" of security, it is no longer possible to maintain the closed format. Sovereignty no longer defines borders. The agencies of security, as we have seen, have expanded into a space that no longer respects sovereign borders. Topology of security in democracies is no longer the elegant cylinder but a complicated form, the Klein bottle.[4] The opening of sovereign borders destroys the security construct of a homogeneous society. Once freedom of movement of persons has been accepted, the construct of the sovereign cylinder is no longer adequate. In this case, freedom is limited by a new security device: the monitoring of minorities and of diasporas. Identity fences replace territorial fences. While people are allowed to move, their identities must be constructed and controlled. To achieve this Klein bottle process, people need to be reduced to the status of a herd that has only the right to bread and circuses (Veyne 1976). However, this fails to take account of the social practices of resistance and of indifference. Nowhere can it accommodate the role of uncertainty, chance, and the fluidity of identities. This transnational program will fail when governments try to enforce it. Flows of persons cannot be controlled by channeling them or filtering them by reference to identity.

Contrary to the Klein bottle process, the Möbius ribbon process can accommodate social practices of flows of people, the practices of the diasporas that open the sovereign cylinder and bind internal freedom with the freedom of movement and residence. Too much freedom does not necessarily harm security, notwithstanding the current discourse to the contrary that demonizes the new freedom for criminals and migrants. It is necessary to achieve a coexistence with the Others inside an infinite and open topology like the Möbius ribbon. Permanent uncertainty should be accepted as normal and not feared. The fact of not knowing on which face of the strip one is located (the internal or the external) is not in itself a danger but can be an opportunity. It is necessary to tame these fears rather than project them onto scapegoats—migrants, asylum seekers, and so forth. Equally, the professionals of security must not become the scapegoats. This is not an easy process. But it is vital to reconciling freedom and security beyond borders.

NOTES

1. Paul Veyne, *Comment on écrit l'histoire* (Paris: Seuil, 1971); our translation.

2. François Ewald, *Histoire de l'Etat providence* (Paris: Grasset, 1996), 17.

3. Approximately one hundred police officers, liaison officers, and department heads in the prevention of terrorism, drugs, and organized crime and other members of the security forces (police with military status like gendarmerie, judges, customs officers, intelligence services, air force, navy, and headquarters of the army).

4. "A one-sided surface that is formed by passing the narrow end of a tapered tube through the side of the tube and flaring this end out to join the other end" (*Webster's Collegiate Dictionary,* 10th ed. [1993]).

5

Borders and Identity in International Political Theory

CHRIS BROWN

Neither modern political theory nor international relations theory has an impressive record when it comes to theorizing the problems posed by borders, frontiers, and identity. In the case of Anglo-American liberal political theory, the dominant tendency is to regard political life as regulated by some kind of contract, and the bounded nature of the society that contains the "contractors" is generally uninvestigated. Nonliberal approaches, on the other hand, focus more explicitly on the community, which, in principle at least, involves a greater awareness of the importance of borders—however, the impact of global social and economic change means that the notion of a bordered, self-contained community that is at the heart of these approaches has become difficult to sustain. The absence of either a liberal or a nonliberal theory of borders has become a major source of embarrassment for political theory.

What is interesting is that international relations theory is also underdeveloped in this area. Certainly, scholars of international relations have studied frontiers, but not in the context of borders and identity. Studying frontiers was the sort of thing that international lawyers did, or global bureaucrats, not international relations theorists. This was because the relevant disciplines (international relations and international law) generally equated borders and frontiers; their practitioners believed they had a pretty good idea what a border/ frontier was in general terms, a dividing line between two states, and disputes tended to be about *where* a specific border was, a subject that raised no important general issues. Broad questions of political citizenship might be involved in a frontier dispute—a Pole could become, nominally, a German and vice versa as a result of changes in a frontier; this might well generate problems, but issues of identity in a deeper sense were not likely to be germane.

Such was the state of play in the 1960s in mainstream international relations, and the move toward the study of "complex interdependence" in the 1970s initially did not change things very much; it increased the range of cross-border transactions studied without asking fundamental questions about the nature of borders as such—the equation of border with frontier remained in place. Perhaps the only major theorist who did raise more profound questions was John Burton, but his apparent lack of interest in economic cross-border transactions isolated him from what has become the major stimulus to thought on borders over the last twenty years—changes in the global economy (Burton 1968 and 1972).

Such changes have operated at a number of different levels and have gradually created a situation in which the study of borders has become a cutting edge within the discipline, and the trilogy of identities, borders, and orders can serve as a valuable focus for research. Some of these levels have been connected with specific political events or institutions. The end of the Cold War and the associated collapse of internal controls on movement in the Soviet-bloc countries raised questions about the status of borders that had been previously suppressed, and the definition of "refugee" that had been forged in the Cold War years became obsolete. Movements within the European Union to create a single market and to facilitate cooperation on antiterrorism reduced the significance of political frontiers within Europe but, perhaps, increased the salience of the border between the Union and the rest of the world. However, the most important shift has been more general—the putative emergence of a global, as opposed to an international, economy. Whereas the world of interdependence of the 1970s was based on the assumption that societies remained separate and discrete, the new emphasis on globalization challenged this assumption (Keohane and Nye 1977; Dicken 1992).

The possibility of a genuinely global economy clearly raises the issue of borders to the top of the agenda—hence the notion of a "border-less world" (Ohmae 1990), and "de-bordering" (Albert and Brock 1996).

This new emphasis on identity and borders chimes with other shifts in the study of international relations. The reawakening of interest in links between political theory and international relations theory has caused attention to focus on the distinction between the political and the international; international relations theory is increasingly seen as constituted by thought on issues of "inside-outside" (Walker 1993) or "inclusion-exclusion" (Linklater 1998). Whereas old-style international relations theory (and, for that matter, more recent rational choice-oriented neorealist theory) took the self-contained nature of the state for granted and thus could afford to sideline questions of identity, the new emphasis is very much on how actors constitute themselves or are constituted, which inevitably involves identities, orders, and borders. Perhaps this involves a return of culture and identity to international relations theory (Lapid and Kratochwil 1996) in the sense that in an earlier period these questions were very much on the agenda, but, in any event, it certainly constitutes a shift from the 1960s and 1970s.

How international political theory understands questions concerning borders and identities is the focus for the rest of this chapter, in which a rough-and-ready classification of international political theory into "cosmopolitan" and "communitarian" categories is employed—an overly simple dichotomy that has the merit of stressing links with earlier traditions of political thought (Brown 1992). Liberals in the broad sense of the term (including social democrats) tend to be, at least in principle, universalists and cosmopolitans, while communitarian, particularist positions have been held by most of the critics of liberalism of the past two hundred years. The opposition between liberal-cosmopolitan and communitarian political theory thus makes some sense as an organizing device, even though, as will become apparent, neither camp can offer a satisfactory account of borders and identity—albeit for different reasons—while changes in the nature of international order, the third term in our trilogy, are actually making the situation more difficult for both camps.

LIBERALS, COSMOPOLITANS, AND THE ARBITRARY NATURE
OF BORDERS

Liberal political theory is Janus-faced in its approach to the political significance of boundaries and identity. On the one hand, liberals are generally universalists who approach politics from the perspective of a belief in a common humanity and whose commitment to notions such as human rights, religious tolerance, the rule of law, representative and responsible government are, in principle, universal.

At a first approximation, liberals are "cosmopolitans." This term derives from postclassical Greece (in the age of the *polis,* the city itself was at the center of political and social life, but Cynics and Stoics, writing in an age when the cities no longer possessed political independence, oriented themselves as citizens of the world, cosmopolites), but was employed as self-description by the protoliberals of the European Enlightenment. Given this general position, the expectation would be that liberals/cosmopolitans will be skeptical of any account of borders and frontiers that attempts to assign to them more than provisional and instrumental significance. Political identity itself has limited significance in the context of a universalist worldview—identity is a matter of language, literature, folkways, and, in a broad sense, culture, without necessarily carrying political weight.

At the same time, the dominant tradition espoused by liberals from Locke to Rawls via Kant has been "contractarian"—based on the idea that political relations between individuals ought to be based on a probably notional contract between them, the terms of which will, of course, vary as between different kinds of liberals. In principle, there is no reason why this notional contract could not cover the whole of humanity, but, until very recently, no liberal has taken such a position—probably because the practical problems are such that even the most hypothetical of contracts looks implausible if the assumption is that literally everyone must be a signatory. Instead, the characteristic move has been to think of a contract as operating within a "society"—being a "social contract"—without necessarily theorizing how that society came to distinguish itself from other societies or what other implications follow from this step. Clearly the only way in which this silence could be justified given the universal, cosmopolitan side of liberalism is if the borders of "society" are of instrumental significance only—simply administrative conveniences of no potential moral importance. Can this position be sustained?

A liberal who wished to sustain this position would presumably promote the establishment of the borderless world of some theorists of globalization, a world in which peoples, goods, and information would flow freely, and frontiers would become of trivial importance. Some do take this position, but surprisingly few. The essays collected in a book with the promising title of *Free Movement* are instructive in this respect (Barry and Goodin 1992). In this collection, which explicitly contrasts different ethical perspectives on the issue of the transnational migration of people, the majority of contributors write from liberal/cosmopolitan premises, but virtually no one endorses the immediate removal of frontier controls and the consequent establishment of actual free movement. The writer who comes nearest to this is Hillel Steiner; as a libertarian Steiner believes that "national boundaries possess no less—and no more—moral significance than the boundary between my neighbor's land and my own" (Steiner 1992, 93). It is all a matter of property rights, and anyone should be allowed to live anywhere they can afford to live—with, of course, no assistance from the state, direct or indirect. For the rest, even Ann Dummett, writing from the "natural law" perspective, tempers her otherwise extremist argument by acknowledging that "it would probably [sic] cause chaos if all borders were instantly opened" (Dummett 1992, 179). The more common position is that although the presumption is for free movement, and the burden of proof rests with those who would impose restrictions, nonetheless "restrictions may sometimes be justified because they will promote liberty and equality in the long run or because they are necessary to preserve a distinct culture or way of life" (Carens 1992, 25).

This is an interesting formulation that captures nicely the dilemma for liberals here; borders can be legitimated solely on pragmatic grounds, but these pragmatic grounds may actually be quite wide— "promoting liberty and equality in the long run" and a "distinct culture or way of life" cover quite a lot of space. In any event, neither phrase is quite as straightforward as it seems. The argument that borders might promote liberty and equality in the long run can take many forms. Onora O'Neill provides a good summary of these forms in one of the best examinations of the political philosophical implications of boundaries in the literature (O'Neill 1994). After examining the ways in which so much of political philosophy is dominated by an uncritical acceptance of boundaries and thus by unspoken assumptions about the limits of moral responsibility, she, nonetheless, specifically rejects the idea that

> only a world without state boundaries could be a just world. Such a world—a world state—might concentrate so much power that it risked or instituted much injustice. The common reasons given for fearing world government and its colossal concentrations of powers seem to me serious reasons. The reasons for thinking that justice is helped by bonds of sentiment between citizens, and can be destroyed by lack of all such bonds, are also strong. The evidence that those bonds are easier to forge when a sense of identity is shared is also considerable. (Ibid., 85)

This seems clear, but, on the same page, O'Neill goes on to say that boundaries are not acceptable when they "systematically inflict injustices on outsiders"; her acceptance that justice does not require the abolition of states is accompanied by the proviso that it does demand "an interpretation of sovereignty that does not constitute an arbitrary limit to the scope of justice" (ibid., 86).

Let us follow the logic of this argument. Take a real-world example, the implications for borders and frontiers of a somewhat idealized version of the social policies of the Scandinavian social democracies, "Norden," as the composite not-quite-accurately portrayed Scandinavian country is sometimes known for the sake of convenience. In Norden there is a strong sense of identity among citizens, and on this sense of identity bonds of sentiment emerge and generate social policies that are generally thought of as effective attempts to create a just society. All this is compatible with O'Neill's first formulation. However, we can still ask whether Norden "systematically inflicts injustice on outsiders." Nordanes believe that although they defend their national sovereignty quite firmly and are skeptical of supranational schemes, they are good international citizens—loyal members of the UN, upholders of international law, with comparatively high aid budgets and generous policies on asylum seekers and refugees. Nonetheless, the extensive system of social benefits they have developed are designed for citizens and invited guests. The Norden welfare state is socially inclusive but excludes those who are not Nordanes, employing the sovereign powers of

Norden to do so. Does this policy set "an arbitrary limit on the scope of justice"?

If the answer to this question is "yes," then it is difficult to see why O'Neill does not simply argue that state boundaries ought to be abolished. Here we have a society that is doing its best to create liberty and equality, and yet the equality it creates necessarily depends on preserving a greater inequality between its citizens and the rest of the world. In the world in which we live, any effective welfare state will have this effect, and no effective welfare state could exist that did not restrict its benefits to members/citizens. If one is serious about the moral irrelevance of boundaries and frontiers, then one ought to be opposed to schemes of social welfare that are restrictive, and indeed O'Neill is critical of, for example, Rawls's theory of justice precisely on the grounds that it takes for granted that justice is to be achieved in discrete societies defined as "schemes of co-operation for mutual advantage" (Rawls 1971, 4). However, in practice, most liberals—apart from Steiner, who is a libertarian, but including O'Neill—do not actually want to abolish welfare states, and so they will try to deny that Norden systematically inflicts justice on outsiders. It is difficult to see on what (liberal, cosmopolitan) basis they can do so. Writers such as David Miller or Michael Walzer certainly defend the capacity of states to restrict their membership on the basis that only thus is it possible to develop socially just societies, but their arguments are explicitly anticosmopolitan (Miller 1995; Walzer 1983).

Things are no easier for cosmopolitans when it comes to the second of Caren's reasons for accepting restrictions on free movement, the necessity to preserve a "distinct culture or way of life"; a similar bind quickly emerges. Carens is a liberal and an egalitarian, but he is also a Canadian and thus engaged in a political culture in which the rights of territorially based minorities is a key issue—hence, no doubt, his sensitivity to the issue. French Canadians in Quebec have been engaged in a long-running process of redefining their relationship with the rest of Canada, a process that may well lead to independence in the not-too-distant future—the vote for independence in successive referenda has moved toward 50 percent, and a "no" vote is regarded by the Parti Quebecois (PQ) simply as a platform for the next referendum. At the same time various of the First Nations—Canadian aborigines—wish to assert greater control over their territories, some of which, interestingly, are to be found in Quebec province. These practical issues raise serious questions about borders and identity, in which, as with the welfare state, liberals and cosmopolitans find themselves torn between the answer they would like to give, and the answer that their overall conception of society tells them they ought to give.

Consider the case of Quebec and the protection of the French language in Canada. Canada already has two official languages— English and French—and anyone wishing a civil service post needs to display proficiency in both, even if they live in a part of the country where the first language is English and the second language is more likely to be Cantonese than French. Cosmopolitan liberals will and do defend this requirement on the basis that without such protection the French language would be marginalized in Canada. However, within Quebec, where the first language is French, local law makes it very difficult to use the English language, banning its employment even in bilingual signs. Is this acceptable for a liberal cosmopolitan? Leaders of the PQ have blamed English-speaking Quebeckers for the "no" vote in the recent referendum on independence—correctly, since French-speakers did, indeed, vote for independence—and critics have alleged that the anti-English language stance in Quebec is designed to encourage the Anglos to emigrate. Is this acceptable? If so, at what point does the right to defend a particular way of life, a distinct culture, cease to legitimate departures from universal norms?

Many liberals support the right of French Canadians to defend their distinctive way of life, but would resist very strongly the idea that French people in France would have an equivalent right to defend their way of life, for example, by instituting stricter controls on immigration or by forcing new immigrants to abandon their own distinctive customs, assimilate, and become French. The practical difference here is clear enough; in the first case we have a minority within Canada defending itself in the only way it can by practicing processes of exclusion; in the second case we have a majority community in France that has no need to behave in exclusionary ways in order to defend itself and therefore cannot claim to be acting, as it were, in self-defense. If we accept the first premise—that communities are entitled to defend their identities—then there is a clear difference between what is morally acceptable behavior from an (apparently) beleaguered minority and what is morally unacceptable from a majority that is not under threat. But why, if we are liberals, should we accept this first premise? If borders and frontiers are morally irrelevant divisions of the human race that should not be allowed to interfere with the achievement of universal goals or the promotion of universal values, then, surely, we should not accept this premise. But if we do not hold that communities in general are entitled to defend themselves, why should we hold that minority communities are so entitled? What is it about being part of a minority that entitles one to special consideration?

We can see the problem even more clearly when we move to the example of the First Nations in Canada. Here we have obvious victims of past injustice who now are asserting—quite successfully in some cases—their right to control the stretches of territory that they managed to hang on to via the system of unequal treaties they were forced to sign with the British and then the Canadian federal government in the nineteenth century. Their aim is to apply their own laws and customs in their territories. The problem is that there can be a clear contradiction between these laws and customs and the rights guaranteed to all citizens of Canada by the Canadian constitution. The First Nations can only preserve their way of life in particular territories by preventing others from acquiring land or settling in the territory, i.e., by strict systems of border controls. Does the fact that the minority in question has "victim" status justify this or other potential social inequalities and patriarchal systems of rule that would not be acceptable in other circumstances?

A common cosmopolitan tactic here is represented by the work of another Canadian liberal egalitarian, Will Kymlicka (1995). He argues that liberals/cosmopolitans ought to recognize a wide range of group-differentiated rights for national minorities as not incompatible with their core commitments to individual freedom and social equality. The capacity of particular individuals to exercise freedom is formed by the culture in which they are developed and some such cultures may need differentiated rights to survive, and (for reasons which seem essentially not liberal but communitarian) Kymlicka believes that cultural diversity is good in itself, and therefore the survival of minority cultures is desirable. However, he then reintroduces universalist, cosmopolitan ideas by defining the group rights he is prepared to accept in such a limited way that actual supporters of the rights of the First Nations would be hard-pressed to accept his argument. The latter are deemed to collectively own land that they cannot alienate, but are only capable of governing the lives of individuals to the extent that individuals are prepared to allow themselves to be so governed; members retain their rights as Canadian citizens and cannot be compelled to accept any customs that violate the Canadian Bill of Rights. In effect the Nations become private associations. The group-differentiated rights he is prepared to give to minorities are not the kind of rights that the minorities themselves believe themselves to be entitled to. It is difficult to see this as other than a set of ad hoc concessions to the political needs of the day.

As with the welfare state, liberal cosmopolitan thought finds itself committed to contradictory positions on the preservation of culture. If one is committed to the view that borders, and especially frontiers, are morally arbitrary divisions of the human race, then the use of "border controls" (in the wide sense of the term) to restrict access to benefits or to preserve distinct identities seems unacceptable, and yet most are unprepared to live with the consequences of this position. One possible way out of this dilemma is offered by Brian Barry, who is one of the few cosmopolitans in the Free Movement collection who prepared openly to sanction the control of movement on the grounds that it interferes with any possibility of progressive social policy (Barry 1992). His argument is that rather than make free movement a matter of principle, one should develop the kind of global social policy that would remove the necessity for large-scale movements of people—for example, by introducing a global basic income. If such a policy were in place—admittedly quite a big if—free movement would become, in effect, a nonissue. In the meantime, we have to acknowledge that exclusion is often necessary if desirable social goals are to be maintained. Although exclusion involves discriminating between locals and "foreigners," such discrimination would be defensible on second-order "impartialist" grounds— any partiality would be justifiable on the impartial grounds that the same right to exclude would be extended to other communities (Barry 1995)—and in general consequentialist terms.

This argument has some similarity with that of liberal communitarians such as Miller and Walzer, but it also, potentially, meets O'Neill's requirements for an acceptable use of sovereign power. There is no "arbitrary limit on the scope of justice" in a policy of interference with free movement when such a policy option is available to all, and, equally, no injustice would be inflicted on outsiders, always presuming that the policy goals Barry outlines in terms of global distributive justice can be achieved. As suggested above, this is a very large presumption, but the general point is surely right that from a cosmopolitan point of view it does not make a great deal of sense to look at borders in isolation from the wider issue of the global distribution of wealth and power. If borders are essentially morally arbitrary, then their significance will be determined by factors of this kind. In an ideal world in which there were no major territorial discrepancies in the distribution of wealth, issues of exclusion and inclusion would take on different forms from those they assume under our present world order. In the meantime, the arbitrary nature of borders can be used to justify a consequentialist approach to policy as easily as it can a deontological line. But while massive worldwide discrepancies of wealth and life-chances exist, a policy of completely open borders would destroy Western welfare systems and social structures without extending any comparable advantage to the inhabitants of the rest of the world—and, of course, the losers thereby would be the poorest inhabitants of the rich countries.

BORDERS AND IDENTITY

As will have become apparent from the above discussion, liberal/cosmopolitan thought on borders and frontiers can take many forms and can even try to take on board apparently quasi-communitarian notions about the value of preserving cultural identities—albeit with some difficulty. Cosmopolitan and communitarian thought shade into each other when it comes to matters such as the right of minority cultures to preserve themselves, although it is noticeable that an essentially cosmopolitan thinker such as Kymlicka is less willing to extend the same rights to majority cultures than even a liberal communitarian such as Walzer or Miller. Where the two approaches really diverge, however, is when it comes to the nature of identity as such.

From a liberal perspective, the only true and foundational identity we possess derives from our common membership in the human race, which might also denote our common status as God's children, although this is not a necessary feature of this position. We might well possess, by chance or choice, a series of other identities (Englishman, academic, music lover, or whatever), but these are essentially secondary. The fact that they are secondary does not mean they are unimportant; as we have seen, there are circumstances where secondary identities can become very important indeed, and it is reasonable that policy should reflect this fact, so long as our primary identity as sharers of a common humanity is not compromised thereby—which is where the sort of debates engendered by multiculturalism kick in. How different can we allow the Inuit to be, or the Quebecois or whoever, without, precisely, compromising this primary identity? Some writers who are often thought of as communitarians think of identity in much the same way. The difference between their approach and that of liberal cosmopolitans is that they would allow a wider latitude to difference; the framework imposed by a common humanity is less of a straitjacket, but the general idea is much the same.

Against this position, a "strong" communitarian will argue two central and interconnected theses. First, it is not possible to be human in any generic sense of the term—one is always the product of a particular background, a particular culture, a particular form of life, and to try to separate out some sense of a common humanity foundational to all these other identities makes sense only in biological, or possibly religious, but not political terms. To attempt to crystallize this common humanity into cosmopolitanism and to oppose it to particularist identities is to make an important mistake; it implies a distinction between primary and secondary identities, which is not valid. We are not human beings who happen to be Inuit or Quebecois; we are Inuit and/or Quebecois, terms that already contain our humanity. A further implication of this point is that identity is, in the broad sense of the term, always political, always shaped by the general terms under which a particular community understands itself, its characteristic way of going about things. One can have more than one identity—just as some people are fortunate enough to be bilingual—but one cannot be without identity, any more than one can be without a language and be fully human. Identities are not something one can pick up, try on, and cast aside; they are defining characteristics of existence.

Already there are clear implications here for the notion of borders and frontiers. From the cosmopolitan perspective, borders/frontiers are essentially arbitrary—they simply enclose a group of individuals and make them part of the same political world in an arbitrary way.

The alternative position is that while communities may well originate in this way—indeed, most boundaries are the product of contingency—they will not survive and prosper unless the individuals they enclose develop a sense of self and become a community of fate and not simply a collection of individuals.

This last point leads to the second thesis of the strong communitarian: identity is not simply a matter of who you are, equally it is a question of who you are not. This negative feature of identity formation is characteristically ignored or underplayed by liberals and cosmopolitans, but it is, nonetheless, quite basic. Any particular identity always exists as one of a set of possible identities and makes no sense in other terms. Identity is about difference. Hegel saw this very clearly—his works, from the *Phenomenology* to the *Philosophy of Right* are about the processes in which individuals and, in the latter work, states become who or what they are by differentiating themselves one from another (Hegel 1956, 1991). In the final pages of the latter work, he offers what is still a powerful defense of the system of sovereign states, arguing that it is not possible to be a state unless there are other states, any more than it is possible to be a human being in the absence of other human beings. A world-state would not be a state; it could not perform the integrative functions that Hegel believes the modern, rational state is designed to perform. Identity is always about difference, borders are about maintaining difference. Thus, the point of being Quebecois is that one is not an English-speaking Canadian—indeed the point of being Canadian is that one is not a U.S. citizen. None of these identities make sense in the absence of their alternatives.

What this means, of course, is that borders and frontiers have a deep significance in identity formation and preservation and that their existence is not a contingent feature of social life. Contrary to the instrumentalism of O'Neill, for whom borders are essentially contingent features of a society that might, in certain limited ways, be made to work in favor of social justice, for the strong communitarian, borders are what make community possible in the first place. Control of "membership" as Walzer puts it (Walzer 1983) is not simply a possible social policy that might in certain circumstances be justified; it is an absolute necessity if a community is to preserve itself and the system of differences upon which it is based. If this system breaks down, then so does the identity of the community and thus the identity of the individual, unless, that is, a new system of differences and identities emerges.

IDENTITY, BORDERS, AND GLOBALIZATION

The strong communitarian account of borders and identity makes it a lot easier to understand why people take borders seriously—as most people obviously do—than does the perspective of the liberal cosmopolitan. However, a key question is the implication of this way of looking at things if we are indeed entering an era of globalization, or, at least, of an ever deeper "internationalization" as some critics of globalization would have it (Hirst and Thompson 1999). If the maintenance of borders is central to identity formation and preservation, within and between communities, and if there are links between the global economy and the global political order—as there surely are—then the alleged phenomenon of de-bordering potentially takes on a significance far beyond matters of political economy. In the extreme case, a borderless world—to take one globalist formulation—would be a world in which human identity itself was put in question. This would be an "end of history" of a sort, although perhaps not the one envisaged by Fukuyama (1992).

From a strong communitarian perspective, here presented in Hegelian terms, the basic problem lies in a potential physical disjuncture between civil society and the state. In the model of identity formation set out in the *Philosophy of Right,* civil society is the location of economic activity, competition, and strife—albeit strife within a legal framework. This competitive environment is a necessity for personal development—if we remain within the unconditional support-structure Hegel calls the family, we will not develop our capacities—but it is also necessary that this process of setting individuals against each other is not the end of the story. A level of wholeness has to be reestablished by the state—a political environment where the inequalities of civil society are countered by the notion of equal citizenship and (perhaps) an equal contribution to the general arrangements of a society. The underlying assumption here is that civil society and the state cover the same terrain—what happens when this ceases to be the case? Can the state still perform this integrative function when the civil society in question ranges over a much wider area than is bounded by the political authority?

The answer seems to be no. If we take the European experience as a guide, we can see how the process works or, rather, does not work. European integration—and trends in the global economy—has created a kind of Europe-wide civil society, but one that operates without the backup of a European state. Thus, for example, British, Spanish, Portuguese, and French fishermen compete with each other for catches in this newly emerging European civil society, but the conflicts this competition inevitably engenders cannot be reconciled by the political process because Europe is still a geographical expression, a territory with a boundary, but not (yet?) a state. There is no European identity that allows fishermen from the Basque region and the West of England to recognize each other as fellow citizens. The institutions of the European Union produce decisions, but not decisions that are accepted as legitimate and authoritative. Instead, the effect of the Europe-wide civil society is to undermine the political authorities that do exist. The British state is unable to satisfy Cornish fishermen, unable to reconcile them to the law, get them to understand that the law, in some sense, represents their will, because the problems they face transcend the boundaries of the British state. Hence the malaise known in Britain as "Euroscepticism"—although this is a misnomer, because the problem is not created by the European Union. Indeed, the Union may be the solution, not the problem. If a genuine European identity were to emerge, then these kinds of disputes would be reconcilable by the political process, and the current lack of a clear sense of the relationship between civil society and polity would come to be seen as the product of a transition period.

However, and this is the most important point, a new European identity forged around a European state might solve these intra-European contradictions, but the process could not be generalized to provide a model for the worldwide disjuncture between global civil society and global political authorities produced by globalization (or internationalization). Identity is about difference. There is no reason why a European identity could not gradually supersede British or French or Portuguese identities, but there is every reason why a global identity could not supersede European or North American or Japanese identities. Such a global identity would have no borders, no frontiers, no sense of the Other. It could do no work for the individual. Instead, the development of a genuinely global economy would create conflicts between individuals while destroying the possibility of resolving these conflicts—unless, that is, the processes of globalization create a new system of identities and difference at the same time that the old one is destroyed.

Looking on the bright side, instead of the physical borders—frontiers—that delimit the old communities, we might see the emergence of new communities, still bounded, but not by physical features. In some of his proselytizing work on behalf of the communitarian movement, Etzioni has argued for the positive significance of "virtual communities," held together by shared interests or employment (Etzioni 1993). The extreme case here is the conversation group established in cyberspace over the Internet. There is a boundary here between members and nonmembers, but it is not a physical boundary and it is a boundary that can be crossed by all who share the interests in question. Perhaps this way of thinking will become more widespread. However, it ought to be clear from the argument of the previous section that this kind of community is not able to do the sorts of things that a community in the full, nonvirtual sense can, and that the sort of identity that would emerge out of this kind of community would not be one that most people would desire.

A more plausible scenario, perhaps, is one in which old identities are destroyed as borders crumble under the pressures of globalization and are replaced by a dehumanizing uniformity. This is one side of the future dissected in Benjamin Barber's snappily titled *Jihad vs. McWorld* (1996). The forces of global consumerism, symbolized by the ubiquitous "M" of the McDonald's sign, cross all borders, undermine all identities, and reduce difference to trivialities. The response generated by "McWorld" is likely to be "jihad"—outbursts of irrational, anomic behavior. As the forces of globalization destroy older, more stable senses of identity, so darker, more primitive ways of being different come to the surface and make war on the new uniformity. "Jihad" is, perhaps, an unfortunate term here with its specifically Islamic connotations—the irrationalism in question is as likely to be found in the West as in the East, just as McDonald's threatens the roadside diner in the American Midwest as much (probably more) than it does the Parisian café. Barber himself remains committed to "strong democracy" as an alternative to either jihad or McWorld, but it is difficult to be optimistic that the forces he portrays so vividly will be manageable in this way—ultimately this is a pessimistic vision of the world, to set against Etzioni's rather facile optimism.

Can we find a way of thinking about borders in an era of globalization that does not fall into either bleak pessimism or resort to implausible technological fixes? Perhaps the beginnings of an answer can be found by investigating a little more closely what kind of borders are required in identity formation. Clearly the borders of a virtual community will not do, but—contrary to the argument set out above—one should also avoid setting up the hard shell of the classic Westphalian territorial sovereign state as the only kind of border within which identities can flourish. A more eclectic approach to political forms may be justified. Hegel and his followers had quite good reasons for regarding the modern state as the pinnacle of human achievement, but it would be a mistake to think that his reasoning will always hold good—given that most of us employ a demythologized version of his thought, we need not be reluctant to tamper with his notion of the unfolding of the "Geist." In any event, the possibility that there might be something beyond the ethical state is held out by Hegel himself at one or two points (1956, 86).

One such approach has been termed the "New Medievalism" by Hedley Bull—although only in an unelaborated passing reference (1977). Whereas the Westphalian state-system (allegedly) standardized political systems into the "like units" identified by Kenneth Waltz as characteristic of anarchical political orders (1979), its medieval predecessor recognized a number of different kinds of political units, none of which was "sovereign" in the modern sense of the term, but all of which possessed a fair degree of political autonomy. Empires, kingdoms, principalities, free cities, cathedral chapters, chartered guilds, or universities—each of these institutions was bounded and conferred identities, each had some independent political power, each was part of a system of differences that gave meaning to the lives of the individuals who composed them. This is a heavily idealized picture of medieval life, and, in any event, the analogy with the European Middle Ages ought not to be taken too seriously; the root idea here is simply the coexistence of a number of different kinds of borders and identities; indeed, it can be argued that the Westphalia system itself has rarely been quite as dominated by the territorial sovereign state as conventional thought on the matter would have it.

It is not too fanciful to suggest that a quasi-medieval range of political forms may be reappearing in contemporary global politics alongside the state form. The state-centric nature of the institutions of contemporary international society will act as a hindrance here, but in recent years even the United Nations—a supremely state-centric body—has sponsored conferences and fora in which nonstate bodies have been given an official role, and some of these bodies appear to attract levels of loyalty and commitment from their supporters at least equivalent to those that others are prepared to give to "their" states. These bodies are "bordered" and operate systems of exclusion and inclusion, even though progressively inclined groups, such as Greenpeace or the International Campaign to Ban Landmines, may be reluctant to admit that this is what they are doing. However, even if such groups become more important as time passes, which seems quite likely, and even if they become the focus for a new, limited kind of identity politics that might help to assuage somewhat the pain inflicted by McWorld and give more substantial content to the new virtual communities envisaged by Etzioni, it is highly unlikely that, for most of the world's inhabitants, they will be able to act as more than supplementary backups for the more traditional identity-conferring territorial units. One of the dangers of writing about this topic is that of mistaking the current political concerns of the literate, intellectual elite of a small group of privileged states for a more general movement. Outside of the advanced industrial world—and for many people within that world—these new forms of political identity are of little significance.

CONCLUSION: IDENTITIES, BORDERS, AND EVERYTHING

The aim of this essay has been to bring to the surface some of the ways in which the subject of borders and identity has been discussed in (international) political theory, a necessary step because neither political theory nor international relations theory has devoted to this subject the attention it deserves. In the case of liberal political theory—the dominant mode of theoretical discourse about politics, in one form or another, in advanced industrial states—there is mostly silence on the subject of borders and identity, possibly reflecting the obvious gap between the cosmopolitanism of liberal theory—the view that borders are of no great moral or normative significance and thus may be replaced, rearranged, and refocused more or less at will—and the anticosmopolitanism of liberal political practice, in which political identities are preserved if not strengthened by the active defense of borders and frontiers. Borders are an embarrassment to liberal political thought.

"Strong" communitarianism has a clearer sense of the importance of borders and of systems of inclusion and exclusion more generally for political life. Political identity is foundational to politics rather than a secondary phenomenon. The problem here is that the account of the state offered by the strong communitarian is undermined by changes in the world economy and the shift away from predominantly state-based civil societies. Opponents have always questioned the extent to which the ethical ideal of a functioning political community bears any relationship to actual political reality—this question becomes yet more germane with the passage of time. However, these same changes do not appear to be working to resolve the contradictions inherent in a more liberal, cosmopolitan approach—if anything, globalization is likely to make the clash between local and global welfare if not more relevant, then at least more readily apparent, and to make the task of determining just how local identities may legitimately be preserved more difficult.

In these circumstances it is difficult to reach any kind of conclusion except the rather trite one that the categories we bring to bear on these issues may be becoming outmoded. The pace of change is such that the normative theories developed over the past centuries seem increasingly to be directed toward a world that is disappearing; at the same time the power of these theories—and of the social institutions with which they are associated—is such that new ideas and institutions are slow to emerge. The best hope—again, rather trite—is that as changes continue to come in thick and fast, so, gradually or perhaps more rapidly, new, unpredictable kinds of thinking will emerge. At the moment we cannot see what they might be; serious thought about these matters is always backward looking, and our age's Owl of Minerva has not yet flown.

NOTE

Earlier versions of this paper were presented at Southampton University in September 1997 and in Aschaffenberg to the IBO group in January 1998. Some of these ideas are further developed in "On the Borders of (International) Political Theory" in *Political Theory in Transition*, edited by Noël O'Sullivan (London: Routledge, 2000).

6

Boundaries, Borders, and Barriers: Changing Geographic Perspectives on Territorial Lines

DAVID NEWMAN

Geographers have traditionally viewed boundaries as lying at the very heart of their discipline. Since geography is concerned with the study of areal and spatial differentiation, the existence of territorial boundaries is taken as normative in the sense that the compartmentalization of social, economic, and cultural space assumes the presence of lines that separate these spaces from each other. The geographic literature in general, and the political geographic literature in particular, is replete with the study of boundaries as a category, building on numerous boundary case studies (Minghi 1963; Prescott 1987). While the bulk of this literature has focused on the international dimension of boundaries, the existence and functions of administrative, municipal, planning, and other forms of localized boundaries have also been studied. Notwithstanding, it is the international boundary that has traditionally been seen as the most distinct of geographic demarcators, separating the sovereign state from its neighbor and, as such, determining the nature of the political and economic development on either side of the boundary. The bulk of this material has been descriptive and case study oriented and has not translated into the construction of meaningful boundary/border theory, either within geography or as part of a wider multidisciplinary debate (Newman and Paasi 1998; O'Loughlin and Kolossov 1998; Paasi 1999a; Newman 1999b; Newman, in press).

As the nature of the territory-state discourse has changed in recent years, so too has the role and function of boundaries. The end-of-nation-state thesis has brought with it a parallel argument relating to the disappearance of boundaries (Guéhenno 1995; Ohmae 1995). The impact of economic globalization, the dissemination of information through cyberspace (Brunn et al. 1994; Morley and Robins 1995; Brunn 1999), and the firing of ballistic missiles into the core areas of enemy countries with scant regard to the location or position of boundaries have greatly reduced the significance of boundaries as barriers to movement—of people, goods, information, and weaponry.

A brief glance at the map of the world shows that, despite the discourse of new world orders, the basic territorial compartmentalization of the globe remains strongly based on the existing pattern of sovereign states. The territorial dynamics of the world map continues to undergo constant change, as it has done for thousands of years, both before and since the advent of the Westphalian state system. In this sense, the territorial compartmentalization of the globe has not changed as much as many commentators have recently argued.

At the same time, the function and role of the lines that divide states have undergone significant change, as transboundary movement is eased and as political and economic interaction takes on new suprastate and intrastate dimensions, in many cases ignoring the state altogether. While some boundaries are being opened up to movement and becoming more permeable, many countries are creating their own new fences of separation in an attempt to establish their own sovereign rights as part of a process through which national and/or ethnic groups attain self-determination as ethnoterritorial conflicts are resolved. The geographical differentiation of boundaries is such that, at one and the same time, some fences are being destroyed while others are being erected.

The objective of this chapter is to partially survey the geographic literature on boundaries in light of the changing territorial realities within the system of states. The study of boundaries is one of the few areas within political geography that continued to be discussed even during the period when the study of political geography was, to a great extent, less than acceptable in most institutes of higher learning throughout the world because of its associations with pre–World War II geopolitics. The renaissance of political geography during the past two decades has brought about a return to geopolitics, in the guise of critical geopolitics, and with it a fresh approach to the study of state territories and, by definition, boundaries (Agnew 1998; Ó Tuathail 1997; Newman 1999a; Eliot and Newman 2000). Two very distinct approaches in the literature can be determined. The first of these is a continuation of the more traditional studies, focusing on particular boundaries, their changing territorial dynamics, and, to a certain extent, a discussion of the way in which boundaries, and their associated frontier regions, can become places of cooperation and contact rather than just iron walls of defense and separation (Martinez 1994). A second approach looks at the multidimensional function of boundaries, not only as fixed territorial lines, but also as social, spatial, and political constructs that are tied up with the politics of identity and in which territorial ordering is a means through which national and ethnic groups form their respective hierarchies of social order and belonging, creating exclusive and inclusive spaces in a world of transboundary movement and virtual spaces and communities (Sibley 1995; Newman and Paasi 1998). This second approach ties in with the IBO approach, with its focus on the multidimensionality and the cross-disciplinary nature of the "boundary" notion, with boundaries as social, spatial, and virtual constructs, creating diverse layers of identities, ranging from the local to the global, and from the territorially fixed to the virtual.

The study of international boundaries is, in this latter approach, just one of many types of lines that can be studied, along with many other forms of boundaries, real and imagined, national and local, all of which perform an ordering process (Albert 1999a). This approach has been characterized by a crossing of disciplinary boundaries as geographers have begun to engage with the other social sciences in their discourses of space in general, and their understandings of boundaries in particular. This chapter briefly describes the movement of geographers into the world of identity boundaries while, at the same time, retaining the importance of territory and space as part of this process or, in other words, the coming to terms with the multidimensional characteristics of the boundary/border phenomenon. The study of boundaries is placed more firmly in the contemporary social critique of society and space and the setting of a new agenda for boundary studies among geographers and other related disciplines.

THE TRADITIONAL BOUNDARY DISCOURSE

Boundary Typologies

Much of the traditional political geography literature perceived boundaries as constituting a normative construct of state-territorial organization. As such, the study of boundaries focused on their internal differentiation as a means of understanding boundary categories. Boundary typologies were a common feature of boundary studies, focusing on their location in and along certain types of terrain or the historic evolution of different boundaries as part of the growth of the Westphalian state system. Notable amongst these studies were those of Boggs (1940), who classified the process through which boundaries are drawn up and implemented on the ground. He discussed the four stages of initial definition, delimitation, demarcation, and administration of boundaries as they move from the stage of initial treaty to the physical demarcation of the boundary and its administration through the erection of fences, customs posts, searchlights. A leading American geographer of his time, Richard Hartshorne, divided boundaries into five categories: pioneer, antecedent, subsequent, superimposed, and relict (1936). He argued that the imposition of boundaries upon a landscape were linked to the process of human settlement. In some cases boundary delimitation would precede the settlement of an area and, as such, determine in advance the way in which settlement would take place and national identities would be formed, while in other cases the line of the boundary would be determined by the existence of settled groups and would take into account their cultural and identity differences. Where the two did not match, this would normally be because of the superimposition of boundaries by external, colonial powers who did not take account of existing cultural and ethnic identities and spatial patterns. In yet another classic descriptive boundary typology, S. B. Jones divided the world's boundaries into five categories: natural, national, contractual, geometrical, and power-political, again focusing on the physical evolution of these lines and the nature of the decision-making process that brought them into being in the first place (1943; 1959). Each of these typologies takes the existence of these state-dividing lines as being part of the normative territorial structure of the state, focusing on their empirical characteristics rather than their functions.

In some ways, this approach largely parallels some contemporary discussions of boundaries as the territorial shape of some states undergo spatial change, especially in Central and Eastern Europe, although this is but one strand within the contemporary debate. The study of boundary typologies and boundary evolution continues to play an important role, not least for diplomats and negotiators, but it is paralleled with alternative modes of thinking about the nature of boundaries in general that spread beyond the specific disciplinary boundaries of the academic practitioners. The traditional geographic debate concerning boundaries can be compared to much of the contemporary debate among political scientists concerning the role of territory in general and the relationship between territory and conflict in particular (Goertz and Diehl 1992; Huth 1997). This is a largely empirical debate, dividing conflicts and their territorial characteristics into types and categories, but lacking a solid theoretical base from which to derive a greater understanding of the dynamic relationship between changing notions of territory on the one hand, and the causes of international conflict on the other.

A rereading of some of these boundary typologies would allow them to be applied to contemporary thinking concerning lines and fences. Hartshorne's use of fluvial geomorphology terms, antecedent and subsequent, to describe the historic evolution of boundary types relative to the presence of settled population can be applied to the way in which sociospatial identities are formed vis-à-vis processes of territorial compartmentalization. It is the chicken and egg question of which comes first—the boundary or the identity? Are boundaries drawn up, as part of the modern state system, as a means of reflecting existing national and territorial identities, or is it the partition of territory in the first place that gives rise, over time, to the development of separate identities? When national groups are divided by boundaries into separate sovereign territories, such as in Korea, Germany after World War II, or Arab-Palestinians after the creation of the state of Israel, does the boundary impact upon them in such a way that identities change? Historical evidence would suggest that the core elements of national identity in such cases remain strong, overcoming the short-term effect of boundary imposition, while in some cases the feelings of mutual affinity displayed by minority populations may be strengthened rather than weakened.

Functionality and Frontiers

Beyond the study of boundaries as constituting physical lines on a map, the impact of the boundary on the surrounding landscape led to the study of frontier regions—not in the Turnerian sense of a settlement frontier in which so-called virgin regions were settled in the western frontiers in nineteenth-century America, but in the direct political sense of the relationship between the state boundary and the surrounding frontier region. In this latter sense, the very existence of a frontier was itself dependent on the prior existence of a boundary, or border, constituting a fault line around which the political frontier emerged. The boundary was differentiated from the frontier in the sense that the frontier constitutes an undefined area either side of the boundary line, within which the nature of spatial and socioeconomic development is dictated, in part, by the presence of the boundary. This could take place on both sides of the boundary, or on one side only, depending on the importance of the boundary as perceived by the respective governments of each state. The nature of frontier development would not necessarily be similar on each side of the boundary, as some governments would pour additional resources into the region as a means of bolstering a presence vis-à-vis the Other side, while other governments could neglect a region if they feared that it could become transformed into a future war zone in which there was a chance of the civilian infrastructure being destroyed. The work of John House was important in this respect, particularly in his focus on the notion of double peripherality and his attempt to study the functionality of frontier regions inasmuch as they are associated with the political line of separation between states (House 1980, 1981; Rumley and Minghi 1991).

A simple but meaningful functional typology of boundaries was the continuum running from "open" to "closed," characterized by the extent to which transboundary movement of goods, people, and ideas was enabled to take place (boundaries of "contact"), as contrasted with boundaries that were impermeable and acted as barriers to transboundary flows (boundaries of "separation"). This was tied in with the nature of political relations between neighboring states, with the interfaces of military confrontation characterized by closed, even "sealed," boundaries, the surrounding frontier region being transformed into a unique military landscape. Open boundaries indicated regions of peaceful cooperation between states with free movement of goods and people. Thus the functional nature of boundaries was seen as an indicator of the relations between states. As these improved or worsened, so they were reflected in the opening or closing of boundaries and the extent to which transboundary flows were allowed to take place. But questions relating to identities were not asked, as these continued to be understood as part of the normative world territorial order. Contextually, notions of movement related to tangible goods, while identities continued to be tied up with specific territories and the way in which these were divided up into states. Identities remained, to a large extent, exclusive of the Other, regardless of whether the spaces were physically compact or virtual. For their part, economic and information flows are now more inclusive, although even these are still controlled respectively by economic and academic elites, who determine the changing nature of the boundaries and the extent to which they simply become more inclusive, but nonetheless retaining certain barrier functions, as contrasted with all-inclusive phenomena that rarely exist.

Just as the military interface between East and West during the Cold War period represented the closed end of the boundary continuum, so contemporary notions of state deterritorialization, the end of territorial absolutism (Taylor 1995, 1996), and the removal of boundaries represent the open end of the continuum. The fact that the "disappearance of boundaries" thesis is largely a Western European and North American discourse reflects the fact that many (although by no means all) of the boundaries in these regions have become increasingly permeable as a result of both technological and political changes that have taken place in these regions during the past three decades. Much of the recent literature on international boundaries has focused on the nature of transboundary cooperation in Western Europe and the way in which this is both an outcome of, and a catalyst for, peaceful relations between states (do Amaral 1994; Galtung 1994; Martinez 1994; Minghi 1991, 1994). In this sense, these studies draw on the functional differentiation of boundaries, but only as lines that have become more permeable, where some of the barrier and fence dimensions have become more flexible, not as social constructs that determine the borders of group exclusion and inclusion at a variety of levels.

Removing or Erecting Fences? A Geography of International Boundaries

The end-of-boundaries thesis is tied in closely with the suggested demise of the nation state (Guéhenno 1995; Ohmae 1995). Globalization impacts have meant that boundaries can no longer act as effective barriers to economic flows or the transmission of information, while even physical movement of people has become easier as a result of greater mobility on the one hand, and the opening up of economic and labor markets on the other. Nowhere is this more apparent than in Western Europe, where the lines separating states have, during the past forty years, been transformed from barriers into points of contact.

But territory remains a basic ingredient of state formation (Driver 1991; Agnew 1994; Johnston 1995; Anderson 1996; Murphy 1996) as well as the means through which governments compartmentalize and control their citizen populations (Taylor 1994, 1995). While boundaries are opening up—even collapsing—in some parts of the world, new fences are being erected in many other areas. This is particularly the case in regions of ethnoterritorial conflict, where minority populations and/or secessionist groups aspire to greater autonomy and independence, expressed through sovereignty in a clearly defined piece of territory, demarcated by the boundaries of separation with neighboring states and national groups (Newman 2000a). This is as true of Israelis and Palestinians as it is of Tamils and Sinhalese in Sri Lanka, Cypriot Turks and Greeks in Cyprus, the many new national groups in the former territory of the Soviet Union, and Bosnians and Serbs in former Yugoslavia, to name but a few of the more prominent cases (Kolossov 1992; Forsberg 1995).

Paradoxically, it is the erection of new national fences and the creation of independent sovereign units that operate as equal units within the world political system that paves the way for the eventual opening up of boundaries in the long term. It is only as equal members of the international community, as countries that do not feel themselves automatically threatened by the country on the Other side of the fence, that states are prepared to enter into transboundary cooperation within economic and information spheres, bringing about the gradual opening of the lines that have been rigidly sealed in the past. Seen from this perspective, the Western European experience during the past forty years is a single model of boundary opening, one that may yet be copied by other countries and regions, but one that has not yet taken place in large parts of the world.

Globalization of information and economic flows has meant, however, that even the erection of new state boundaries that mark out the sovereign territory of the state do not have the sort of impact that an "iron curtain" between East and West Germany, or a "green line" between Israel and the West Bank have had in the past. The transmission of information through satellites and cyberspace has played a major role in the willingness of states to open their boundaries, due to cultural awareness and/or economic necessity to be part of the global village (Brunn 1999). The days in which the United States would attempt to erect a transmission station for the Voice of America broadcasting station in Israel's Aravah desert as a means of transmitting through the back door of the Soviet Union are long gone.

Territorial lines remain partial barriers to the physical movement of people. Fences, walls, and customs posts retain their function of preventing the movement of people who do not possess the correct documents or are defined as undesirable elements, although this, too, is changing as the technology of transportation becomes increasingly sophisticated, as borders are removed from the territorial periphery of the state into the heart of the main metropolitan airfields, and as the global economy creates an increased demand for cheap migrant labor, who, having arrived in a host country, are loathe to give up their new status and return to their countries of origin. This results in the creation of new ethnic minorities, minorities who do not even benefit from the minimum obligations of the state to its citizens. As such, the relationship between the territorial boundary and its citizenship, while remaining more closely in tandem than the relationship between the boundary and the national identity of the individual, is also undergoing substantial change (Soysal 1996).

THE BOUNDARIES OF IDENTITY: LINKING THE SPATIAL AND THE SOCIAL

The formation of national and group identities is closely linked to the notion of boundaries (Wilson and Donnan 1998). The relationship between spatial boundaries and the formation of ethnic and national identities has, until recently, been inferred at the best, normally through the existence of the state system and the formation of regional identities that often result in demands for autonomy and/or secession (Knight 1982, 1994). Not only do the social and ethnic boundaries that enclose groups create the Us and the Other, but so, too, do territorial boundaries as the lines within which state activity takes place and that determine the spatial locus around which national identities are formed through processes of social construction (Paasi 1996). Territory itself becomes part of the national identity, with places and spaces taking on historical and, in many cases, mythical significance in the creation of the nation's historical narrative.

But boundaries of identity and territorial boundaries do not always overlap in such a convenient fashion. The superimposition of territorial lines in areas in which a single regional identity has already been formed may result in the fragmentation of these groups into a number of state territories, within each of which they are transformed into an ethnic/national minority. Alternately, the superimposition of lines, often by colonial outsiders, brings together a number of groups possessing clearly differentiated national identities into a single territory, giving rise to internal struggles for power and, in some cases, civil war, ethnic cleansing, and even genocide. One only has to look at the impact of boundary superimposition on Africa during the past century to understand how tribal identities, based as they were on territorial flexibility, have been caught up in the colonial demand for territorial fixation. Even as African peoples are still coming to grips with the imposition of the nation-state idea, the past colonizers are now suggesting that these boundaries should be broken down in a new world of shared identities, multicitizenship, and flexible territories.

The postmodern discussion of territory suggests a more flexible framework through which territorial boundaries and identity boundaries can live side by side without the need for the demarcation of absolute entities (Newman 1999a, 2000a; Paasi 1999a, 1999b). The opening of boundaries does not necessarily mean the dilution of national identities, but it enables such identities to operate within a looser spatial framework, one that is not so tightly bound to the territorial demarcation of state sovereignty. The permeability of territorial boundaries enables freedom of movement, dissemination of ethnic and national cultures, and, for some favored groups, multicitizenship. But it does not mean that virtual identities are necessarily aspatial or divorced from notions of territory and space. In many cases, it enables members of diaspora groups to identify with distant territories, territories they learn about through the Internet and the satellite media, thus strengthening their territorial attachment while not necessarily residing therein. This, in turn, causes new problems associated with the extent to which these groups undergo successful processes of absorption into their new surroundings and/or the extent to which their host society accuses them of having dual loyalties.

Important in this respect has been Paasi's study of the Russian-Finnish boundary. Paasi notes the importance of socialization narratives as part of the process through which the specific territorial attachments and identities of the populations on each side of the boundary have evolved over time (Paasi 1996). I have discussed similar processes in studies of the "green line" boundary between Israel and the West Bank (Newman 1994, 1995), itself part of a wider process through which the formation of Jewish national identity in the modern state of Israel is part of an ongoing process of territorial socialization to which the Jewish people were subject during the two thousand years of the Diaspora and that has been transformed into concrete policies aimed at controlling territory as a result of the establishment of the state of Israel.

Thus a study of contemporary boundaries requires significant reconceptualization, which can take account of the diverse scales of territorial analysis, from the global to the local, as well as the extent to which these different boundaries allow for greater or lesser contact as they become more permeable and easier to cross. The relationship between identity and borders is, to a great extent, a function of the degree to which sociospatial ordering takes place, undergoes territorial reconfiguration, and is maintained for any significant period of time. It is the fluidity of boundary change that has to be taken into account as part of this ordering process, rather than erroneously assuming that such fluidity automatically brings about the eradication of a structured spatial ordering.

IDENTITIES, BORDERS, ORDERS IN ISRAEL AND PALESTINE

The Israel-Arab conflict in general, and the Israel-Palestine conflict in particular, are good examples of the way in which the concept of boundaries has changed over time and provides a good example of the need to understand the multidimensionality of the border/boundary notion for a deeper understanding of the conflict in general. Geographers have traditionally viewed this conflict from a territorial perspective, focusing on such issues as the demarcation of physical lines, the impact of boundaries on changing settlement patterns, and the position of boundaries in relation to strategic sites and/or scarce water resources. Conflict and peace discourses have both traditionally focused around the notion of territorial boundaries and the need to demarcate lines of territorial separation that meet the various security, resource, and settlement needs of the respective sides. But increasingly the search for "good" boundaries (Falah and Newman 1995) has demonstrated the need to equally take into account the need for boundaries that satisfy the identity requirements of both Israelis and Palestinians, over and beyond the simple lines of territorial demarcation. These become complex as national territories and identities do not overlap in such a way as to enable each side to create lines of maximal separation, resulting in the residual of national minorities residing in the territory dominated by the Other. The formation of national identity for both Israelis and Palestinians is strongly tied up with the nature of territorial separation and sovereignty, each demonstrating, time after time, their preference for respective nation-states rather than a single binational entity in a single, small territory.

The demarcation of territory has been a very fluid process in Israel-Palestine during the twentieth century. From the period of the Ottoman Empire through the British Mandate, the establishment of the state of Israel and the partition of Palestine, the Six-Day War and Israeli territorial expansion, the Camp David Peace Accords with Egypt and territorial contraction, followed by the most recent phases of Palestinian autonomy and Israeli territorial withdrawal, the map of the region has been constantly changing (Newman 1998a). Despite the mental images of a map made up of Israel and the West Bank, it is forgotten that the West Bank only came into being as a separate territorial entity in 1949 and that its boundaries were removed/opened after only eighteen years in 1967; since then it has continued to function as a separate administrative, if not sovereign, territory under Israeli control. The future lines of territorial demarcation lie at the heart of the Israel-Palestine peace process, although attempts to move beyond the stage of cheeseboard autonomy, consisting of exclaves, territorial corridors, bypass roads, and Palestinian territorial discontinuity, into a stage of territorial compactness and the establishment of a two-state solution is proving to be a difficult task (Newman 1998b).

Some studies have demonstrated the importance of space for an understanding of demography (Soffer 1984; Romann 1989), but only in the sense that the nature of the demographic problem changes according to the geographic scale studied. This ranges from the microlevel of regions within the state, the entirety of the sovereign territory of the state, to the state and the Occupied Territories. From a purely descriptive perspective, it is deduced that the most favorable demographic ratio in terms of state control is that of the sovereign territory of the whole state, such that the boundaries of the state act as an important territorial container and agent of control. Reducing the spatial scale to regions within the state or increasing the scale to include the Occupied Territories displays demographic ratios that are less favorable to state (Israeli) control, and, as such, spatial policies of control and development are put into effect as agents through which that state control is enhanced (Yiftachel 1991, 1992), normally justified in terms that the state has to ensure its security and safety.

The notion of Israel as a state without borders is interesting in this respect. Jewish residents of the Diaspora, as far away as Miami, can sometimes have more rights than Arab-Palestinian citizens of the country who have lived there uninterrupted for generations. While for Israeli settlers in the West Bank there is no boundary separating them from citizenship and participation in normal daily life in the Israeli core, for Palestinian residents of the Occupied Territories (the same area) the "erased" boundary has a major impact (Newman 1994, 1995). They are not citizens of Israel and are subject to different laws than their Israeli settler neighbors. From this respect, the West Bank is one of the most interesting territorial issues still to be resolved. Unlike virtually all other territories, even contested ones, the West Bank does not have any formal jurisdiction or sovereignty. It is not part of sovereign Israel, neither is it part of neighboring Jordan. As such, the Palestinian residents of this region do not face that same contradiction of international law in which the right to self-determination for national groups is recognized, while the right to secession from the state is not. In the case of the Palestinians, there is, legally, no problem of secession, because their territory is not part of an existing sovereign state. Given the mutual desire to reach a political solution, the main problem to be solved is the demarcation and delimitation of the boundary in a situation where there is no such thing as an optimal boundary, one that lines up the territorial and identity dimensions of both sides to the conflict. This assumes, of course, a situation where both peoples continue to reject the notion of a single territory in which there is a binational state for both Israelis and Palestinians.

But the question of boundaries and identity do not only relate to the Israel-Palestine conflict. They also relate to the intra-Jewish diversity and growing heterogeneity of Israel's citizen population. Groups that were previously marginalized, through a combination of socioeconomic inferiority and spatial segeregation, have undergone significant empowerment in recent years. Ashkenazic secular hegemony is being lost as the voices and growing electoral power of Mizrahi (Sephardic) and religious groups are coming to the fore. Other marginalized groups include those that are spatially segregated (such as the Arab-Palestinian citizen population, 20 percent of the country's total) and those that are not (such as women) as issues of citizenship and identity become more complex within a post-Zionist society. As a single-state ethos, Zionism displayed a clear identity between territorial homeland and national identity. As a state of all its citizens (rather than an exclusively Jewish state) a post-Zionist Israel would be less focused on territory, to the extent that territory is a spatial construct within which people reside but does not necessarily possess deep symbolic values contributing to identity formation (Newman 2000b). Thus the relationship between territory, boundaries, and identity is undergoing significant changes as Israel enters into its next fifty years of existence.

CONCLUSIONS: FROM BOUNDARIES TO BORDERS

The discussion has raised questions concerning the nature of boundaries/borders as constituting both spatial and social constructs at one and the same time. While it may be no more than a play on semantics, the discussion also raises a terminological question as to whether boundaries and borders constitute the same phenomenon. The geographic literature has distinguished between the boundary and the frontier but has assumed that the boundary and the border are interchangeable—they constitute the line of separation, as contrasted with the frontier, which is the area affected by the existence of the line. The dictionary definition of these terms simply describes the boundary as "the limit line," while the border encompasses the notion of boundary and is described as "distinct edging or... definition round anything." It is this transition from the study of the line per se to the social and spatial functions of those lines as constructs that defines the nature of inclusiveness and exclusiveness, which would appear to characterize the contemporary debate concerning boundaries and borders. While boundaries have been penetrated, borders retain their essential characteristics as constructs that define the nature of exclusion and inclusion. The point of contact is to be found where ethnic and national groups desire to erect their new borders and fences of separation but at the same time benefit from the permeability of boundaries in the economic and information spheres of activity, in other words, the forces of globalization. The extent to which the latter will not, eventually, affect the former is one of the most interesting questions facing geographers, political scientists, and international relations scholars in their study of the boundary/border construct.

This review of the study of boundaries/borders within political geography has demonstrated a significant move from a traditional, descriptive approach to a conceptual approach that recognizes the fluidity of the boundary concept—both in territorial and social terms. Rather than view the geographic line from a deterministic perspective, it is clear that the territorial compartments and the social groups therein are part of a mutual feedback relationship in which the local, regional, and virtual identities of a group are responsible for creating the boundaries within which they are enclosed and that form hierarchical processes of ordering. In this sense, the geographic study of boundaries cannot be fully understood without recourse to the sociological and political literature appertaining to this topic, while neither sociologists nor political scientists should ignore the importance of the territorial component in the formation of identities and in the spatial compartmentalization of human groups.

II

*Rethinking the "Political":
Democracy, Citizenship, and Migration*

Rethinking the "Political": Democracy, Citizenship, and Migration

YOSEF LAPID

Recognizing international relations as a subdivision of a broader field of political disciplines invites an interesting reformulation of John Ruggie's puzzle. The question now becomes: "What makes the world hang together in the political sense?" Three observations make this question timely and relevant to our current concerns. First, recent developments have been no less, and perhaps more, cruel to the "political" than to the "international." Long recognized as an essentially contested concept, scholars now wonder if even this minimal recognition is still warranted. "[I]s politics condemned to incoherence, and is political science condemned to incoherence, in a crosscutting, globalized world?" asks, for instance, Philip Cerney (1999, 152). The question is anything but rhetorical. It denotes a massive and still growing confusion as to the proper definition, location, and parameters of the political (Hey and Marsh 1999). It represents the price tag of a perhaps understandable, but intellectually unsustainable, mainstream reluctance to seriously engage with the question of the political in an era of epochal transition (Walker 1995). And it anticipates the inevitable collapse of would-be proprietary claims by various political fields over this elusive subject matter (Parekh 1999). In short, to the extent that our world still hangs together in the political sense, we need a very different understanding of the political (i.e., more globalized, less territorialized, more processual, less formalistic, more reflexive, and less nationally bounded, etc.) to make theoretical sense of this observation.

The second point takes us further down the road in the same direction. Upon closer examination, it turns out that some of the major problems now afflicting the political derive from similar origins and lend themselves to largely similar solutions as those encountered in our previous discussion of the international. The main culprits, in both cases, are orthodox positions that unreflectively declare themselves satisfied with pregiven actors operating in preconstituted and clearly demarcated "inter" and/or "intra" arenas. The limits of such formalistic, nominalistic, and parochial understandings of the political are well exposed by Colin Hay and David Marsh (1999) who take their clue from Adrian Leftwich to develop a more processual and contextual definition of politics. As well put by Leftwich (1984, 10), "the single most important factor involved in influencing the way people implicitly or explicitly conceive of politics is whether they define it primarily in terms of a process or whether they define it in terms of the place or places where it happens, that is, in terms of an arena or institutional forum."

Thirdly, whereas a processual understanding of politics allows the political to unfold in any and all social locations, an identities/borders/orders approach directs us to the contested historical processes likely to determine the specific shape, scope, and location of the political in any given situation. For, as aptly noted by Richard Devetak, "political space is never simply 'present,' but only takes effect after boundaries have inscribed and demarcated different domains" (1995, 30). With Devetak, it is essential to emphasize that the political is already present in acts of boundary inscription that subsequently shape its forms and manifestations. More generally perhaps, this insight needs to be expanded from the borders/bordering element to the entire IBO construct. For it is at the intersections of this triad that the historically variable shape of the political comes to be (momentarily) fixed and unfixed. To that extent, the IBO triad offers an excellent entry point to the study of how different worlds come to hang together in the political sense. It follows furthermore that the ability to imagine new forms of politics (and new forms of justice) is intimately related to the ability to conjure new IBO configurations (Dillon 1999).

In different ways, the chapters included in this section demon-strate that thinking through the political using IBO terms is currently tantamount to rethinking it. In the context of IBO discussions of different topics such as democracy, human rights, and citizenship, the political gets stretched, pulled, and bent in new and surprising ways. Depicting a world of increasingly unbundled and free-floating identities, polities, and territories, David Jacobson subtly touches upon most of these issues. Geography is depicted as a big loser in the late modern game, with a variety of "social spaces" moving into the vacuum left by the weakened logic of Westphalian territoriality. As a result, the global landscape—now vastly complexified and ju-dicialized—is reconfigured as a "skein of myriad social, territorial, political, and economic 'spaces.'" Politics is forced to respond to and partake in these developments. As Jacobson puts it, "It is at the interplay of these spaces or 'territories'—moral, social, physical, economic, and so on—that we can discover incipient political forms with consequences for both domestic and international politics." The new political forms that Jacobson finds most interesting are in-cubated under his expansive notion of judicialization, which cuts across the traditional internal/external distinction. The IBO triad plays an important, if tacit, role in this analysis, demonstrating its versatile applicability to all the thematic issues included in this sec-tion (i.e., migration, citizenship, and democracy).

The possibility that we might be facing some new fundamental transformations in democratic political practices as they cross terri-torial borders is Antje Wiener's main concern in the eighth chapter. One major purpose is to highlight what happens to democracy as the regulatory and problem-solving capacities of territorialized po-litical orders are gradually declining. Her broader objective, how-ever, is closely associated with David Held's ambitious "democracy for the new millennium" project (Buzan, Held, and McGrew 1998), seeking to imagine democratic institutions beyond the nation-state. In this spirit, Wiener creatively appropriates, adapts, and deploys the IBO triad, putting the mutually constitutive interplay of political practices and structuring norms at the center of attention. This di-alectical interplay is relied upon, in turn, as the main driving force behind Wiener's "process-oriented approach" to modern and post-modern polity formation. Her analysis suggests that "postmodern democratic substance is based on contested access to participation in changing identity, borders, orders constellations." Noteworthy also is Wiener's insistence on moving discussions of democracy from political theory and comparative politics into international relations. For insofar as contemporary democratic politics are hybridized along medieval or postmodern lines, the scientific tools used to engage such phenomena must undergo a corresponding process of hybridization.

In chapter nine, Rey Koslowski invokes currently expanding state practices that allow dual nationality to explore possible changes in the manner in which both our international and political worlds hang together. Challenging both traditional notions of political identity and basic assumptions of the modern European interstate system, dual nationality and/or dual citizenship can be readily analyzed in IBO terms. Koslowski takes full advantage of this potential to address some hidden complexities entailed in his case study. Particularly interesting is the author's refusal to indulge in a simplistic equation of dual nationality/citizenship with dual or multiple identities/loyalties. "Dual nationality," notes Koslowski, "may be indicative of a step in political identity transfer from home to host state, retention of home state identity, a desire to maintain multiple political identities, a reluctance to choose a political identity, or it may have nothing to do with political identity at all." However, rather than concluding from the above that dual nationality can have only weak or remote ramifications for international order, Koslowski opts for the opposite conclusion by calling attention to the "constitutive nature of citizenship" and to "the role of nationality law in 'bounding' states." By moving swiftly from a potentially problematic identities-to-orders (I-to-O) argument to a more plausible borders-to-orders (B-to-O) hypothesis, Koslowski highlights one of the important advantages offered by our triad.

In chapter ten, Martin Heisler makes migration the focal point of the interrelated dynamics of identity, borders, and orders. To be sure, the combination of the IBO framework with the migration subject matter constitutes a perfect match for scholarship and reflection. For, as aptly put by Heisler, "When migrants cross borders...they enter not only the territory of a (more or less) sovereign state, with predominant legal powers within its boundaries, but also that maze of social relationships and institutions." In other words, migrations involve all the intersections of the IBO triad and are hence likely to deeply impact political dynamics in both domestic and international arenas. Issues of citizenship, democracy, and human rights are greatly complicated by contemporary waves of internal and external migrations. To make these points, Heisler takes his readers on a vast comparative journey across time and space with well-targeted crossings of domestic/external and modern/postmodern intersections. The end result leaves no doubt that in the foreseeable future one cannot possibly hope to understand the political without due attention to the migrant (Weiner 1996; Castels 1998).

In the closing chapter of this section, Neil Harvey registers an explicit plea to conceive of the political as a "constitutive rather than merely reflective" of identities, borders, and orders. Subscribing to an understanding of the political that is heavily shaped by postmodernist, poststructuralist, and feminist sensibilities, he locates the political in a wider social, economic, and cultural context. Given his expressed desire to sensitize the IBO framework to the needs of "marginal sites" in world politics, it is hardly surprising that Chiapas, rather than Westphalia, becomes the empirical referent for the IBO construct. In addition, Harvey advocates the use of discourse analysis as a preferred methodology for IBO studies. Note, however, that these analytical and methodological choices do not denote a reluctance to engage with mainstream positions in area, comparative, and/or international studies. On the contrary, Harvey's endorsement of the IBO framework partially derives from the proved ability of this framework to bring together scholars subscribing to profoundly divergent worldviews.

7

The Global Political Culture

DAVID JACOBSON

The social organization of the world, it is now apparent, has become much more complex. Bordering has become more multifaceted of both geographic and nongeographic forms, of social, political, and economic characters. Political regimes (like human rights or the European Union) and ethnic or other forms of community and territorial states are no longer necessarily coextensive or congruent. Borders, in this broader sense, also designate inclusion and exclusion and, particularly with ethnic, religious, and other such communities, moral proximity and moral distance. It is at the interplay of these spaces or "territories"—moral, social, physical, economic, and so on—that we can discover incipient political forms with consequences for both domestic and international politics. Administrative and judicial rules, I argue, are becoming ever more significant in mediating and regulating the kaleidoscope-like complexity of the world. These are mechanisms of control that become tighter, not looser, with growing complexity, just as any organization requires more regulation with growing specialization, differentiation, and complexity. Thus it is no accident that international law has become much more "dense" with growing global complexity (just as domestic law historically became more extensive and more specialized with industrialization). Similarly, the logic of rights is at least complementing, and increasingly constraining, the logic of popular sovereignty and its political philosophical base—civic republicanism—and its institutional expression, the legislature.

In terms of the IBO framework, identities, borders, and orders or, as I would put it, the communal, territorial, and political threads of the human condition, which were a single braid in the nation-state, so juxtaposed as to be indistinguishable, are being rethreaded in a uniquely different way. The IBO components are, of course, still intrinsically related to one another, but in fundamentally different ways. Social solidarity can take many forms—it does not have to be the *Volksgemeinschaft* or other territorially defined forms of nationality, of the nation-state. And territoriality and politics do not—obviously—disappear, but take on distinctly different castes. I have examined issues to do with social solidarity and political community elsewhere; here the primary concern is the political (ordering) and, to a lesser extent, the bordering dimensions of the IBO triad.[1]

In this chapter, I will schematically examine the global political (and, to some extent, the social) forms coming to the fore in the wake of the unbundling of the nation-state. Particular attention will be paid to the role of law for both methodological and substantial reasons. Methodologically, law is an observable and measurable means for tracking political and social changes. Substantially, I argue, a robust legal-institutional framework of immense regulatory importance frames the global changes we are witnessing. Globalization, in the economic, social, or cultural sense, is not taking place in an anarchic environment.

The changes we are witnessing also pose fundamental normative issues: Are these changes good or bad? Can social order and peace be maintained in this much more multicultural framework? Let me point out that certain structural and "moral" changes are, empirically, taking place, and I believe that they are not likely to be fundamentally reversed, whether they are "good" or "bad." I think we can examine these changes independently of what we think of them (though some of my friends in political theory will disagree)—my argument here is not a prescriptive one. If asked, I would say I believe some of the changes are welcome; others raise concerns. However, in this chapter, that is neither here nor there. One can say, nevertheless, we are not descending into a chaotic world any more than it has been in the past—the key word is "transformation," not "fall."

NEW BORDER CUSTOMS

In recent decades, if not in recent years, some remarkable developments have taken place in what can be broadly referred to as the "global political culture" (or, alternatively, developments leading to a global political culture). Let me note some political and social "snapshots" that, I shall suggest, are indicators of significant changes in the way political identity is constituted and in the place of the state in the international order.

From the end of World War I, there was a steady accumulation in the number of multilateral international legal treaties and a dramatic increase after World War II. In 1950, there were 187 significant multilateral treaties in force; by 1988 there were almost 800 significant treaties—evidence of an increasingly dense global legal environment (Bowman and Harris 1993).

In the last two decades (and, more rapidly, in the last five years) countries that account for the bulk of foreign populations in the United States and Western Europe—such as Mexico, Turkey, Italy, the Dominican Republic, Russia, El Salvador, and Columbia—have legalized dual citizenship or nationality.

The term "human rights" is referred to in 19 U.S. federal court cases before the twentieth century, 34 cases from 1900 to 1944, 191 cases from 1945 to 1969, 803 cases in the 1970s, over 2,000 times in the 1980s, and, at the present rate, will be cited in over 6,000 cases through the 1990s. In the European Court of Human Rights, the caseload jumps from 11 cases in 1959 through 1973 to 395 cases in 1974 through 1992.[2]

Foreign and immigrant populations have changed the ethnic hues of Western European and American social landscapes in recent decades. In France and Germany, with the largest foreign populations in Western Europe, there were about 9 million foreigners, accounting for more than 7 percent of the total population, compared to 3 percent in 1960. In the United States, the foreign-born population was 90 percent white in 1970, compared to 50 percent in 1990. The Hispanic share among the foreign born jumped from 15 percent in 1970 to 40 percent in 1990. Asians account for another 25 percent of the foreign born in the United States today.

These collective "snapshots" both reflect and reinforce what is one of the most striking developments in the international structure since the Treaty of Westphalia in 1648: the disaggregation of the nation-state. The political, communal, and territorial components of the nation-state, once thought so intertwined as to be unremarkable, are being unbundled. Territory no longer constitutes identity, in that a territory and a people are no longer viewed as being inextricably linked. Diasporas and transnational identities are increasingly common. Citizenship no longer designates "belonging-in-space" and decreasingly answers the question "Who am I?" (Goodwin-White 1998; Habermas 1992a). The state itself is also being "rebranded," to use that curious phrase of the present Labor government in the United Kingdom; new transnational, international, and regional political entities, from international human rights institutions to the European Union, are constraining the state in some respects and enhancing its role in others.

This does not suggest the state is in decline; on the contrary, its bureaucratic role is enhanced.[3] The marriage of nation and state, however, is in question. Similarly, borders and their control remain significant, but the form and functions of regulation are changing— who can and cannot be admitted is more constrained by international norms than has been the case up to now and is no longer the sovereign prerogative of states. Thus the dichotomies that are presented to us—"states' rights versus human rights," or "open borders versus closed borders" hide, if I may so suggest, more than they reveal. Similarly, the tendency to think linearly—the state is in decline or is reasserting itself, or globalization is in opposition to a world of states—is false; the process we are witnessing is of a much more dialectical character. Finally, the developments described here are much more characteristic of the Euro-Atlantic arena; ironically, trumpeting human rights in the West brings a reassertion of Westphalian sovereignty in many parts of the Third World, notably China.[4] Still, there is an underlying logic to human rights—their imputed universality—that creates constant pressure to extend that regime worldwide.

In this paper I explore how in recent decades migration has contributed to the restructuring of the international order as well as the state itself by, in effect, decoupling the organization of identity from the state. Migration is referred to only as an illustrative (if important) case; research along these lines in other areas is, of course, warranted as well. What we see emerging, in essence, are different forms of "bordering"—in addition to territorial and state borders, ethnic, religious, and social groups are defining themselves, their boundaries, in ways that are not necessarily coextensive with physical borders. This creates—from the perspective of the modernist—a dissonance between physical and social spaces. In addition, we have other spaces being formed that may cut across or aggregate boundaries, both territorial and social. Those spaces include economic zones or regional organizations like the European Union (EU) or open-ended arrangements like the European Convention on Human Rights or the Organization for Security and Cooperation in Europe (OSCE) or, for that matter, the all-encompassing yet instantly linked space— a hyperspace, if you will—of the global economy. The questions, or problems, become: Are these spaces linked or organized? What is the role or place of the state in this context? One response is the poststructuralist—to purport a decentered world, with constantly contested meanings with no clear direction. This is not the case. Indeed, the world, and especially the northern half, shows a remarkable degree of structure and, so to speak, logic.

What is interesting about this skein of myriad social, territorial, political, and economic "spaces" is that it is matched by a growing density of law—not just domestic, but international law. And that international law is characterized not only by its quantitative growth, but certain qualitative developments as well. Central is the growing importance of law where the object of the law is the individual, not the state. Second, there is the growing specialization of the law in specific domains like commercial law. Third, in tandem with specialization is the expansion of international law issue areas into cognate concerns (like GATT, in its most recent round, or NAFTA, making explicit reference to migration issues). Fourth, there is the visible presence of tribunals, arbitration mechanisms, and other legal entities that deliberate independently of states and even allow nonstate actors to arrive at agreements or arrangements independently of these states (Sassen 1996). In addition, we see many more actors internationally; the case of transnational corporations is well known, but this is matched by actors of all kinds on the global stage, such as international nongovernment organizations or INGOs (see Boli and Thomas 1997). Transactions across the international arena, from economic to social to communications, are becoming, likewise, much more multitudinous. So not only do we have many more "dissonant" spaces, the series of transactions that take place at various levels and between levels across the world landscape are much more extensive. Similarly, we have a global division of labor that at one and the same time unites the globe into a singular orbit, a single society if you will, while at the same time creating increasing specialization and differentiation. What, in the context of this differentiation and "uncoupling" is the anchor, the organizing principle that "makes the world hang together" in Edward Teller's now famous phrase?

The answer, in part, is a contractual framework, emerging not in the microeconomic sense but in a Durkheimian sense—that is, we do not have free-floating rational actors arriving at mutually self-interested agreements, but a social and political framework of immense coercive power mediating between different spaces using the logic of contractual law. It is a contractual logic that is also anchored in certain moral assumptions of the dignity and the privileging of the individual (and private property) over all other ideological arrangements, that assumes collective identities are legitimate only insofar as they reflect certain voluntarist understandings, and that reinforces a tendency toward privatization of property and of identities.

International human rights law and the idiom of human rights, rooted in presumptions of the inviolability (with some limits) of the individual, is one critical, emerging mechanism for mediating the multitude of social spaces no longer necessarily delimited by geographic demarcations. In fact, international law generally expands dramatically; as the forms as well as the multiplicity of interactions increase (between states, between states and nonstate actors, between transnational nonstate actors, and so on), so the rules enabling and mediating contact multiply. Law of a contractual nature, furthermore, becomes all the more evident as the taken-for-granted assumptions, the collective consciousness, wanes—or was not very strong to begin with, as is the case on the international playing field. To paraphrase Durkheim (1984, 24–25), the number of social or economic relationships is proportional to the legal rules that enable them, and furthermore, if social life generally is to have any regularity, it becomes organized, and law is that organization in its most precise form. The expansion of human rights, with its contractual-like underpinnings—the dignity of the individual, the notion that community is or should be at the voluntary acquiescence of the individuals concerned, and the idea that the individual and his or her community inhabit an autonomous space that needs to be mutually agreeable with other like individuals and their spaces—is associated, not surprisingly, with the emergence of global production and division of labor, with which it shares a certain moral affinity.

A preliminary analysis of international law trends reveals, in this context, some interesting developments. First, international law treaties have steadily increased since after World War I, but they increased especially dramatically after World War II (Bowman and Harris 1993). Second, international human rights law in its present formulation begins with the Universal Declaration of Rights in 1948, but makes its most significant entrance in case law in Western Europe and—with some ambiguity—in the United States in the 1970s and 1980s, confirming the individual as an object of international law. Third, treaties on economic issues, like NAFTA and the later rounds of GATT, began to deal with cognate areas like migration in the 1980s and 1990s. What is interesting about these developments is that it is in this period, roughly the last twenty-five years, that we begin to see bubbling up to the surface, as it were, activities that cannot be neatly "packaged" in the confines of self-contained nation-states or in relations between states. This is the period when foreign populations were becoming recognized as permanent phenomena in Western Europe, when diasporas were becoming more than marginal phenomena, and when illegal immigration came to be viewed as a crisis in the United States. In other words, since the 1970s, homogeneous nation-states have no longer been taken for granted, and we began to witness the phenomenon of the bifurcation of membership in the state from membership in the nation (Hammar 1990). Transnational corporations, no longer wedded to any particular state, replace multinational corporations with their imputed ties to specific national interests (Reich 1991). In other words, borderings became much more multifaced and nuanced, of a nongeographic as well as of a geographic character, in the sense described above, at roughly this time.

Let it also be noted that states enforcing transnational and even autonomous bodies of laws are not entirely new even in the West over the last several hundred years (even if highly accentuated in recent decades and years), nor is this phenomenon limited to human rights. The law governing international commercial transactions (*lex mercatoria*) is in essence a transnational body of law that grew out of contractual practices and customary understandings of a community of international merchants, bankers, and others in the shipping and insurance industries. *Lex mercatoria* is, notes Harold Berman (1988, 298), "an autonomous body of law, binding upon national states." It is a law that precedes the emergence of the nation-state system by some centuries. States have rarely sought to modify it, and have mostly incorporated the law merchant into their national legal systems. Disputes can be brought before an autonomous International Chamber of Commerce, whose decisions are viewed as binding on states (see also Dezalay and Garth 1996).

The question is, if there is no global state, how does such an arrangement work? Furthermore, in a world of presumably sovereign states, how did such a set of circumstances arise? How is the state to be characterized in this regard?

THE GLOBALIZATION OF LAW

No global government exists in the sense of a global bureaucracy with a monopoly on the means of violence or even means of coercion. What we do see, as I noted, is an increasing global network of legal arrangements and ties, arbitration mechanisms, regimes, institutions, and the like. One could go so far as to say that "globalization" (as a shorthand for the web of global activities that parallel and transcend states) is rule driven. Thus there is no "felt identity" on the global level, but law is becoming the common language, so to speak. In Durkheimian terms, I have referred to this as a restitutive or contractual legal framework; it is not repressive or hierarchical. This globalization of law, to use Martin Shapiro's (1993) phrase, is motored by the globalization of the economy on the one hand, and state responses to cross-border activities and phenomena like migration and the environment on the other.

So we have an increasingly dense web of legal relations, ties, regimes, and the like, but we do not have any world government with a legislature to rule and an army to enforce its will. In what sense do these global legal institutions and ties have significance? How are they played out or enforced? The answer is judicially and administratively. And the state remains critical in this regard: it is the judicial branches of states, for example, that enforce international human rights law, and it is through the states that environmental protections are administered. Even decisions by regional courts, such as, notably, the European Court of Human Rights, are realized (or not—this process is clearly contested) through state actions. The growing judicial and administrative role of states is, of course, not entirely new in the domestic sphere. But now states find themselves more accountable to international laws on human rights and in other areas as well, such as the environment. If courts traditionally, particularly in Western Europe, deferred in international matters to the other branches of government, this is now less the case (though the extent of this development differs between different countries). It is through the courts—and, by extension, the legislature—that international norms are mediated. It is through the courts that individuals and nonstate actors can shape and contest understandings of human rights.[5] The role of the courts is particularly striking in the area of human rights; in other areas, such as international understandings on the environment, enactments by legislatures and administrative rules by government agencies may be more important (see Wapner 1996).

But this process of the growing judicial and administrative role and character of the state cannot be reduced to court cases or litigation. International laws and understandings are cascading downward, leading to (and reinforcing domestic trends of) a surge of rule making and regulations not only in government agencies, but in private and corporate institutions, often responding to larger national, regional, and international judicial and administrative exigencies. Thus the state is playing the role of mediator, defining "social spaces" in the process of delineating peoples' (human) rights. This process goes beyond high-profile court cases: it is explicit in public and private organization rules on diversity, hostile work environments (regarding both ethnic and sexual matters), or sexual harassment. It is in this larger sense we must understand the judicialization and the massive growth in administrative rules and the overarching role of human rights, rather than narrowly focusing on actual litigation and the actual litigants (though that is, of course, centrally important). Hearings within private and public organizations have surged as well, though less noticeably, alongside (and in response to) growing judicial review in Europe, as well as in the United States. This process is paralleled by the near end to presumptions of assimilation, that we "should" all melt into a common, homogeneous culture.[6]

This is not a top-down process whereby a global normative order scripts the activities of state and nonstate actors; international norms evolved as states reacted to structural challenges, changing themselves in the process.[7] State responses to transnational challenges bound the state into a set of institutional relationships and obligations that would not, given foreknowledge, have been viewed as desirable—in part, we see here the law of unintended consequences. Let me elaborate on this process in the area of migration and on the changing character of the state.

As I have written elsewhere, in the 1970s and 1980s, governments in Western Europe and the United States found themselves confronted with large foreign populations who, it had become apparent, were permanent. Furthermore, they—primarily guest-workers and undocumented immigrants—were not viewed initially as immigrants who would ultimately assimilate into their host societies nor, for that matter, were they populations that were viewed by the host countries as positively desirable immigrants, as they did not belong to the ethnic, political, or even economic categories of regular immigration criteria. In the case of guest-workers the assumption was always, by the migrants as well as the host governments, that they would return to their home countries, such as Turkey and Algeria. They lay in a legal limbo between citizens and outsiders, unwelcome except as cheap labor, but no longer could they be collectively expelled.[8] It was in this context, in good part, that states in the Euro-Atlantic arena began to take international human rights law seriously, though states differed significantly to the extent they turned to international human rights law—the American case being much more ambivalent than, say, the Germans. International human rights law, in contrast to national law, recognizes the individual as an object of rights regardless of national affiliations or associations with a territorially defined people, and thus was a useful institutional mechanism to account for "resident" foreign populations. Thus states turned in a piecemeal and incremental fashion to international human rights law (such as the UN human rights instruments or the European Convention on Human Rights). States increasingly had to take account of persons qua persons as opposed to limiting their responsibilities to their own citizens (see, generally, Jacobson 1996).

For migrant populations, human rights—with its stress on personhood rather than citizenship or nationality as such—was a means of making claims on the state without presuming assimilation (even if possible) into the host community. In addition, states had to legally account for these populations by extending to them social, economic, and even political rights (short of the national vote). Thus states were populated with people with a variety of statuses. The concept of nationality was, in effect, being recast, from a principle that reinforces state sovereignty and self-determination (by giving the state the prerogative of defining its nationals) to a concept of nationality as a human right; the state was becoming accountable to all its *residents* on the basis of international human rights law. Of major significance in this was the bifurcation of membership in a state from membership in the nation—hitherto viewed as synonymous, legally at least, as in the nation-state (Hammar 1990).

Much has been made of the "backlash" against immigrants, the assumption being that the nation-state is reasserting itself. But this stems from an unfortunate tendency in the social sciences, as well as in popular thinking, to think in linear terms. The state does react (again) to certain challenges, such as migration crossings and foreign populations, but the state today is reacting in a different institutional environment than in the past (for example, Germany's and France's early 1970s responses to guest-workers, or the U.S. reaction to illegal immigration in the 1970s and 1980s). The irony is that much of the more recent state responses to fears about the apparent dangers of migration in the 1990s reinforced the process of decoupling between territoriality and identity, between nation and state; for example, when Germany cracked down on the many apparently false claims of asylum status (in terms of the strict definition of "refugee" of the UN protocol on refugees, which certainly excludes economic hardship as a basis for asylum), it was just as important for the international protocols on refugees as it was for Germany. The U.S. Congress, enacting laws that predicated certain welfare benefits in 1996 on citizenship status, prompted many major immigrant-sending countries, such as Mexico and the Dominican Republic, to legalize dual citizenship or nationality (with the United States itself looking more kindly on dual citizenship as well).[9] No longer was citizenship the nucleus of a singular loyalty. Political and social change is taking a much more dialectical course, where states can loom large while taking new forms, where citizenship can be reinforced while it is shorn of former meanings, where human rights legal codes that are rooted in national constitutions and the birth of nation-states can transform states (Jacobson 1997).

Thus the very process of seeking to reverse circumstances associated with foreign populations ("loss of control" at the borders, and so on), has heightened the salience of international legal institutions and helped weave the threads of sociolegal transactions and of international law on the global level more tightly. The developments related to the migration issue have also contributed, in a fundamental way, to the "character" and interrelationships of all three components of the IBO triad.

THE (GLOBAL) POLITICS OF IDENTITY

We know that rights—political, social, economic, and so on—have steadily expanded. And we know more and more groups have been bestowed with rights. We also know that the legal protections and enumerations of rights in constitutions and statutory law have expanded and become more extensive over time around the world (see Boli 1987). This is a phenomenon that has been primarily within the domestic orbit of states but has now burst territorial boundaries in the form of international human rights law. That law has been expanding steadily since 1948, with the Universal Declaration of Human Rights. That law was at first largely ignored, but since the 1970s and 1980s it has become much more significant in the Euro-Atlantic arena. (I discuss the reasons for this in Jacobson 1996.)

This globalization of law—in the absence of a global government or legislature—is being realized, as I noted earlier, primarily through administrative rules and judicial rulings (and through states enacting laws to comply with or incorporate international laws, which are then subject to judicial and administrative review). This legal framework draws on a contractual presupposition, but one rooted in certain moral assumptions privileging the individual over other moral or ideological arrangements to regulate and mediate a world of multifarious actors.

Thus in this global legal order claims are made that are of a contractual nature—not only in the economic sense, but in the sense of "rights" claims. In some sense, this is inherent in the process of globalization. So, for example, foreign residents make claims on states on the basis of their international human rights, say, as Turks in Germany or France. They do not claim or wish to be Germans or

French. They do not wish to become French, necessarily, to *civically participate*. This is the right to be apart, separate—freedom *from* rather than freedom *to*. The judiciary places bounds on the actions of government vis-à-vis the individual; it delineates personal distance, between the state and individuals or groups and among individuals and groups themselves. The idiom of judicial (or constitutional) politics is one of "rights." Globalization—here in the sense of making claims on the basis of international law—in part is judicially driven. Legislative politics, in contrast to judicial "politics," is about the collective, public interest, where commonalities (or at least majorities) are stressed. Thus, the increased importance of the judicial branch is very significant for civic, republican ideals of collectivities determining their social and political life.

The state is being transformed in this process. The model of the sovereign nation-state was reinforced by an international legal system that recognized the state as the only actor with agency on the international stage. This made nationality critical; only thus did an individual have a status of legal standing—but only states could determine who its nationals were. Internally, sovereignty was expressed through the idea that the one compulsory association, universal in its grasp, was the state (see Hinsley 1986). In this respect the state embodied the body politic, the nation—it was a nation-state. That "nationness" could be defined ethnically, as in the German case, or politically, as in the American case (or some mixture of the two).[10] Thus the state was not simply a bureaucracy but the embodiment of a primordial identity, providing place in the world, metaphorically as well as literally. Citizenship, the designation of belonging and membership in the state, answered the question "Who am I?"

For better or worse, the globalization of law is unraveling this understanding (again, in the Euro-Atlantic core of the world order). Consider the area, especially, of international human rights law: Insofar as individuals and groups can make claims on the state on the basis of their "personhood" and not on the basis of "belonging" (as Americans, Germans, or Frenchmen, for example), the state as the embodiment of a national community is compromised. Furthermore, with growing dual citizenships and diasporic identities, the state ceases to be "the one compulsory community." And as the state becomes accountable to international law and norms, it becomes a mediating mechanism of (international) norms rather than a primordial source of such norms. And when talking of human *rights*, and the protection of rights, it is specifically the judicial arm that adjudicates and decides. When the state recognizes international legal safeguards in the area of human rights or incorporates such protections into domestic law, the relationship between the state, its residents, and international institutions are reconfigured (Sikkink 1993).

The state as a bureaucratic entity, gradually stripped of primordial content, is reinforced not only in its judicial role but in its administrative role as well. States become the administrative mechanisms of rules and ordinances that are formed at a regional (like the European Union) and international (such as different regimes) levels—for example, legal protections against environmental degradation, consumer protections, and occupational health and safety. Government is cast in increasingly technocratic and legalistic terms. The upsurge of legal rules, laws, and regulations reflects at one and the same time the bureaucratic or administrative state *and* the gradual loss of taken-for-granted assumptions of a unitary, singular political culture. When the unitary quality is lost, law—explicitly defined rules and procedures—becomes all the more critical. And administrative bureaucracies generate rules and regulations much more quickly than legislatures. Max Weber's description of the bureaucracy—rule-bound, "value-neutral," impersonal—comes to epitomize (ironically) the *post*modern state (Weber 1956). And bureaucracy and regulations add to the significance of lawyers and the courts. Globalization, the bureaucratic state, and the rising significance of the judicial process are interlinked phenomena. Lawyers are needed to defend rights and interpret contracts, and judges are needed to arbitrate between conflicting claims (see discussion generally in Shapiro 1993).

What we witness, then, is not a zero-sum relationship between the state and the international institutional order where the state "gives up" authority to a supranational polity. While state legitimacy increasingly comes to rest in international human rights standards, the state itself is critical in advancing human rights. Furthermore, the human rights regime enables, as well as constrains, state action— for example, it provides ample room for states to resist claims of refugee status that do not fit the specific definition under international law.[11] Thus the process described here, involving the relationship between the state and international institutions and law, is a dialectical one: the state is becoming the mechanism essential for the institutionalization of international human rights. The state and the international order are, consequently, mutually reinforcing. This relationship applies in other areas as well, such as in the international commercial law described above (Jacobson 1996).

NEW BORDER CONTROLS

It was noted earlier that in the international order, or at least in its Euro-Atlantic core, we have a developing social and political framework that uses the logic of contractual law to mediate between different groups. International human rights law and the idiom of human rights is crucial in mediating different *social* groups (along ethnic, religious, or other such distinctions) through the courts and through other administrative rules that now saturate organizations, both private and public. The premise of assimilation is dying, and the state—now almost bereft of its role as the symbolic center of a (no longer) unitary people—increasingly mediates a world of potentially conflicting spaces between groups fully aware of their "rights." The question becomes more critical as social "space," no longer geographically demarcated, has to be constantly negotiated. The everyday rules that govern daily interactions—neutral, and demanding no sense of a felt commonality—are, when taken to a higher level, a way of adjudicating a society where an overarching sense of community is fading (Jacobson 1997; Goffman 1971; Simmel 1950).

Less noticed, however, is the immense coercive power and *constraining* aspects of human rights. An ethnic group (or its imputed representatives) can make claims on states in terms of its "human rights" (for example, to wear traditional religious scarves in public schools)—in this sense human rights are *enabling*. In doing so, a set of contractual demands are being made—here, the social contract of human rights that privilege individuals and voluntary collective identities. Through such claims, we (an individual, social group, or a state) bind ourselves not only in the nominal sense of a contract, but structurally into a set of institutional scripts and rules. Even if the initial action is voluntary (e.g., claiming human rights), "our voluntary cooperation creates for us duties [that we may] not have [initially] desired." Thus the "law confers rights and imposes duties upon us as if they derived from a certain act of our will" (Durkheim 1984, 161). For all the talk of multiculturalism, for example, the degree of diversity that will be tolerated in the name of human rights is, in certain respects, remarkably constrained—constrained by the *voluntary* and *individualist* (moral) presumptions inherent in human rights. Thus the threat of female circumcision is a legitimate basis for claiming asylum; similarly, arranged marriages cannot be forced (and child brides are legally out of the question) on unwilling parties, whatever the traditional culture may desire. Human rights change the nature of identities, and contracting into human rights when it is at a party's advantage has, as noted, certain possibly undesirable outcomes. The same applies to regimes on human rights: states may have contracted into human rights when the regimes were explicitly state-centric, but with changing circumstances individuals have increasingly been able to make claims on states, thus contributing to changing the identity of the states themselves. Yet states have not—not in a single case, at least in the West—withdrawn their participation in such human rights regimes. *Raison d'état* in the Euro-Atlantic arena has become, in many respects, *raison de droits d'homme*. The state has become enmeshed, unwittingly, in a set of institutional arrangements that define what it means to be, so to speak, a (legitimate) state. This has implications for notions of security—collective security and societal security—as Wæver and his colleagues (1993) note.

CONCLUSION

The multilayered character of the postmodern world is hard for us to comprehend, particularly the unbundling of the nation-state such that territorial, political, and communal components of it are no longer coextensive or congruent. But we need to be cognizant of a couple of factors: when viewing recent developments against the background of the nation-state, which for us has a taken-for-granted quality, we tend to view changes as either suggesting some kind of incipient disintegration (such as the "Jihad vs. MacWorld" variety) or as abnormal, in the sense of straying from the norm. Yet we need to realize that the nation-state, where notions of community, territoriality, and polity were so intertwined and so clearly and integrally bounded, is historically the exception, not the rule. From the Middle Kingdom's notion of being an unbounded, culturally superior center, extending out to ever more barbarian lands (for Confucian China recognized no other civilizations, just barbarians), to Imperial Russia's conflation of nation and empire, ever on the war march, to American Indian tribes with fairly expansive collective identities but with political authorities very much at the local, village level, we find cultures and civilizations in sharp contrast and relief to the nation-state (see Ulam 1974; Fairbank 1968; Wallace and Adamson 1952).

Furthermore, we can learn from these other civilizational constructs, in this case the Indian example just alluded to: in some respects what we are witnessing is the development of a global (if still limited to the northern hemisphere) political culture based on human rights—which is demarcated (in principle) in nonterritorial terms and, in its domain, is distinct from territorial states (the local political authorities). Yet it is through these states that human rights are institutionalized, both domestically and internationally. And this brings us to the second point: the new political and social framework, primarily organized around human rights, is highly structured. The IBO triad is not a set of disparate entities but a highly interlocking and mutually reinforcing framework. State, international institutions, communities and identities of various kinds, and in many ways the fulcrum of all this, human rights, are complementary elements in the emerging international order. This does not mean that there won't be conflict—common principles can often *generate* conflict (witness the effects of the principles of sovereignty and national self-determination shared by Irish Catholics and Protestants, or Israelis and Palestinians alike)—but that we can witness a reasonably clear trend and "patterning" in international and domestic relations.

NOTES

I am deeply grateful to John Boli, David John Frank, Peter Katzenstein, Arjun Appadurai, Mathias Albert, Saskia Sassen, John Meyer, Thomas Risse, James Holliefield, Jamie Goodwin-White, Yosef Lapid, Dietrich Jung, Ole Wæver, Thomas Diez, Barry Buzan, Thomas Berger, Martin Heisler, Christopher Rudolph, Zeynep Kilic, and different seminar participants for their comments and suggestions. This chapter benefited from presentations at colloquia at the University of Chicago, Arizona State University, UCLA Law School, and the New School of Social Research. A visiting fellowship at the Copenhagen Peace Research Institute facilitated work on part of this chapter. A different version of this chapter appeared in the UCLA *Journal of International Law and Foreign Affairs* 3, no. 2 (fall/winter 1998/99): 443–62.

1. I discuss the communal dimension in chapter 7 in Jacobson (1996).

2. When these figures were first reported in Jacobson (1996) from a database search in 1995, it appeared that "human rights" would be cited in over 4,000 cases through the 1990s at the (then) present rate. A search in mid-1999 reveals that, in fact, human rights will be cited in over 6,000 cases—reinforcing the impression of a dramatic shift.

3. For the literature on the decline of the state or nation-state, see, for example, Sassen (1996) and Guéhenno (1995).

4. The Chinese case, in both its Confucian and Maoist incarnations, is striking given its historical antipathy to the Westphalian states system. For the Middle Kingdom, "the West" did not constitute a civilization, let alone represent principles worthy of emulation. Western countries lay in the shadowlands of barbarism. Mao, in turn, developed elaborate ideologies to demarcate the purity of the Chinese and proletarian peoples, such as "Three Worlds" and "people-to-people" relations (in contrast to state-to-state relations), from imperialist and corrupt Western concepts like the state and the states system.

5. The impact of the courts goes beyond the formal process of judicial review—some legislatures now formally, others informally, have a process of "pre-legislative scrutiny" to ensure a proposed law would pass, for example, in the European Court of Human Rights in Strasbourg.

6. This analysis draws from Friedman (1994), though Friedman focuses primarily on domestic U.S. law. On the international level, see Shapiro (1993).

7. The Stanford sociological institutionalists have rightly taken center stage in the study of the world polity, in part by illustrating the remarkable isomorphism of states, reflecting in turn a powerful "global culture." Their writings have been a cogent response to microeconomic-inspired rational choice models of international relations (see Meyer et al. 1997; Boli and Thomas 1997). However, I would differ with them in their top-down approach and what appears as a wholly normative stress. Structural factors and the role of actors—state and nonstate—in shaping the international normative environment need to be considered. A certain realism and consideration of structural pressures and the role of actors can complement a study of normative possibilities and constraints.

8. The reasons for this are discussed in Jacobson (1996).

9. With regard to the "backlash" against immigration, see also the Illegal Immigration Reform and Immigrant Responsibility Act of 1996 (IIRIRA), Pub. L. No. 104–208, 110 Stat. 3009 (codified as amended in different sections of 8 U.S.C.).

10. The most cited distinction on the attribution of citizenship is between *jus soli,* or citizenship on the basis of birth within the territorial boundaries of the state, and *jus sanguinis,* or citizenship on the basis of blood-descent from a specific people or nation.

11. It should be stressed that "specific" does not mean "fixed." Thus definitions of "refugee" are understood to be legitimate insofar as they are of a universal character—the definitions should not discriminate on the basis of national origin, race, sex, and so on. However, the definition and interpretation of all human rights codes, including those on refugees, evolve— primarily through court cases—to include, for example, social groups once excluded from human rights protection, such as homosexuals, or old cultural practices, such as female genital mutilation, now viewed as a human rights violation.

8

Crossing the Borders of Order: Democracy beyond the Nation-State?

ANTJE WIENER

> As substantial areas of human activity are progressively organized on
> a regional or global level, the fate of democracy, and of the indepen-
> dent democratic nation-state in particular, is fraught with difficulty.
> (Held 1997, 251)

> Is democracy in the national state, then, destined to meet the fate of
> democracy in the city-state? . . . In the same way that the idea and
> practice of democracy were shifted away from the city-state to the
> larger scale of the national state, will democracy as an idea and a set
> of practices now shift to the grander scale of transnational govern-
> ments? (Dahl 1994, 27)

As processes of democracy are spreading across national borders,
justifying authority as the main political function of democracy has
become increasingly difficult to organize (Walzer 1983). Representative democracy within a political entity and based on a system of
constitutionally entrenched shared values has become less feasible
as processes of policy shaping and implementation, production, financial markets, and communication are no longer exclusively based
on either national constitutions or international treaties. It is now
increasingly problematic to draw on the norms embedded in the institutions of the liberal nation-state that have provided a stable framework for a principled relationship between a collectivity and a polity.

Instead of asking what is the model of democracy, I propose to pursue the question of democratic legitimacy as an interplay between process and procedure that gives rise to an institutional setting. This setting in turn secures the balance between the collectivity (the people) and the polity (the state). The focus is thus on an interactive process-oriented approach to polity formation and, more specifically, on the norms that are constitutive for democratic polities. Democratic theories identify different approaches to democratic legitimacy such as "interest-based model of democracy" and "deliberative democracy" (Young 1996, 120). While the interest-based model has proliferated in most current liberal democracies, the deliberative model has received increasing attention among scholars who seek to address deviations from formal institutions such as the focus on accommodating differences on the one hand, or on new forms of policy negotiations on the other.

Currently, two types of change in global politics challenge core assumptions about democracy. The first change is the changing shape and pattern of polities. The modern nation-state appears to present medieval traits such as a pluralist conglomeration of polities, overlapping authority, and divided loyalties (Ferguson 1996a; Ferguson 1996b; Held 1997, 261). The second change refers to the shape and behavior of political actors. International relations scholars have found that global politics is increasingly shaped by nongovernment actors whose action has an impact beyond the limits of national borders. This pattern of acting across borders has an effect on the performance of both domestic and international politics (Clarke et al. 1998; Jacobson 1996; Soysal 1994; Tarrow 1998; Wapner 1995). These practices undermine the familiar perceptions of democracy as "an idea and a set of practices" (Dahl 1994, 27) established on the limited site of the nation-state and raise doubts as to whether or not "the nation-state itself can remain at the center of democratic thought" (Held 1997, 252). Both challenges move the theoretical debate over democratic political order beyond the nation-state. As this chapter argues, this does not just trigger a critical rethinking of modern concepts. The necessity of approaching the subject of democratic political order beyond bounded political communities (Held 1992) has led to a new interest in debating democracy—beyond the boundaries of political theory and comparative politics—in international relations (IR) theory.

This chapter attempts to do two things. First, it points to a conceptual problem that evolves from state-centric approaches to democracy at a time when the regulating and problem-solving capacities of territorialized political orders are gradually declining. Second, it suggests shifting focus from (state-centric) models of democracy toward practices and norms of democracy. While models are familiarly based on principles and procedures, practices and norms are assumed to be mutually constitutive of creating the *substance* of democracy.[1] Two approaches sustain the focus on substance. First, IR scholars, and the various strands of constructivists in particular, have begun to explore the impact of *norms* as the immaterial structures that are constitutive for agency behavior. Second, critical theorists have introduced the concept of deliberative democracy in an attempt to link the liberal principles of fair justice and equal rights to guide the relationship between citizen and state with the republican principle of participatory governance by means of deliberation (Benhabib 1996; Cohen 1996). Both facilitate a view on democracy that is based on *practices*. If it is true that practices are constitutive for changing norms and institutions (Koslowski 1994; Kratochwil 1989), then this opening is crucial. It facilitates a way of addressing the middle ground of institution building that has been found lacking in much of recent constructivist theory building (Checkel 1998, 335, 340).

In agreement with social constructivists, I point to the crucial impact of norms on politics notwithstanding borders of national polities. Yet, drawing on historical institutionalism, I argue that while socially constructed norms have a structuring aspect on political processes, political practices equally influence the construction of norms and institutions. I suggest that this dialectic between norm construction and structuring politics can be fruitfully assessed within the framework that is provided by the identities, borders, orders triangle (see the introduction to this volume by Lapid). In other words, while changes of identities, borders, and orders have been pointed out as crucial and dramatic challenges to politics, the changing constellation of the three corner points of the triangle is approached via the substantive practices at its core. They are taken as the basis of democratic rule. While this perspective ultimately aims to identify new institutional ties between the collectivity of citizens and changing types of polities, this chapter is limited to identifying conceptual shortcomings of state-centric approaches and raising propositions for alternatives. The debate over the "democracy deficit" in the European Community, and now European Union, is taken to illuminate the point.

This chapter is organized into three sections. The first section points to the two major caveats of state-centric approaches to democracy and their application to postmodern polity patterns. The second section turns to the example of the democracy deficit debate in the European Union (EU) and singles out the two major strands in the debate. The third section suggests that postmodern democratic substance is based on contested access to participation in changing identity, borders, orders constellations. In conclusion, the chapter points out that while fading democratic legitimation presents a dilemma for state-centrically framed approaches to democracy, debates over access to participation in changing polities offer a theoretical access point for alternatives.

BEYOND MODERN BORDERS OF ORDER: CHANGING THE TRIANGLE

The growing tension between the classic democratic ideal and the actual circumstances of democratic practice has been characterized as developing between the rhetoric of "great cosmopolitan charm" and a practice that is "pretty thin on the ground" (Walker 1993, 141; cf. Dunn 1979, 2). This section advances a perspective on *practices* and *norms* as two mutually constitutive factors for modern democratic political order. Both are crucial for assessing the tension between theory and practice. It proceeds to discuss the mutually constitutive role of practice and norms in constructing the discourse of political order. I argue that if social practices and norms are interdependent, it follows that the prevailing constitutive norms that were influential for establishing modern democratic polities might be affected in an equal—yet different—way by postmodern practices. Studying these practices would subsequently facilitate an insight into the construction of postmodern democratic norms.

Both practices and norms are identified as the substance of democracy and hence deemed central factors for assessing changing democratic order. One crucial indicator of democracy, and its stability or deficit, is therefore the tension between ideal assumptions about and practices of democracy. A cursory review of day-to-day political discourse shows, indeed, that political actors usually resort to the ideal in order to legitimize their actions. Thus, both international and national authorities refer to the principle of majoritarian rule in the attempt to legitimate their authority. Despite a growing distance between collectivity/ies (the people) and polity/ies (the state) on the ground, world leaders such as the former Secretary General of the United Nations (UN) Boutros Boutros-Ghali and the fifteen signatories of the Treaty of European Union (TEU) maintain that their style of governance is democratic because the treaties that frame their political practice have been signed by the people's representatives. The UN Secretary General's understanding of the category "people" as a bearer of democracy, as well as the EU's intention to bring "peoples" together, represent that phenomenon. He states, for example:

> The word *democracy* does not appear in the United Nations Charter, but its opening words are "We the peoples of the United Nations." The notion of democracy—that political legitimacy derives from the people—is therefore central to the foundational document of the United Nations. (Boutros Boutros-Ghali 1995, 3)

Representatives of states are familiarly taken to speak on behalf of the people. This representative function is seen as a sufficient condition to legitimize political action within democratic contexts. However, while both the UN Charter and the Treaty of European Union have been signed by representatives of peoples, from the act of signing it is not possible to draw conclusions about democratic order. While the procedural aspects defined by the text of the treaty are evident, the practices and norms that are at the core of the substance of the particular democratic order are not. In other words, while, historically speaking, it remains hypothetical whether or not the people's consent to a particular text could actually be guaranteed, the democratic legitimization of politics is based on precisely that assumption. Perspectives on democracy—be they cast from the EU, the national, or the global level—are derived from experiences with and expectations of democratically organized states and the expectations they produce, while not paying much attention to the actual practice of democracy.[2] Indeed, as R. B. J. Walker writes, "to ask what democracy could possibly be in relation to 'the people' in general or to structures of global power is to engage with the great silences of contemporary political discourse" (1993, 146). To break the silence, we need to go beyond an assessment of what democracy means in formal terms and address *how* democracy is practiced and *who* makes claims to *which* political institution.

In the following, the political consequences of changing norms and practices are sketched within the framework provided by the triangle of identities, borders, and orders. The basic assumption is that modern democracies have established a balance among the three corner points of the triangle (see Figure 1). Key to this stable balance was the institutionalization of central political authority resting on shared norms, routinized practices, and formalized procedures. As practices change and, inevitably, if more slowly, norms are redefined, the triangle loses its balance, and, in the process, the democratic political order is challenged. For remedies, it is suggested to take the middle ground of the triangle, i.e., the changing practices and norms, as the point of departure, not the corner points. This procedure rests on the assumption of territorialized conceptual caveats that are inherent in all three corner points, yet which appear to be more easily circumvented in the middle ground of practices and norms as the substance of democracy.

In modern times the framework of democracy has come to be characterized by the territorially bounded nation-state, a constitution and a *demos* as the *pouvoir constituant* that conferred legislative power to the government as the *pouvoir constitué* (Grimm 1995; Held 1992). The nation-state with its definition of belonging and rights—expressed by citizenship—as the central political institution with power and authority on the one hand, and formal election procedures as the practices that attributed legitimacy to it on the other, were constitutive of the liberal democratic norm of justice and equality. Together they provided sufficient means for building and maintaining democratic legitimacy. The understanding of citizenship as generating identity and offering rights sustained this normative framework (Brubaker 1992; Soysal 1994). The constructed belongingness attached to a myth of national identity provided the strong territorialized border for this democratic order (Anderson 1991).

In the second half of the twentieth century, the modern democratic context had changed. While the institutional settings of national states including constitutions remained largely unchanged, the citizenry and the borders of nation-states had undergone major changes. Most visibly two developments contributed to the perforation of borders of the collectivity and (national) polities respectively. First,

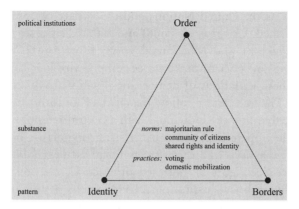

Figure 1. Democratic order in modern nation-states.

border crossing by a variety of nonstate actors such as interest groups, as well as transnational movements and migration flows, have challenged the perception of a shared national identity as the building block for the *demos.* Second, international interdependence expressed by institutional arrangements that went beyond international treaties, such as regimes and much more strikingly the pooling of sovereignty among states in the European Community and now Union, has challenged the sovereign power of the (national) polities. Both processes have contributed to nonstate actor mobilization on a global level around policy-shaping processes of international organizations, e.g., nongovernment organizations' (NGO) networks aim to influence the World Trade Organization (WTO). Local social movements and interest groups have begun to successfully apply globally developed human rights discourse as a resource in local community disputes. And in the EU, lobby groups, NGOs, legal advisers, and a number of unidentified political actors have formed policy networks as new actors on an intermediate level within the Euro-polity (Bromberg 1996; Mazey 1993; Peterson 1995).

In other words, a variety of political actors who are often characterized as forming part of a global civil society (Macdonald 1994; Shaw 1994; Wapner 1995) mobilizes around policy issues such as trade, the environment, and social policy. Their motivation can be summed up along two different sets of transnational practices. One focuses on interest groups demanding a say in policy processes that stretch beyond national polities; the other uses international institutions such as the United Nations and the variety of conferences it has established (Clarke et al. 1998) and global discourses on human rights (Blacklock and Macdonald 1998; Klotz 1995; Menschenrechte 1998) in order to make states comply with locally raised demands. These variations of democratic practices have one thing in common: They do not all follow the channels of formal democratic procedure that link the individual with a centralized political entity. Instead, they operate on a flexible basis, acting across boundaries, addressing demands to a variety of political entities and/or levels of governance (see Figure 2). Both sets of practices focus on new ways of accessing political institutions. They express a shift in political action as a reflection of new types of polities that constitute the space for a "politics without a centre" (Della Sala 1999).

The societal and political changes that follow from these practices of border and order crossing challenge the substance of democracy in a way that leaves no easy answers on the basis of formal institutional innovations. Indeed, they shed light on the limits of democratic procedures and access to participation in postmodern polities. However, they do not simply challenge the validity of modern democratic norms beyond the nation-state; they also contribute to the gradual redefinition of central. Different from studies that focus on the effects of global norms that penetrate national politics (Menschenrechte 1998; Klotz 1995), I seek to also assess the impact of actors on the construction of norms. The focus is on changes in state-society relations that are enhanced by globalization. The leading empirical question is: how does the essence of identity and order hold under the challenge of globalization, which brings about, for example, medieval-like polity patterns and postmodern citizen behavior?

The booming literature on citizenship and migration is one expression of emergent cracks in the once successfully established democratic norms. In other words, the modern "crystallization" of citizenship rights and state building is losing its balance. As a discourse that reflects and sets the "borders of order" (Kratochwil et al. 1994) and a core institution to the construction of modern polities, citizenship has long been challenged by political actors. Social movements, as well as advocacy groups and interest groups, have taken issue with the twofold pattern of citizenship consisting of *rights* and *identity* by struggling for *access* to participation. The changing global political scenario suggests that this basic pattern of citizenship

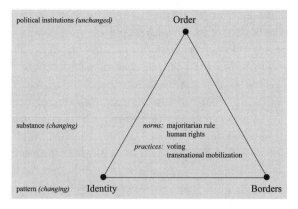

Figure 2. Substantive changes within modern nation-states.

is now further challenged by processes of globalization that enforce the stress on access even more. With the fading overlap of identity and political borders, the access problematic enhances the problem of democratic deficit. It can therefore be concluded that the practice of border crossing involved in current interest politics and migration flows highlights the dissonance between democratic principles and democratic practice. The substance that ties both together is, however, shifting, and therefore requires further examination.

I argue that the crucial theoretical and empirical problem posed by this transformation is the conceptual mismatch between the medieval pattern and modern substance. While the pattern of current polity constellations may be medieval, i.e., the form of political entity varies according to overlapping borders, the substance of these polities bears the experience of modernity. It is entrenched in historically constructed institutions and socially constructed norms. Although subject to change, the traits of history including modernity will not disappear because democratic substance is marked by historicity. It follows that any research on the principled articulation of political space within and accordingly among these polities stands to incorporate a tension between pattern, i.e., changing constellation of units, and substance, i.e., norms constituted through practice. The pattern of differently structured and shaped polities without fixed boundaries challenges modern assumptions about democratic substance that are best characterized by the triangle of identities, borders, and orders (see Figure 1).

With increased border crossing, this triangle has lost its balance; the substance has changed. To address the substance, two issues need to be addressed. One is the effort to identify the style of a specific democratic setting on the basis of shared norms. These norms express, for example, expectations about equal voting rights and the principles of justice that have been central to liberal democracies. The other issue is the acknowledgment of practices that are guided by norms and contribute to the creation of norms. Such practices have been made visible most clearly, albeit not exclusively, by work that focuses on contentious struggles over political rights (Tarrow 1998; Tilly 1975). This process, which I have elsewhere called "citizenship practice," has contributed to the forging of institutionalized terms, i.e., the norms, of citizenship (Wiener 1998). It has therefore been found to acquire a central role in processes of state building. It follows from these observations that the mutually constitutive role of practices and norms shed light on the substance of democracy in different contexts. As analyses of democracy in a post-Westphalian nonstate cannot rely on the rhetoric of cosmopolitan charm derived from the classic democratic idea, they must turn to the messy situation on the ground to focus on the empirical facts about new forms of constructing democracy. From these facts and from expectations and experiences of democracy, insights about the social construction of new forms of sovereignty and citizenship may be conceptualized. In order to assess democracy as a meaningful concept for post-Westphalian polities, we need to establish new coordinates at the crossroads of dissolving sovereignties and newly emergent identities in the form of new political institutional links. This task involves studying emerging democratic norms in context.

THE DEMOCRACY DEFICIT DEBATE IN THE EUROPEAN UNION

Students of global politics have observed the emergence of a new pattern of polities in postmodern[3] times. Crucially, they argue this pattern differs from the core realist assumption of an international system of (nation-)states. Instead, it shows medieval traits presented by a pluralist conglomeration of polities "the essential characteristics of which was a system of overlapping authority and divided loyalties" (Held 1997, 261). However, "while students of democracy have examined and debated at length the challenges to democracy that emerge from within the boundaries of the nation-state, they have not seriously questioned whether the nation-state itself can remain at the center of democratic thought; the questions posed by the rapid growth of complex inter-connections and interrelations between states and societies, and by the evident intersection of national and international forces and processes, remain largely unexplored" (ibid., 252). Indeed, debates over how democratic order might be established within a polity that does not match the pattern of modern nation-state polities suggest that the theoretical capacity to imagine democracy within a nonstate polity remains limited at best.

The EU's extensive and largely inconclusive discussion of the "democracy deficit" is a case in point. It suggests that, conceptually speaking, an answer to Dahl's question of whether or not we are about to reinvent the city-state above the modern national state as a context for democracy is more often than not a "yes." This chapter contests that answer by elaborating on the theoretical and empirical consequences of a negative answer to Dahl's question. It contends that while modern democratic institutions have adapted to and been formed by the concepts of liberal or communitarian styles of democracy, this sort of adaptation has yet to take place with a view to democratic polities after modernity. If it is true that global politics is currently undergoing a large transformatory change toward postmodern or, for that matter, medieval patterns of organization, then we need to address the substance of this sort of organization and its ability to recontextualize modern democratic concepts. The following summary of this debate points to the fact that both approaches miss the target of establishing democratic legitimacy because they operate on the assumptions of the modern triangle of political order (see Figure 1), based firmly on fixed identity and formal procedures.

In comparison with the centrally organized liberal democracies of nation-states, the EU represents a dramatically deviating case. As a polity that is neither an international organization nor a national state, the EU does not encompass the formalized democratic institutions of national liberal democracies. The Euro-polity is a political arena that is not fixed but in a continuous state of construction. Its incremental character is specified in the TEU that establishes the determination of its fifteen signatories "to maintain the *acquis communautaire* and build on it" and to "create an ever closer union among the peoples of Europe."[4] While comprising a supranational bureaucratic apparatus and a highly sophisticated system of economic integration, no familiar concept of governance applies to the EU. Even though the EU is considerably more than an international regime, it is still less than a fully fledged polity (Wallace 1996). In this political entity, the process of governing and being governed stretches across various levels, it is polycentric, and citizens are entitled to fragmented citizenship rights and practices. As a result, voting and "tangible policy change" (Wendt 1996, 62) appear increasingly disconnected.

In this context the democracy deficit has been defined as a "gap between formal legitimization and material democratic deficiency."[5] To address the deficit conceptually or politically requires some framework of reference that defines the core normative and institutional characteristics. Finding such a framework is made exceptionally difficult by the undefined character of the EU's polity.[6] For studies of the relation between potentially emerging collectivity/ies and polity/ies in this context, it is important to consider that this developing relation is placed within the context of a "new practice of governance beyond the state" (Jachtenfuchs 1995, 115). The actors who influence policy changes appear in a new variety of shapes and with new fragmented and diffused patterns of territorial affiliation identified as policy networks that act across multiple levels of governance. While it is entirely possible to speak of the EU as a system of governance encompassing a broad spectrum of supranational policies, institutions, and a constitutional framework, this system differs from modern nation-states. The polity fits within the perception of a new "medieval" pattern of global polities (Ferguson and Mansbach 1996a) (see Figure 3). The EU has, for example, taken steps toward building institutions that establish a principled relationship between a collectivity and a newly emergent polity including the step-by-step expansion of a quasi-constitution (integration through law), the stipulation of political citizenship rights, and the pooling of sovereignties in various policy areas. These institutional innovations are tied together by the concept of subsidiarity. Together these changes give a new postmodern character to the Euro-polity.

These institutional innovations notwithstanding, or possibly precisely because of these significant challenges to modern experience and expectation, the Maastricht treaty has renewed the debate over democracy (Everson 1998; Grimm 1995; Weiler 1997, 1999; Zuleeg 1997). Two major strands have developed in the course of this de-

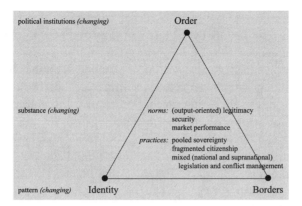

Figure 3. Changing the IBO constellation toward a postmodern democratic order?

bate. They reflect the twofold set of norms that have so importantly contributed to the meaning of modern citizenship, i.e., rights and identity. Accordingly, the first strand focuses on the establishment of formal political institutions in order to establish legitimacy within the multilevel Euro-polity. I term this approach the *procedural approach* because formal political procedures are considered the primary factor for establishing democratic legitimacy. The other strand discusses the possibilities of developing a European *demos*. Contributors to this line of thought draw on constitutionalism, legal thought, and political theory in particular (Grimm 1995; Preuss 1998). I call this model the *identity approach* because a shared identity is considered a necessary condition for democratic legitimacy. While the European *ethnos* based on nationality is not necessarily required, a shared European identity in a republican or communitarian sense is expected nonetheless.

The former model focuses on the formal conditions of democracy such as establishing centralized democratic organs including a stronger European Parliament, an elected Commission, a bicameral Council of Ministers, as well as a stronger constitutional basis of democratic institutions, for example, citizenship (Monar 1998). Thus, for many observers, the lack of appropriate institutions is the main cause of the democracy deficit, "the lack of a responsible EU parliament and the lack of a European polity" (Anderson and Eliassen 1996, 3), exemplifying its core. The latter has produced an ongoing debate on

"Who is the demos?" of the EU (Weiler 1996). This debate was crucially pushed to the fore by the German Constitutional Court's Maastricht Judgment of 1993 (Zuleeg 1997). In contrast to the procedural approach, the identity approach puts an emphasis on the collectivity, the *demos* that is built on shared identity. As Dieter Grimm points out, if it is agreed that a homogeneous identity based on a common ethnos is not a required basis for democracy, then the focus remains on a European identity derived from a collective identity developed by the European *demos* according to a republican logic (Grimm 1995; Habermas 1992c). Developing this identity does, however, crucially depend on the existence of a public sphere. "What obstructs democracy is accordingly not the lack of cohesion of Union citizens as a people, but their weakly developed collective identity and low capacity for transnational discourse. This certainly means that the European democracy deficit is structurally determined. It can therefore not be removed by institutional reforms in any short term. The achievement of the democratic constitutional state can for the time being be adequately realized only in the national framework" (Grimm 1995, 297).

The European debate over democracy has been characterized by the search for a missing public sphere, which would ideally form the birthplace for a European *demos* built on a collective European identity (identity approach) on the one hand, and the absence of political issues that would mobilize voter interest on a European level (procedural approach) on the other. Propositions to overcome the democracy deficit have subsequently included Europe-wide referenda (Grande 1996) and improving the conditions for representative democracy in order to stabilize the formal link between Euro-politicians and the electorate, for example, by electing the Commission (Hix 2000). As Renaud Dehousse has critically pointed out, such a majoritarian avenue toward tackling the democracy deficit would, however, involve identifying shared issues of European political interest to establish a political substance similar to that of national politics (Dehousse 1995, 120). The former hinges on a shared language, which has so far not developed; the latter requires further sovereignty pooling toward the creation of a European center, an unlikely development after the recently increased intergovernmentality of EU politics.

In sum, debates over how democratic order might be established within a polity that does not match the pattern of modern nation-state polities suggest that the theoretical capacity to imagine democracy within a nonstate polity remains limited at best. The EU's extensive and largely inconclusive discussion of "democracy deficit" is a case in point (Grande 1996). Indeed, the thrust of this discussion suggests that, conceptually speaking, an answer to Dahl's question "Will democracy as an idea and a set of practices now shift to the grander scale of transnational governments?" (Dahl 1994, 27) is currently still hard to imagine in other than state-centric terms. The temptation to reinvent a state above the modern national state as context for democracy persists despite the serious theoretical challenges, pointed out by European integration scholars in particular (Armstrong and Bulmer 1998; Joerges and Neyer 1997; Ladeur 1997; Majone 1994; Schmitter 2000).

TOWARD A PROCESS-ORIENTED APPROACH TO POLITY FORMATION

The previous section shed light on the temptation to reinvent the nation-state beyond its own borders based on the example of the democracy deficit debate in the EU. In the remainder of this chapter I argue that the deterritorialization of politics, i.e., the rupture of political institutions, practices, and principles from the concept of the modern nation-state,[7] cannot be successfully met by focusing on questions of formal democratic procedures or identity politics alone. As insights from constitutional theory suggest, the institutions, practices, and principles of a constitution and its respective impact on democratic rule depend on a set of historically contingent practices that construct the meaning of the constitution (Bellamy and Castiglione 1996). They contribute to the construction of regulative and constitutive norms. The practices and norms are hence mutually constitutive for the substance of democracy. This substance is historically contingent; it is reflected in the institutionalized state-society relations. However, it changes according to place and time. As political institutions are increasingly decentered, yet still require legitimation for decision making, and political processes extend beyond borders, it is no longer obvious how to organize political order. Efforts to address this problem in the EU have, so far, resulted in bringing back the two main conceptual pillars of democratic rule, the concept of a *demos* with a shared identity as the collective basis of democratic governance on the one hand, and majoritarian rule as the necessary political procedure on the other.

Speaking of a deficit always includes a comparison with something else. From the literature on the EU's democratic deficit, we can conclude that the EU's state of democracy is usually measured against perceptions of democracy that have been formed on the basis of either the experience or the philosophically formed expectations of nationally defined frameworks of democracy. That is, both the ideal and the really existing democracy on the ground are firmly linked with the institutional arrangements of the modern nation-state. If this understanding of democracy is the yardstick for democracy in the EU, then any measure to overcome the deficit is implicitly directed toward the establishment of democratic elements similar to the national experience.[8] Speaking of a democracy gap in the EU therefore means addressing the deficit between supranational and the national models of democracy. The *democracy deficit* then indicates European shortcomings vis-à-vis national models.

This way of approaching the EU democracy deficit includes two caveats. The first caveat is based on the observation that national democracy has become a largely contested concept itself. It has been pointed out that the material appearance of democracy on the ground has long differed from the classic ideal of people governing themselves in the Greek city. Instead, the relationship between the "normative although impossible ideal" and the "concrete, yet quite different, contemporary reality" (Green 1993, 30) has been found to develop into a growing tension between the two poles of the democratic ideal and democratic practice. With popular sovereignty becoming increasingly fragmented, access to democratic participation has become equally diffused. One result of this fragmentation of democratic practices is that democracy has become a generally contested concept. In other words, the democracy deficit is not restricted to the EU polity. Secondly, the state-like development of the Euro-polity seems unlikely.

The second caveat therefore involves the application of state-centric analyses to a polity that will not develop into a state. This does not necessarily prohibit insightful work on the democracy deficit, quite to the contrary. As this chapter argues, to overcome the democracy deficit requires finding ways to overcome state-centric analyses. This chapter argues the need to reformulate the question about the democracy deficit in the EU. Instead of trying to identify the proper model of democracy based on modern concepts, it is suggested that the question of how democracy is addressed by social and political actors be pursued. Thus, the impact of substance provides an empirical access point to reach beyond the concept of formal democracy characterized by procedural and institutional attributes. A view on substantive democracy then offers analytical potential to address the silence about the people based on the inclusion of the Tocquevillian notion of the "societal condition toward equality."[9] The fit between collectivity/ies and polity/ies is measured against expectations and experiences of citizens that have been shaped over time as a result of contentious political struggle over citizens' rights.

Two aspects about this relationship can be singled out. One aspect is that of process. It highlights the way in which the substantive aspect of democracy is created, bringing the process of claims making, discursive struggle, and identity building to the fore of the analysis. Studies of constitution building and citizenship have pointed to the fact that democratic change can take place either in a revolutionary or evolutionary way with both modes of change implying a different concept of the citizen-regime relationship or, in other words, of citizenship. In the former case, transformatory moments of democratic change are singled out (Closa 1995); in the latter case, democratic changes evolve over time through the day-to-day practice of constitution making. The second aspect is that of concepts. It focuses on formal democracy, that is, the institutional and procedural framework for democracy as it is established by the assumption of the state-people relationship of classical democratic theories. It involves a critical reconceptualization of the state and the people both defined by and interrelated through different forms of sovereignty (state sovereignty and popular sovereignty). Work on global politics has pointed out that state sovereignty has been socially constructed. Indeed, as Thomas Biersteker and Cynthia Weber write, state sovereignty is "an inherently *social* concept. States' claims to sovereignty construct a social environment in which they can interact as an international society of states, while at the same time the mutual recognition of claims to sovereignty is an important element in the construction of states themselves" (1996, 1–2).

Similarly, the people—and more specifically popular sovereignty—as the other part of this relationship and the crucial contributor to democratic legitimacy have been challenged by two debates that are interdependent but have usually been led apart; one is rooted in comparative constitutional studies, the other in critical historical as well as liberal feminist studies of citizenship. For example, comparative constitutionalism has highlighted the problematic two-step assumption about the transfer of power from the people to the constitution[10] and noted that the actual experience of sovereignty on the ground is that popular sovereignty has become liquidized (Habermas 1992c, 626). It has therefore become difficult to locate the democratic roots of legitimate governance within a polity. In most modern democracies, sovereignty is indeed not transferred to the institutions of government in a moment akin to the ideal Rousseauian moment of classical democratic theories, but it has become proceduralized instead. It may be examined as discourse about democratic legitimacy that is spread over the manifold discursively shaped steps of decision making within the institutions of a polity (Habermas 1992c, 621–29). This development entails a move of the people further and further away from the government. Citizens are represented by and through a plethora of democratic institutions that define the democratic state of affairs within a polity.

The perception of both state sovereignty and popular sovereignty as socially constructed introduces an important conceptual doubt about the people and the state as reference points for democracy. This perspective situates the inquiry about the democracy deficit in nonstate polities within a conceptual framework with two loose ends. Since both concepts are subject to deconstruction, their use as methodological reference points needs to be handled with care. Since it is beyond the framework of this chapter to pursue both aspects of democracy, that of process in its different real existing formations of evolutionary and revolutionary changes toward constitution making and that of concept within the interdependent global politics and citizenship debates over contested concepts, it must suffice here to state the importance of both interrelated aspects for our thinking about democracy.

I propose to scrutinize the understanding of input-legitimated democratic rule to include a more complex notion. While the notion of input is familiarly restricted to voting as the central element of majoritarian rule within a representative liberal democracy, I argue that it also involves the communicative processes that precede the act of voting. These communicative processes are crucial aspects of democratic input because they are formative for public opinion *and* identity formation. Both are determining factors of electoral behavior (Lazarsfeld et al. 1944). In other words, input legitimation entails discursive input apart from votes. While the former is usually granted by the constitution and enacted according to formal procedures of electoral law, the latter needs to be established as *access* to participation in processes of deliberation. It is often part of informal processes of communication that are not exclusively situated in the public sphere. Indeed it has been suggested that, instead of hinging on formal democratic institutions that provide the institutional framework for an interest group model of liberal democracy, institutional settings for democracy beyond the nation-state would seek ways of establishing citizens' *access* to a "plurality of modes of association" (Benhabib 1996, 73).

If this access were established, then input-oriented legitimation of governance could be understood to be communicative. It would ideally entail a two-step process of communicative interaction: electoral issues among citizens and at the ballot box through the act of voting. Yet, it has been demonstrated that the expansion of governance beyond the constitutional limits of national borders has weakened the potential of input-based democratic legitimation (Scharpf 1995, 1999). Majoritarian rule based on the citizens' right to vote as the prime characteristic of political participation loses its legitimizing function under conditions of a crumbling national identity. This development shifts the focus of political legitimacy toward an output-oriented model of democracy stressing the efficiency of political and economic performance (Majone 1997) over political procedures and national identity as the familiar pillars of input-oriented democratic legitimation.

CONCLUSION

This chapter highlighted crucial changes within the modern triangle. To that end it drew attention to the implications of the mutually constitutive interplay of practices and norms on the triangle of identities, borders, and orders. If the goal was to identify the substance, not just the form, of the medieval polities that emerge in postmodern times, democratic institutions—and the rules, procedures, and norms attached to them—need to be addressed as a function of principles contested by practices. This implies that change does not appear at the corner points of the triangle but needs to be analyzed as a function of changing practices and norms. These changes are best identified by the interplay of change in both state-society relations pushed by actors and norms that structure political behavior.

The chapter raised conceptual and methodological questions with a view to contributing to the larger project of imagining democratic institutions beyond the nation-state. To that end, it suggested focusing on the tension between practice and norms of modern democracy, which trigger postmodern interest group behavior and medieval polity formations in global politics. Both were found to challenge the limited organizing capacity of modern democracies, including the formal procedures and shared norms. Border-crossing activities of a variety of social actors point to the shortcomings of modern democratic norms and procedures within a postmodern or, for that matter, medieval context. The argument built on both, the observation of medieval patterns in global politics and the suggestion for an associative model of deliberative democracy. Both approaches agree from the different viewpoints of global politics and critical theory on a new pluralism that challenges conceptual and territorial boundaries. They offer new insights into the contextual and conceptual changes that are spurred by the large transformatory process from modern to postmodern polities. While both approaches offer substantial theoretical improvements in their respective subfields of political science, they still leave the question of how to apply deliberative democratic principles in postmodern/medieval polities unanswered. The emerging gap between pattern (medieval polities) and concept (ideal deliberative democracy) remains to be bridged by empirical work.

NOTES

While this final version is the responsibility of the author, for comments on earlier versions of this chapter I would like to thank Mathias Albert and Karin Fierke; the participants of the Workshop on Identities Borders Orders: New Directions in IR Theory, Aschaffenburg, 10–12 January 1998; the Seminar Series of the Sussex International Relations and Politics Group, the University of Exeter European Politics Workshop, 19 January 1998; as well as the Lunch Time Seminar at the Robert Schuman Centre, European University Institute, February 1998.

1. For the focus on substance and procedure in democratic theory, see Cohen (1996).

2. For example, Weiler, Haltern, and Mayer find that in the European discussion, "Typically and endearingly there is an implicit projection onto Europe of a national self-understanding of democratic governance" (1995, 2).

3. I use the term "postmodern" to indicate a difference from things "modern." This use of the term is purely temporary. It does not entail epistemological claims.

4. See Article B(5) TEU and Article A TEU respectively. The *acquis communautaire* entails the shared legal and procedural properties of the EU. It lies at the core of EU governance since it reflects the shared norms, rules, and procedures at any time (Wiener 1998).

5. Weiler 1995, 11. Weiler takes issue with seemingly unreflected assumptions about democracy when he states, "An interesting feature of the democratization discussion in Europe, especially the blueprints for change, concerns the very understanding of democracy. Very rarely, if at all, is there more than cursory acknowledgement of the uneasy co-existence of competing visions and models of democracy which, in turn, should inform both diagnosis, prognosis and possible remedy of democratic shortcomings" (ibid., 2).

6. This led some students of the democracy deficit to state that "the problems of democracy, legitimacy and effectiveness in the EU can never be solved within the present set of constraints placed upon it by the member states. The only logical solution from a strict democratic point of view is to strengthen the EU Parliament at the expense of member states, which implies moving towards some form of federal system" (Andersen and Eliassen 1996, 11). Others have, however, begun to wonder about alternative ways of thinking about this polity.

7. The term "modern nation-state" refers to a territorialized concept.

8. Subsequently, "From a normative democratic point of view the lack of a unified polity is the most serious democratic deficit, since the legitimacy of the parliamentary institution as such is based upon voters having at least a common frame of political reference. The formation of such a common identity is at best a long term project" (Andersen and Elliassen 1996, 7).

9. Drawing on Tocqueville, Mary Kaldor and Ivan Vejvoda (1997) point out that the distinction between formal (procedural) and substantive democracy is crucial for transitional processes.

10. This perspective on the "how" is based on the relationship between the citizen and the regime. Constitutionalists have identified it as "the perennial problem of the proper fit between citizens and regimes" (Murphy 1995, 237).

9

Demographic Boundary Maintenance in World Politics: Of International Norms on Dual Nationality

REY KOSLOWSKI

It is commonly assumed that the world's population is divided among 189 states, each with its own passport used by individuals to prove his or her nationality[1] when crossing the border between one state and the other. Well, not exactly. People can be deprived of their nationality and become "stateless," or they may acquire two or more nationalities. Individuals may acquire dual nationality at birth, through marriage, by claiming ancestral lineage, or through naturalization. Individuals with dual nationality may take advantage of the resulting conflicts of laws between states or suffer the consequences. Dual nationality often gives individuals full access to two labor markets, property rights that are reserved for nationals, and certain tax shelters, but it also raises the potential of double taxes on income or inheritance. Extension of the political rights of citizenship to emigrants abroad or permitting newly naturalized immigrants to keep their first nationality may strengthen ties to the homeland polity or facilitate immigrant political incorporation. At the same time, the resulting dual nationality may also raise the dilemmas of double voting and multiple political loyalties. Individuals with two passports may find international travel easier; however, dual nationals may also have multiple military obligations and risk being drafted on trips to their ancestral homeland.

In facing these practical problems, jurists have traditionally argued against dual nationality. Justice Felix Frankfurter commented, "no man should be permitted deliberately to place himself in a position where his services may be claimed by more than one government and his allegiance be due to more than one" (Frankfurter 1958). The German Constitutional Court has made similar arguments (*Bundesverfassungsgericht* 1974, 254–55). Most states do not, in principle, endorse dual nationality, and some states have entered into multilateral agreements aimed at international cooperation on naturalization and expatriation policies in order to minimize its occurrence. The development of a set of international legal norms against dual nationality over the past century helped delineate what parts of the world's population belonged to which states—they in effect grounded a demographic boundary maintenance regime.

More and more states are changing their laws to explicitly permit dual nationality (e.g., Switzerland and Mexico), newly formed states are adopting the principle into their nationality laws (e.g., Russia), and other states whose laws ostensibly forbid dual nationality often tolerate it in practice (e.g., Germany and the United States). For the most part, domestic politics rather than the international environment is driving these changing state practices that have undermined the demographic boundary maintenance regime and led to growing numbers of dual nationals. The phenomenon of dual nationality challenges traditional notions of political identity and challenges basic assumptions of the classical European states system. In terms of the IBO conceptual framework, such changes in demographic boundaries reflect as well as reproduce increasingly complex political identities and international orders.

I make this argument in three steps: First, I will review the development of international norms intended to minimize the occurrence of dual nationality and offer explanations for why recent state practices regarding dual nationality are changing. Second, I will suggest several interpretations of what dual nationality may indicate about the political identification of individuals and consider the implications of dual nationality for traditional understandings of political identity in general. Third, I will assess the consequences of the declining demographic boundary maintenance regime for the existing international order.

RISE AND DECLINE OF THE DEMOGRAPHIC BOUNDARY REGIME

Conflicts of laws among states regarding nationality are rooted in differing principles governing nationality. As modern nationality laws developed throughout the nineteenth and early twentieth centuries, states adopted either the *jus sanguinis* (ancestral lineage) or the *jus soli* (birthplace) principle, thereby delineating which inhabitants of the state were citizens. Since both *jus sanguinis* and *jus soli* were internationally recognized as legitimate principles for the ascription of nationality, it meant that cases of dual nationality would be unavoidable (e.g., when a national from a *jus sanguinis* state has a child in a *jus soli* state).

Although the terms "dual nationality" and "dual citizenship," as well as "nationality" and "citizenship," are often used as synonyms, they are not quite the same. In terms of international law, nationality encompasses subjects as well as citizens (Oppenheim 1955, 642–43). Nationality refers to the status of being subject to a state's laws, its taxes, and military conscription while enjoying the right of protection by the state even when abroad. Citizenship refers to a bundle of civil, political, and social rights possessed by individuals (Marshall 1964). Moreover, as Weis notes, "every citizen is a national, but not every national is necessarily a citizen of the State concerned" (1979, 5–6). Ships, aircraft, and corporations (i.e., legal persons) possess nationality, as well as individuals, but only individual human beings can be citizens. A felon may lose his or her citizenship rights but still retain his or her nationality. States may also permit dual nationality without dual citizenship. For example, Mexico now gives passports, diplomatic protection, and civil rights to its emigrants who have become nationals of another state, but it does not extend political rights (Lizarraga Chavez 1997).

Dual nationality has historically led to serious international disputes and even military conflict. Following the doctrine of "perpetual allegiance," Great Britain considered naturalized American sailors born in Great Britain to be subjects of the British Crown and impressed them into military service, thereby triggering the War of 1812. When emigrants naturalized and became U.S. citizens, they often found themselves possessing two nationalities and two sets of military obligations. France, Spain, Prussia, and other German states routinely drafted naturalized Americans when they visited their homelands.

The problem of multiple military obligations associated with dual nationality became a preoccupation of George Bancroft, the German-educated historian who became the first U.S. ambassador to the North German Federation in 1867 (Handlin 1984). In 1849, Bancroft argued that states should "as soon tolerate a man with two wives as a man with two countries; as soon bear with polygamy as that state of double allegiance which common sense so repudiates that it has not even coined a word to express it" (Bancroft, 1849). As the U.S. ambassador in Berlin, he negotiated a treaty in 1868 with the North German Confederation in which U.S. naturalization was recognized and German nationals secured a limited right of expatriation. Soon thereafter, the Grand Duchy of Baden, Bavaria, the Kingdom of Wurtemberg, and the Grand Duchy of Hesse all concluded similar bilateral treaties with the United States (Flournoy and Hudson 1929, 660–67). Additional bilateral treaties recognizing U.S. naturalization and limiting dual nationality were negotiated between the United States and Great Britain, Austria-Hungary, Belgium, Denmark, Norway, and Sweden during the last decades of the nineteenth century (Bar Yaacov 1961, 163–66). In total, the United States entered into twenty-six such bilateral agreements, which collectively became known as the "Bancroft Treaties." Although most major sending states entered into agreements with the United States, some states continued to draft naturalized American citizens when they returned to their country of origin as, for example, Italy and Switzerland did during World War I.

The proliferation of bilateral treaties regarding nationality during the latter half of the nineteenth century accumulated into a set of norms against dual nationality in customary international law. The project of codifying customary international rules began in 1925 when the League of Nations began to prepare for an International Codification Conference. The continuing conflicts between states over their nationals during World War I helped raise the issue of the regulation of nationality to become the first of three areas under consideration (Harvard Law School 1929). The conference produced the 1930 Hague Convention on Certain Questions Relating to the Conflict of Nationality Laws,[2] which stated that "it is in the interest of the international community to secure that all members should recognize that every person should have a nationality and should have one nationality only" (League of Nations 1930d, preamble).

Continuing the project of codifying international customary law after World War II, the United Nations's International Law Commission drafted a Convention Relating to the Statelessness of Persons in 1954 and a Convention on the Reduction of Statelessness in 1961. In the post–World War II era, states take on a duty to extend nationality to those who would otherwise be stateless: "All persons are entitled to possess one nationality, but one nationality only" (International Law Commission 1954).

For the most part, however, postwar international cooperation to reduce dual nationality by treaty moved from worldwide to regional efforts, most extensively in Europe. According to the Council of Europe's Convention on the Reduction of Cases of Multiple Nationality (Council of Europe 1963), a national of one participating state who gains the nationality of another should lose his or her previous nationality, and an individual with nationalities of two participating states should be able to renounce one state's nationality. France, Austria, Denmark, Germany, Italy, Norway, Luxembourg, Sweden, and the Netherlands ratified the Convention while the United Kingdom, Ireland, and Spain agreed only to chapter 2 of the Convention, "Military Obligations in Cases of Multiple Nationality."

International norms against statelessness and dual nationality helped establish an international system of nation-states by delineating its parts in terms of population. Just as states conclude border treaties that delineate their jurisdiction geographically, states delineate their jurisdiction demographically. Just as multilateral boundary conventions provide international rules for delineating geographic borders, states have entered into multilateral conventions on statelessness and dual nationality in order to both legitimate their competencies over defined jurisdictions and to minimize conflicts. These multilateral efforts reduced the number of cases of statelessness and dual nationality and instituted a regime for the resolution of conflicts over the remaining cases.

As long as the number of remaining cases that persist stays relatively small, conflicts of nationality law can be marginalized in relations among states given that the consequences of statelessness and dual nationality are ultimately borne by individuals, whose interests can all too easily be disregarded should they conflict with the interests of the states concerned. Increased international migration places pressure on this demographic boundary-maintaining regime of the states system by increasing the number of people who find themselves caught between two states and suffering adverse consequences because of it. In conjunction with increasing migration, many states have recently relaxed their policies on renunciation of previous citizenship for resident aliens who naturalize as well as on automatic expatriation of their nationals who naturalize elsewhere. Such policy changes have undermined the international regime dedicated to reducing cases of dual nationality.

Thomas Franck has interpreted this change in state practices regarding dual nationality in terms of the emergence of a "new personal right to compose one's identity" in which "Self-determination evolves from a plural to a singular entitlement, from a right of peoples to one of *persons*." He argues that loyalty has become more a matter of personal choice and that "enlightened legal systems" are increasingly permitting it (Franck 1996, 359–60, abstract). While this is a very good first cut at explaining the phenomenon, its subtext is the triumph of liberalism, with the expansion of personal rights being recognized by increasing numbers of "enlightened" legal systems. This depiction is somewhat problematic because the norms against dual nationality were in large measure the outcome of, first, a compromise between American liberals and German conservative nationalists to coordinate their nationality laws so as to reduce the numbers of dual nationals, and then the codification of international law to minimize conflicts between states over their nationals that embodied the liberal ideal of rule of law in the international realm. In the nineteenth and most of the twentieth centuries, the political actions of liberals produced norms against dual nationality; at the end of the twentieth century, the liberal position is increasingly in favor of permitting dual nationality. The liberal embrace of dual nationality perhaps says more about the evolution of liberalism than the spread of liberalism says about states' embrace of dual nationality.

A very different way of explaining these changing norms and state practices is to understand them in terms of one dimension of the formation of a "security community" (Deutsch et. al 1957). Due to the development of postwar European integration and the extension of North Atlantic security structures toward the East with the end of the Cold War, there is a decreased probability of war within Europe and North America. It could therefore be argued that the probability of multiple loyalties being put to the test in war has decreased, and the problem of dual nationality lessened. Moreover, since the end of the Cold War several states are considering or have announced that they are abandoning conscription in favor of all-volunteer military forces, thereby reducing the instances of multiple military obligations. While the permissive context of a security community provides an additional insight into understanding these changes, a security-driven explanation is insufficient, in and of itself, because most of those states that have relaxed their prohibitions on dual nationality have done so for nationals of all states, not just to those of countries within the security community. Indeed, French practice negates this thesis. France is a party to the 1963 Council of Europe Convention, and, in accordance with its treaty commitments, it does not permit dual nationality for nationals from the other signatory states. However, France does permit dual nationality to nationals from all other states (Council of Europe 1995, 47).

If spreading liberalism or decreasing security threats do not sufficiently explain changing state practices and international norms on dual nationality, then what does? Unfortunately, international relations scholars must enter the messy realm of domestic politics to understand these changes, and there are at least four domestic political factors contributing to changing state practices, depending on the state concerned.

A major factor for increasing cases of dual nationality is the postwar rise of women's movements (Hammar 1985). In the development of nationality law in the nineteenth and early twentieth centuries, states that followed the principle of *jus sanguinis* generally followed the additional practice of patrilineal ascription. That is, legitimate children received the father's nationality; illegitimate children received the mother's nationality. This practice reduced the number of dual nationals because the child of a marriage between nationals of two *jus sanguinis* states would then have the father's nationality and, if born out of wedlock, the mother's—but not both. Essentially, the pervasiveness of patrilineal ascription yielded an informal coordination game among states. This informal coordination was effectively sanctioned by the 1930 Hague Convention on Nationality given that attempts to institutionalize a principle of gender equality in nationality laws failed (Brown Scott 1931). Nevertheless, in response to widening women's suffrage and subsequent movements for equal treatment of women under the law, many states gradually abandoned patrilineal ascription in favor of gender equality in the transmission of nationality to children. The more states that ascribe their nationality to children of mixed marriages, regardless of the citizen parent's gender, the greater the possibilities that children of mixed marriages will be born with dual nationality. Although the struggle for women's equality can be viewed as a chapter in the triumph of liberal ideology, the actual increase in cases of dual nationality arising from mixed marriages was not a matter of the state's acceptance of the individual's right to choose dual nationality, because the ascription of nationality is not a matter of choice. Rather the increase in dual nationality in such circumstances is the unintentional outcome of a declining informal international coordination of nationality laws.

The second domestic political factor is primarily operative in migrant-sending states, such as Columbia, the Dominican Republic, Ecuador, Turkey, Italy, and Mexico, which recently began to permit emigrants to maintain their nationality after naturalizing to another state. Most of these sending states changed their policies in large measure due to the lobbying of emigrants who wish to retire or invest in the homeland and as a means of retaining emigrant identity. In many cases, sending states are permitting dual nationality among their emigrants in the hope that, as citizens of host countries, they might form stronger ethnic lobbies that can work to change host country foreign policies in favor of the home states' interests (S. Dillon 1996; Özdemir 1996). In such cases, the arena of domestic politics has been globalized by migration (Koslowski 1996), and one can understand policy changes in terms of emigrants pursuing their interests and policy makers redefining the national interest in the area of nationality law from the primacy of singular loyalty to the state to a strategy using dual nationality to further state interests.

Similarly, historic sending countries of Europe often maintained postcolonial ties by explicit agreements on dual nationality with former colonies or through more informal toleration of the practice. For example, in 1949 the United Kingdom changed its law on dual nationality, permitting its nationals to gain the nationality of Canada, Australia, and New Zealand after these former colonies established their own citizenship laws (Goldstein and Piazza 1996, 521). Similarly, between 1958 and 1969 Spain negotiated a series of bilateral agreements permitting dual nationality for nationals of Chile, Peru,

Paraguay, Nicaragua, Guatemala, Bolivia, Ecuador, Costa Rica, Honduras, the Dominican Republic, and Argentina (Council of Europe 1997c).

New states emerging from the collapse of the Soviet Union and Yugoslavia also opted to permit dual nationality, if only as a possibility for emigrants and their descendants. As the Soviet Union collapsed, twenty-five million Russians found themselves outside of Russia. Russian politicians quickly championed the cause of Russians in the "near abroad" and insured that the new Russian citizenship law permitted dual nationality (Council of Europe 1997c, 142). Members of the "Croatian nation" that do not reside in Croatia may acquire Croatian nationality without renouncing their existing nationality, and Slovenia permits dual nationality for Slovenians who naturalize elsewhere (Council of Europe 1997c, 30, 151).

The third domestic political factor is primarily operative in states experiencing net immigration, i.e., receiving or host states. Many receiving states have relaxed their prohibitions on dual nationality in order to facilitate political incorporation. In 1977, Canada changed its law to explicitly permit dual nationality for immigrants who naturalize as well as for Canadian nationals who naturalized elsewhere. Australia does not require renunciation of previous citizenship for those who naturalize; however, Australians who naturalize elsewhere automatically lose their Australian nationality. The U.S. government officially "discourages" dual nationality but permits it in practice because it is restrained by Supreme Court decisions striking down involuntary expatriation as a violation of the Fourteenth Amendment. Also, naturalized Americans routinely keep their previous nationalities and passports because the renunciation clause of the oath of allegiance is not strictly enforced (Goldstein and Piazza 1996; Spiro 1997). In 1990 Switzerland stopped requiring renunciation of previous nationality of those who naturalize (OECD 1995, 163, 165), and the Netherlands changed its policies in 1991 so as to permit those who naturalize to retain their previous nationalities in certain circumstances (Council of Europe 1996, 22). Since France only requires renunciation by naturalization applicants from states who have signed the 1963 Convention, and this group forms only a small fraction of the French immigrant population, well over a million naturalized French citizens maintain dual nationality (Hammar 1990, 111).

A related fourth domestic political reason for loosening restrictions on dual nationality is operative in countries that have historically been net migrant-sending states and have recently become net receiving states. Permitting dual nationality among emigrants undermines laws that do not permit it for immigrants. For example, Switzerland's removal of its renunciation requirement was not just a matter of increasing naturalization rates. Switzerland has long maintained a policy that Swiss nationals residing abroad who naturalize in their host state do not lose Swiss nationality. Given that approximately 70 percent of the 500,000 Swiss nationals residing abroad maintain dual nationality (*Neue Zürcher Zeitung* 1993), it became difficult for Swiss politicians to argue in principle against the dual nationality on the grounds of divided loyalties without alienating a significant constituency (D'Amato 1997).

Germany's Christian Democratic Union (CDU)–led government rebuffed calls to eliminate the renunciation requirement until its defeat at the polls in September 1998. Nevertheless, the German government tolerated dual nationality among ethnic Germans from Eastern Europe and Russia, children of mixed marriages, and draft-age foreigners, if the home country required military service in order to be released from its nationality. Already in 1995, Cornelia Schmalz-Jacobsen, the Federal Government's Commissioner for Foreigners' Affairs, estimated that there were over two million German citizens with dual nationality (TWIG 1995). Essentially, Germany followed the example of France in practice and violated the spirit, if not the letter, of the Council of Europe 1963 Convention. In early 1999, the newly elected Social Democratic (SPD)–Green coalition government proposed citizenship law reforms eliminating the renunciation requirement. After an electoral setback in Hesse, which was credited to a petition campaign against dual nationality, the government settled for a modified version of the reforms that went into effect on January 1, 2000. Dual nationality is permitted to those born of foreign parents; however, they must choose between German nationality and their other nationality by the time they become twenty-three years old.

Although international norms intended to decrease cases of dual nationality had been most fully developed within the Council of Europe, by the beginning of the 1990s it became clear that increasing migration had put them under significant pressure (Heilbronner 1992,

92–98). Changing nationality laws, evasive treaty interpretations, and contradictory administrative practices on the part of European states undermined these norms and have led to the deterioration of Europe's demographic boundary maintenance regime (for elaboration, see Koslowski 1994). By the late 1980s, the Council of Europe began to reconsider the 1963 Convention, prodded by a French parliamentarian's concern for a constituent's ambiguous legal status (Miller 1989, 949). Interestingly, "French efforts were driven by government officials and French immigrant groups who bemoaned the inequities of the legitimate dual national status of Franco-non-Europeans, such as Franco-Algerians, and the problematic dual national status of a Franco-European, such as a Franco-German, whom they considered 'culturally closer'" (Feldblum 1998, 237). Eventually, the Council of Europe diluted the 1963 Convention with a 1993 protocol that permits dual nationality in certain cases "in order to encourage the unity of nationality within the same family" (Council of Europe 1993, 2).

In 1997, the Council of Europe's Committee of Ministers adopted a new European Convention on Nationality that allows states to permit dual nationality or not to permit it, to require renunciation or not to require it.[3] Nevertheless, the new convention does not abrogate treaty commitments made in 1963 (Council of Europe 1997b), most signatory states retain prohibitions against dual nationality in their nationality laws, and most EU member states still required renunciation of first nationality by naturalization applicants when the European Convention on Nationality was signed in November 1997 (Netherlands changed its policy back to requiring renunciation on October 1, 1997).[4] As Germany relaxes its renunciation requirement, however, whatever is left of the international norm against dual nationality becomes a somewhat moot point as an overwhelming majority of Europe's population of resident aliens will become able to maintain a second nationality.

In sum, changing state practices to permit dual nationality are primarily driven by domestic politics; however, these changes are facilitated by a permissive international security context. Formal international norms are gradually, but persistently, following changes in domestic laws and administrative practices. Increasing gender equality has probably been most responsible for the growing numbers of dual nationals over the past few decades, but recent changes

in expatriation policies by sending states and the elimination of renunciation requirements in receiving states have drastically increased
the potential pools of dual nationals. It is estimated that some five
million people can potentially gain both U.S. and Mexican nationality. If increasing numbers of dual nationals may be anticipated in
the future, what are the broader theoretical and practical implications of this trend?

THE MEANING OF DUAL NATIONALITY FOR POLITICAL IDENTITY

It is tempting to interpret the meaning of increasing dual nationality
in terms set out by Zygmunt Bauman's suggestion that "if the modern 'problem of identity' is primarily how to construct an identity
and keep it solid and stable, the postmodern 'problem of identity' is
primarily how to avoid fixation and keep options open" (Bauman
1996, 18). That is, modern states try to construct solid and stable
identities for individuals while postmodern individuals "keep their
options open" by acquiring a second nationality. In many cases this
depiction of the situation may be quite appropriate; however, as a
general rule it falls short. Part of the problem is that dual nationality is not simply a matter of individual choice, but rather the confluence of state laws and policies regarding the ascription, acquisition,
and renunciation of nationality. The fact that states are increasingly
permitting dual nationality may have quite different implications
with respect to policy-makers' expectations or concerns regarding
individual political identification. Likewise, the act of migrants and
their descendants taking on or retaining two nationalities may have
different meanings to each individual. Dual nationality may be indicative of a step in political identity transfer from home to host
state, retention of home state identity, a desire to maintain multiple
political identities, a reluctance to choose a political identity, or it
may have nothing to do with political identity at all.

Even when dual nationality is accepted in principle by states, it
has been commonly viewed as a marginal and transitory feature of
migration and naturalization. This view is largely based on the classical model of assimilation based on the nineteenth-century experience of immigration countries such as the United States, Canada,
and Australia, in which the political identity of migrants and their
descendants was understood to shift in one direction—from home
to host country. It was generally assumed that eventually the mi-

grants' descendants, if not the migrants themselves, would come to consider the host country to be their home country, and they would lose interest in the politics of the ancestral homeland. The transfer of migrants' political identity from one country to another was usually marked by the act of renouncing home country citizenship and taking an oath of allegiance during naturalization.

Sending countries often view such assimilation in terms of a demographic and national "loss." In response, countries experiencing great out-migration tended to base nationality primarily on *jus sanguinis* because it encouraged emigrants to retain their nationality and pass it on to their children, which facilitated their return and closer ties with their homeland (Koslowski 1997). The tug of war between receiving and sending states over the political identity of migrants increased the instances of dual nationality, whereas the norms against dual nationality helped make citizenship in the host or home country a clear line of distinction of political identification.

Interestingly, receiving states that expect permitting dual nationality to increase naturalization are also permitting residual homeland political identification, thereby making the act of naturalization no longer one of political identity transfer. Apparently the hope is that homeland political identity would fade with time after naturalization; at the same time sending states hope that emigrants will maintain strong homeland political identities despite their newly acquired nationality. That is, states may permit individuals to "avoid fixation and keep options open" but do so with the objective of furthering their modernist projects of constructing stable identities. Contrary to the designs of sending and receiving states, the migrant's act of taking on two nationalities may be indicative of neither assimilation nor homeland political identification, but rather of multiple political identities, an ambivalent political identity, or even an apolitical identity.

The same migrants that express their feelings of political identification with the ancestral homeland often voice similar feelings toward their new country of residence when on visits "back home." Such expressions may be a manifestation of a strong desire to maintain a multiple political identity—to simultaneously be both a "good American" and "good Cuban," a "good Canadian" and "good Italian," etc. The political identity of individuals may even switch back and forth over their lifetimes as expressed in the objectives of their political actions (see, e.g., Blejwas 1995). The internal logic of nationalism may militate against the notion of political identification with two nation-states, nevertheless, individuals defy this logic by expressing multiple political identification through their actions (including voluntary military service to both states). Hence, when an individual maintains or acquires dual nationality, it may be an actualization of multiple political identification.

An ambivalent political identity can be thought of in terms somewhat similar to multiple political identity. However, individuals may be less proactive in efforts to maintain and express both host and homeland identities and more reactive to their host and home country environments. For example, the immigrant who actively tries to leave his or her homeland behind may feel spurned by host country social and political associations and then defensively retreat toward a halfhearted affiliation with homeland political organizations. Similarly, the migrant who returns to the homeland may identify with his or her new country of residence not because he or she wishes to actively maintain that identity, but because homeland compatriots may not fully accept, or may even reject, the emigrant's expressions of homeland identification. When migrants feel rejected by both host and homeland societies, the retention of dual nationality may be more the expression of indecision between political identities rather than the affirmation of both. Retention of dual nationality may also be a self-protective move for fear of being rejected after renouncing one of the two nationalities.

While many may equate dual nationality with multiple political identities (whether fearful conservatives or hopeful multiculturalists), the individual's act of acquiring or retaining a second nationality may have no deep political significance at all. Dual nationality is often viewed in utilitarian terms of having a second passport for easier travel and gaining access to business and employment opportunities for which citizenship is required. For example, Dominica sells its citizenship for a cash contribution of $50,000.[5] In one year, Dominica sold sixty-eight passports for $3.5 million—half to Russians or nationals of other Soviet successor states, over twenty to Chinese and Taiwanese, and about a dozen to Americans (Fineman 1997). Wealthy Russians apparently do not want immigration officials to know about their international movements and investments because such information is sold by corrupt officials to criminals who use it for extortion. Taiwanese and Chinese dual nationals use their second passports to circumvent strict visa requirements in the West (for example, the United Kingdom, Canada, and Australia require no visas for bearers of Dominican passports).[6] Americans primarily use their Dominican nationality to reduce or avoid taxes. St. Kitts and Nevis, the Cape Verde Islands, and Belize offer similar programs, while Ireland and Portugal have offered investment-linked citizenship programs in the past. When individuals treat citizenship as a commodity through the purchase of a second passport in this manner, the resulting dual nationality is apolitical, if not antipolitical, in nature.

The apolitical meaning of dual nationality need not be as blatant. Increasing dual nationality among nationals of certain states with decreasing rates of political participation may simply be indicative of more general trends of decreasing interest in politics. Dual nationality may also simply be a manifestation of ignorance or apathy. Many individuals do not know that they became dual nationals at birth and, as is frequently the case for American-born children of Greek or Turkish parents, they only become aware of their dual nationality after receiving a draft notice from their ancestral homeland. Even if they do discover that they are dual nationals, many, especially those who do not face complications with military service obligations, simply do not bother to renounce one of their two nationalities.

Multiple, ambivalent, and apolitical identities are just as much a part of diasporic existence as strong homeland identities or the transfer of political identity to host states. These alternative political and apolitical identities can also be considered part and parcel of the economic and political dynamics of globalization. As such, we can expect that as the economic and technological processes of globalization intensify and states increasingly permit dual nationality and other forms of multiple membership, members of diasporas will increasingly sustain such alternative transnational identities that transcend undivided loyalties, assumed to exist with singular nationality in sharply delineated nation-states.

BLURRING BOUNDARIES, MULTIPLE POLITICAL IDENTITIES, AND CHANGING INTERNATIONAL ORDERS

The dilemmas of multiple loyalties incumbent in dual nationality led international relations theorist Raymond Aron to consider multiple citizenship as a contradiction in terms (1974), which is incommensurate with the logic of the states system. Given the institutions of the nation-state and a system of states, dual nationality should not exist, and when it does exist, it is unsustainable. But what if the phenomenon of dual nationality not only persists, but cases of dual nationality increase dramatically? What does this say about the state and the states system?

Aron dismissed multiple citizenship by arguing that, historically, the nation-state informed the development of citizenship and that it was unlikely that the practice of citizenship, including both the exercise of political rights as well as the fulfillment of duties such as military service, could ever take place outside of the singular relationship between the individual and the state he or she was a member of. Aron argued that European institutions of democracy, military service, the principle of equality were all organized around the nation-state. Citizenship is the connection between individual and state, whereby with popular sovereignty citizenship defined the state and, as a fundamental aspect of sovereignty, the state determined who its citizens were and obliged them to fulfill the duties incumbent in their exercise of rights. Along such lines of thinking, multiple citizenship is theoretically inconsistent.

The theoretical contradiction, however, only rings true given the history of a set of actors' practices that have settled into institutions. For their reproduction these settled practices depend on constitutive and regulative norms. For example, the differentiation of world politics into an international system of states is made possible by constitutive norms such as "everyone belongs to a state and only one state," and the reproduction of system-unit differentiation is facilitated by regulative norms such as "minimize cases of dual nationality through requiring renunciation of previous nationality" and "permit renunciation of nationality by those who naturalize in other states." If the international system is understood in terms of settled practices that are constituted and regulated by norms, then changes in practices can lead to changes in constitutive norms, which in turn reconstitute the system itself. Moreover, since the reproduction of the practice of international actors (states) depends on the reproduction of the practices of domestic actors (individuals and groups), then changes in domestic politics can transform international systems.

Dual nationality is an "abnormality" within the classical state system because it contradicts the system's constitutive norms. If the incidence of dual nationality increases because domestic politics forces state practices in the international arena to depart from the constitutive and regulative norms of the existing international system, these new state practices can either be dismissed as being anomalous and ephemeral, or they can be viewed as precedents in the establishment of a new set of international norms and as indicative of a transformation of the international system. Aron viewed EU-member-state practices of extending civil and economic rights to nonnationals as anomalous and unlikely to expand into the political realm. One can similarly dismiss the increasing state practice of permitting dual nationality as anomalous and bound to be reversed. In contrast, one could view changing practices of states toward the implicit toleration, if not explicit sanction, of dual nationality as part and parcel of the development of a new set of constitutive norms incumbent with the replacement of the classical European states system with the emergence of a new form of polity, particularly in Europe. What kind of polity could a new norm of permitting dual nationality be indicative of?

When considering the potential alternative to the contemporary states system, Hedley Bull described a secular "new medievalism" or a "system of overlapping authority and multiple loyalty" (Bull 1977, 254). By blurring the boundaries of authority of states over their subjects and increasing the potential for multiple loyalties, increasing dual nationality may be indicative of one dimension of a transformation of the international system in Europe toward such a new medievalism. Gidon Gottlieb furthers this reconceptualization of international society by advocating that the existing territorially delineated international system be adjusted for overlapping authority and dual loyalties through the international recognition of nonterritorial political associations (Gottlieb 1993). Gottlieb distinguishes citizenship that is tied to the state from nationality that is tied to the nation[7] and advocates the idea of a "national home," distinct from the state, to which nationals could belong regardless of their residence. Given that a state's acceptance of dual citizenship legitimates migrants' residual political identification with another state, the acceptance of dual citizenship on the international level would be a first step to international recognition of national homes and an international system of what Gottlieb calls "states plus nations."

This formulation of "states plus nations" conjures the image of a matrix of homeland nationality superimposed onto a territorially organized citizenship of the classical European states system. Within this matrix of nationalities and citizenships, individuals would have dual nationalities in which the rights and duties of homeland citizenship would become recessive upon naturalization in a new state, whose citizenship would be active. Should those who naturalize return to their "national homes," the process would reverse. Although overlapping authorities and multiple loyalties would proliferate, the breakdown of undivided loyalties, assumed to exist with singular nationality in sharply delineated nation-states, need not result in divided loyalties that are uniformly divided between two states. That is, much as in medieval Europe, authorities and loyalties could easily become functionally differentiated (Guetzkow 1955). Sets of rights extended by the home state and duties owed to it may be quite different than rights and duties of the state of naturalization.

Such a disaggregation of unitary nationality and citizenship that the plurality of nationalities incurs is indicative of a parallel disaggregation of unitary authority into a set of overlapping authorities. In this sense, the movement toward a norm permitting dual nationality can be considered part of what Ole Wæver calls "a collective redefinition of sovereignty." As Wæver points out, at one time sovereignty "meant the ability to decide the religion of one's subjects. Although this is no longer included in sovereignty, states have not become less sovereign. Religion and the state have both changed" (Wæver 1995a, 417–18). Likewise, sovereignty once meant the ability to unilaterally determine who one's subjects were and then extend rights to and impose duties upon them. In the context of migration, the development of popular sovereignty, and the growing international acceptance of human rights principles, state sovereignty in the determination of nationality and the content of citizenship rights and obligations is being redefined. As international norms governing nationality are changing so as to exclude certain unilateral prerogatives, nationality and the state are both changing as the classical state system is transformed.

CONCLUSION

The current trend among states to permit dual nationality undermines the demographic boundary regime based on international norms that have developed over the past century. The demise of the demographic boundary maintenance regime demonstrates the relationships among identities, borders, and orders in a rather peculiar way. In this case, changes in demographic boundaries, rather than geographical borders, have complex implications for political identities and generate consequences for international orders.

Although dual nationality can easily be interpreted in postmodern terms of the avoidance of fixation and the desire to keep options open, this interpretation only captures one possible interpretation of the increasing number of cases of dual nationality in terms of political identity. This depiction cannot be generalized in large part because dual nationality is not simply a matter of individual choice, but rather the confluence of state laws and policies regarding the ascription, acquisition, and renunciation of nationality. State expectations regarding the political identification of dual nationals and the meanings individuals give to their dual nationality may also vary widely. Therefore, dual nationality may just as well be a matter of the retention of homeland political identity as it may be political incorporation into the host society; it may signify the possession of multiple political identities or the lack of any political identities at all.

Whereas the general association between dual nationality and political identity may be very commonsensical, the meaning of dual nationality for political identity is not as simple as it may at first appear. The bearing of dual nationality on international order may at first appear very remote, but it becomes pertinent if one is willing to consider the constitutive nature of citizenship and accept the role of nationality law in "bounding" states. Given that international norms against statelessness and dual nationality were constitutive of an international system of nation-states, the decline of the demographic boundary maintenance regime and the concomitant increase in cases of dual nationality is indicative of a transformation of the international order toward a "new medievalism," particularly in Europe.

This changing international order has policy implications for taxation, voting, and military service that are beyond the scope of this chapter. I plan to explore these policy implications at length in the future and will only briefly mention them at this point. Second nationalities enable economic elites to avoid taxes and conceal international travel. As nationalities of convenience are combined with offshore banking and the anonymous electronic money transfers of e-cash, even the most sophisticated states may confront obstacles to effective tax collection. Dual nationality also raises the prospect of individuals voting in two states. When combined with spreading democratization, the easing of prohibitions on dual nationality means that the potential of double voting could grow significantly. Perhaps most importantly, more dual nationals increase the potential for multiple military obligations. If international cooperation to minimize dual nationality is coming to an end, new forms of international cooperation on taxation, voting, and military service will become necessary in order to preempt the problems that prompted the development of international norms against dual nationality in the first place.

Given that the emerging order is characterized by a diffusion of authority from clearly delineated nation-states, with whom will one cooperate? That is, if readily identifiable and coherently organized nation-states are unavailable to address the policy challenges incumbent with increasing dual nationality outlined above, will viable alternatives to states emerge to fill the breach? If states, the international regimes and organizations that states form, or some sorts of political alternatives to them cannot develop effective means of dealing with the "externalities" of increasing cases of dual nationality, we may expect dual nationality to become an increasing point of controversy and potential conflict among centers of political authority as these centers compete for the allegiance and loyalty of individuals within a complex system of polities with overlapping identities and authorities. In effect, it is not at all clear that the seemingly benign new medievalism is completely immune from eventually replicating the kind of internecine political conflicts and perhaps even the violence characteristic of the old medieval world.

NOTES

This chapter is based on research that I conducted while on a postdoctoral fellowship at the Center for German and European Studies at Georgetown University during 1996/97. I greatly appreciate the financial support and the intellectual stimulus provided by the Center. I thank the editors, fellow chapter contributors, as well as Rainer Bauböck and David Martin for their helpful comments on a previous draft.

1. In this paper, I follow the Council of Europe's definition, which is standard in international law: "'nationality' means the legal bond between a person and a State and does not indicate the person's ethnic origin" (Council of Europe 1997b, Article 2).

2. As well as an additional three protocols: one dealing with "Military Obligations in Certain Cases of Double Nationality" (League of Nations 1930a); one regulating "Statelessness" (League of Nations 1930b); and one dealing with a "Certain Case of Statelessness" (League of Nations 1930c).

3. Council of Europe 1997a. As of June 15, 1999, seventeen member states have signed the Convention and two have ratified it. See Council of Europe, European Treaties, Chart of Signatures and Ratifications, http://www.coe.int.

4. Dual nationality would be permitted in only a very limited number of cases (Muus 1998).

5. For details on Dominica's Economic Citizenship Programme, see http://caribcats.com/citizenship.htm.

6. Ibid.

7. Here "nationality" is used in a different sense than defined at the outset in note 1, and I will follow Gottlieb's definition only through the discussion of his work.

10

Now and Then, Here and There: Migration and the Transformation of Identities, Borders, and Orders

MARTIN O. HEISLER

If, as Rosenau (1997) has argued, our age is characterized by the interplay of globalism and localism, then transnational migration not only bestrides but also links these two forces.[1] It is at once a hallmark and catalog of the stresses, frustrations, and opportunities indwelling the forces of integration and fragmentation. Transnational migration significantly affects individual and collective identities, and it creates new identities. It can change the forms and meanings of borders within, as well as between, states; and it increasingly challenges, and sometimes recasts, domestic and international orders. Migration affects people and institutions at all levels, from the individual or psychological to collectivities of various kinds and sizes, and even the putative global system. This makes it especially useful for viewing the ongoing transformations of identities, borders, and orders, both in societies and in international relations. These qualities provide powerful arguments for viewing changes in social and international life through the optics of migration.

Migration not only highlights tensions and connections between centrifugal and centripetal forces but often also generates them. Like the elements in Rosenau's "fragmegration,"[2] changes often move in opposite directions simultaneously, even when driven by the same forces. Thus, migration is associated with globalization in the world economy (Sassen 1991, 1996, 1998; Ohmae 1995), the emergence of international society (Bull and Watson 1984; Elfstrom 1990, chapter 4), and the growing number of enclaves, diasporas, and new ethnic minorities (Appadurai 1990; Barkan and Shelton 1998; Rath 1991). The circumstances that give rise to migration change rapidly, as do the facts and perceptions it produces in the places of origin and destination. The difficulties in pinning down the nature, meaning, and sources of such changes contribute to the perception of "turbulence" Rosenau (1990) and others (e.g., Bigo and Haine 1996) have associated with world politics in the post–Cold War period. Given the complexity of these forces, it is not surprising that they appear difficult to manage.

But taken simply as a process or phenomenon, migration is not a sufficient analytic tool for understanding such changes. That understanding is more likely to follow from the study of the interplay of migration with the ever-shifting frameworks of identity and social and political order at different levels of activity and analysis. That, in turn, calls for multidimensional contextual analysis that is broadly comparative, across time as well as types of situations (Heisler and Peters 1977).

Multidimensional contextual analysis is the best way to understand the effects of migration on matters of identity—that of migrants, members of host societies, and often even those who stay behind in the places of origin—as well as its influences on borders, changing their meanings in some settings and preserving or reinforcing them in others. In some parts of the world migration is a bordering and rebordering force that affects identities and, not infrequently, creates new ones. Migrants may establish temporary, if long-term, enclaves on the edges of the host society, or they may enter it as smoothly and quickly as possible by assimilating. Migration often raises contentious questions about civic order in receiving countries (or host societies) and about relations between them and the countries of migrants' origin. It is sometimes taken to be a sign of the successful and desirable permeation of the borders of states; in other circumstances it leads to redoubled efforts to close or fortify borders.

In the next section I note some recent changes, both "real" and perceived, in the relationships between transnational migration and issues of identities, borders, and orders. Those changes are analyzed along a temporal-developmental dimension. Synchronic comparisons of manifestations of migration and the treatment of migrants show significant differences at any given point of time in the interplay of identities, borders, and orders in different types of societies and polities. This is the principal meaning of the "here and there" distinction in this chapter's title. Diachronic contextualization allows us to see less obvious effects over time and stages of historical-structural development. Comparing the approach of liberal democracies ("here") to migration and migrants in the past ("then") with how they do so "now" helps to understand the behavior of contemporary societies and regimes that are not firmly established and institutionalized liberal democracies. Migration policies and the treatment of migrants in these countries ("there") may reflect stages in development through which countries "now and here" have passed. (It is also possible, of course, that the particular conjunctures of conditions and circumstances experienced by Western democracies in earlier decades or centuries will not occur in other places in the future.)

In the next section I sketch some changes in transnational migration and its key contexts—in particular, domestic governance and international relations—in the latter part of the twentieth century. I then turn to some of the salient effects of migration on the interplay of identities, borders, and orders. This is followed by a brief consideration of some of the roles migration plays in the construction of collective political and psychological spaces. The conclusion notes some insights into ongoing societal and international changes gleaned from the preceding contextual analysis.

MIGRATION AND PERCEPTIONS OF CHANGE AFFECTING IDENTITIES, BORDERS, AND ORDERS

The changes associated with transnational migration contribute to *the growing preoccupation with personal and collective identity* evident in much of the world today. They fuel "the politics of recognition"[3] so important now in many places. Even dominant majorities in societies with many migrants show such culture-focused behavior (see, e.g., Fialkowski et al. 1991). Other important issues, such as the debates revolving around community, citizenship, and individual and collective rights (Walzer 1997); social and political demands expressed in terms of ethnicity, religion, and gender (Elshtain 1995; Glazer 1997); and the securitization of person, job, and culture (see, e.g., Wæver 1995b; Krause and Williams 1996) are also related.

Even where transnational migration is implicated in some of these concerns, the ways and degrees of its connections are far from clear. Mere covariation, rather than causation, may be involved.[4] Some elements of modernity, noted below, militate in favor of increased emphasis on identity, independent of migration. It may be that the growing concern with migration is an artifact of increased interest in identity, rather than the other way around. The tools of social science are not sharp enough to determine the direction of causal arrows or, for that matter, whether causal links exist between migration and the salience of identity issues. But the extent, or even existence, of unambiguous causal relationships is less important than the widespread and growing tendency of people to infer such links. Perceptions become realities, and in societies under stress they can be used to mobilize various sorts of political resources for both domestic and international purposes. The relationships between migration and migrants and the sorts of issues just noted are at least in part artifacts of social and political construction.

Migration is often blamed for *order-disrupting changes* in host societies. When people who seem very different appear in one's accustomed spaces, they are readily associated with differences in established ways of life. What used to be taken for granted—the languages heard in public, gestures and other mannerisms, styles of dress, sounds, smells—can no longer be navigated on culturally ingrained autopilot. These differences complicate the processing of new experiences through the assumptions on which we all depend to make our way through the complexities of modern life. Assimilation to the dominant culture is the preeminent mode of preserving established order, but it has lost much of its normative force in Western democracies. "Integration" implies mutual adaptation by natives and newcomers, and it also suggests adaptations of the old order, to accommodate migrants. This is especially problematic in traditional non-Western societies and in nondemocratic regimes, nor, of course, was it historically common in what are now democracies.

Migrants do not seem to belong; their presence requires explanation and justification. These can be interest-based ("we must import foreign workers because our own people will not do these low-status, low-wage jobs"), moral ("they helped to build our economy, so we owe them decent consideration"), humanitarian ("these poor, persecuted people have nowhere else to go"), or sympathetic ("they are only trying to better themselves and make a better life for their children"), or some mixture of these. Regardless of their content, once such arguments enter public discourse, they become issues in domestic and foreign politics. Publics in host societies often divide politically into pro- and anti-immigration or pro- and anti-immigrant factions. But migration may be little more than a scapegoat or shorthand for broader psychological and ideological differences. Sometimes it is an imputed cause of such undesirable changes as increased crime or unemployment or a declining quality of schools attributed to polyglot overcrowding. It has been implicated in the growing dissensus in the effective, authoritative delineation of societal values, and in many countries it calls attention to distinctions between the society and the total population.[5] It may be seen as a threat to societal security[6] and to the environment. Some deem it a barrier to the achievement of equality for historically disadvantaged (native) populations. It has been blamed for declining civility and for floating anxieties about economic and personal security.

One reason migration enters political agendas with greater frequency and salience now is that, at least in some host societies, it *disturbs the sense of boundedness.* Migrants call attention to what is increasingly seen as a permeability of borders. They enter previously delineated and structured social, economic, cultural, political, and, of course, physical spaces. They are outsiders, "different" simply by virtue of being newcomers, even when their differences are not very obvious. Members of host societies find it more difficult— or are told they should, by those who would mobilize them around migration-related issues—to anchor their lives and expectations in what used to be more comfortable and controllable places. Yet, at the same time, normative developments in at least some receiving countries and international fora militate against excluding migrants from the enjoyment of many or most of the social and political, as well as economic, benefits of belonging.

CHANGES IN CONTEXTS

Some new or newly significant developments are changing the meaning of migration and its import for governance and international relations. Three of these are particularly relevant to the concerns at hand. One is found in the opportunities for and modes of migration, and a second in a series of relatively recent normative developments in many Western democratic host societies. Third, there is an opening in the study of international relations, manifested in the movement away from privileging state-centric theorizing and a rigid adherence to the domestic-international divide and toward perspectives anchored in social theory writ large.

Changing Patterns of Migration

The first development entails changes both in the nature of migration and how we view it. There has been a shift from *im*migration to "semi-settlement" (B. Heisler and M. Heisler 1986; M. Heisler 1998/99). Immigration historically connoted settlement—exchanging one home society for another—and, in the conventional view, carries assumptions of assimilation. Such expectations and assumptions need to be reexamined in many or most cases of transnational migration. Technological, economic, and other factors make it less likely that migrants will—or expect, or are expected by those in the host societies—to settle. In other words, they are less likely to become immigrants. Semisettlement often gives rise to transnational communities, and the dynamics between the communities of origin and places of destination foster new and complex identities among both the migrants and those who stay behind (Kearney 1995; Faist 1997; Pries 1999). It also affects the self-concepts of people in host societies who come into contact with migrants. One formal acknowledgment of these new patterns can be seen in the decisions of a growing number of countries to accord dual citizenship to their nationals living abroad. They belong both here and there, and their identity is officially shared or split.

Multicultural Norms

A second development reinforces these changes in Western democracies: the acceptance, and sometimes the enthusiastic promotion, of *norms of multiculturalism*. These norms impel host societies in the same direction as the diffusion and progressive incorporation of human rights concerns (Jacobson 1996; Sassen 1996), and they alter status and power relationships between hosts and newcomers in many ways. Perhaps the most important is that justifications for faulting migrants for being different have been substantially weakened. Cultural, linguistic, and other traits or, for that matter, the disinclination to naturalize or settle in the host society are less acceptable justifications for discrimination, either formally by the state or informally in social relations, than in the past. The expectation that migrants will assimilate has been weakened in most Western host societies, and in such countries it is becoming less legitimate to demand assimilation (cf. Walzer 1997; Glazer 1997). These are some of the more important reasons for eschewing the use of the term "immigrant," with its built-in assumptions of settlement and assimilation, and for using the term "migrant" instead, since it does not carry such expectations.

The Changing International System

The third development is the opening of international relations theory to non-state-centric orientations and to a perspective Didier Bigo characterizes as a "Möbius ribbon" (Bigo, in this volume). There is a growing inclination to view the internal and external as intertwined aspects of a whole (also see Rosenau 1997; Walker 1993). This is portentous for the future of international relations practice and theory and makes it possible to consider transnational migration free of the assumptions just noted. For a nontrivial number and category of people (migrants), states' borders are no longer the only, or perhaps even principal, determinants of identity, order, or rights. Remaining excluded is no longer the only alternative to assimilation or even, perhaps, substantial adaptation to the state. More to the point, the notion inhering to the Westphalian state model that the state may—indeed, should—manage its population through assimilation and cultural coherence in order to ensure loyalty and internal stability is being brought into question in some, though not most, countries. Aspects of citizenship may also be affected by international agreements on migration, international human rights doctrines and practices, and, in some countries, domestic norms supportive of foreigners' status (see Koslowski, in this volume, and Juss 1998/99).

The trend toward the institutionalization of international human rights in domestic legislation and judicial practice, identified by Jacobson (1996; Jacobson, this volume), Poulter (1998), Sassen (1996), and others, reinforces and is reinforced by the shift in some countries from underlying norms of assimilation to multiculturalism.

What is crucial for the future of international relations is that such norms are gaining ever-wider acceptance in Western democracies but are resolutely resisted or even rejected in many other places, especially in East and Southeast Asia (M. Heisler 1998). This divergence may signal fundamental differences that give rise to tensions in world politics, akin to Samuel Huntington's somewhat fanciful notion of a "clash of civilizations" (Huntington 1996).

Viewed in light of these three sorts of changes, the import of my argument for international relations theory can now be restated succinctly in terms of this volume's central theme. Two types of states are evident at the dawn of the twenty-first century.[7] In one, mostly Western and democratic, migration is a catalyst for transforming the identities of migrants, at least some members of host societies, and, sometimes, of those who remain in the sending countries. Migration affects virtually all manners of borders—personal, local, societal, and even legal and territorial. It may also necessitate reconsideration of conventional notions of sovereignty. Migration tends to bound relationships, creating or reinforcing social, political, and economic systems that are either smaller or larger than the state. In such settings we can speak of the permeation of Westphalian borders and the erosion of classic formulations of sovereignty (see, e.g., B. Heisler 1986; Sassen 1996).

Migration produces ethnic or cultural minorities of varying sizes and kinds in states' populations. Because migrants may be protected by agreements between the sending and receiving states and by international laws and conventions, they can maintain their qualified apartness as minorities for long periods, perhaps indefinitely, even without citizenship (B. Heisler and M. Heisler 1986; cf. Rath 1991).[8] Thus, the social, and especially the political, borders of the majorities in host societies are likely to be drawn not at the territorial limits of the state but, rather, between the society and the other segments of the population. Formal citizenship status may be a partial demarcation line, but, as noted elsewhere in this and other essays in the present volume, the increasing availability of dual citizenship, including qualified or limited citizenship in the European Union (EU) (Wiener 1997), may serve to blur even that line.

There are migrants in the other major type of state as well, but they seldom benefit from international human rights or strong norms of tolerance for cultural differences in the host societies. Most of these are relatively new or newly autonomous states, such as former colonies, successor states to the Soviet Union, or states in Eastern and East-Central Europe that had long been under the sway of the Soviet Union. They zealously guard their claims to exclusive control over territory and population or, in Robert Jackson's terms, freedom from external intervention as a function of "negative sovereignty" (R. Jackson 1990). They are more resistant to suasion to internalize international human rights norms, even when such cajoling is accompanied by inducements from international institutions such as the EU (B. Heisler 1992). The principles of Westphalia, including the drive to delegitimize subsocietal identities and loyalties, seem more relevant for such states than ever before.

SENSIBILITY TO VARIATIONS ACROSS TIME AND PLACE

Reactions among large segments of the populations, political elites, and opinion makers in contemporary Western democracies to the entry and presence of large numbers of foreigners differ in important ways from reactions in the past. They also differ markedly from reactions to such occurrences in most other parts of the world today. We need to differentiate between conditions and values now and those prevalent before the middle of the twentieth century ("then"). We also need to distinguish contemporary Western democracies ("here") from most of the relatively new states that are intent on guarding their sovereignty and on nationalizing their populations ("there"). Currently mature democracies approach migration and the treatment of migrants (and minorities) very differently even as recently as two generations ago. The "here and now" differs markedly from what prevailed or was deemed appropriate in the past.

Current approaches to migration and migrants in many Eastern European, Asian, and African states ("there") resemble Western practices in the past ("here then"). Those approaches are associated with the establishment of new states or the radical alteration of old states. The exclusion of outsiders and transmutation of minorities to outsiders is a frequent concomitant of what Rogers Brubaker terms "nationalizing states" (1996). Imposing the values and norms of dominant cultural majorities and jealously guarding the prerogatives of sovereignty is often justified but, of course, not necessarily justifiable by the need to mitigate fissiparous tendencies in such settings.[9] Failure to meet those needs has led to continuing discrimination against minorities and resistance to the institutionalization of international human rights in many new or substantially recast states.

Another observation follows from a major paradox in the political philosophical underpinnings of Western democracies. Multiculturalism and the protection of human and/or minority rights are increasingly embedded in the institutional, legal, and policy fabrics of such states. Multiculturalism recognizes, and in varying ways and degrees legitimates, subsocietal group identities and ascriptive ties. These norms are also diffused through international institutions, particularly in Europe.[10] The EU is establishing common external borders and dismantling historic ones between member-states, while its regional programs and policies often have the effect of creating transstate regions and of reinforcing subsocietal regional borders.

But the principles of Western liberal democracy accord rights and obligations to individuals rather than to subsocietal collectivities. And for at least two hundred years, the compact between the state and individuals has focused on the former's responsibility to protect the latter—even from the subsocietal groups or social institutions to which they belong. It is not clear if, or how, Western democracies can circumvent that bargain as they try to accommodate resident foreigners without, at the same time, vitiating it vis-à-vis their citizens. Arguments for preserving the cultural integrity of immigrant or, for that matter, indigenous minorities confront these individual-focused tenets of liberal democracy.

This paradox often leads to equivocation and tension in foreign relations. The human rights–related exhortations Western democracies direct toward nondemocratic countries and regimes putatively in transition to democracy demand, simultaneously, the recognition of the status of collectivities (multiculturalism) and the observance of civil liberties (liberal democracy). It is not clear, however, if these two sets of goals can be realized at the same time. Historically, civil liberties and democratic political practice in Western states were built on the ruins of subsocietal, particularistic identities and loyalties.

These and related observations point to significant differences along synchronic and diachronic lines. If attitudes and policies toward migration and migrants vary across types or classes of societies and across time, such differences need to be understood in terms of variations in perceptions and contexts. In the sections that follow, I view the temporal dimension through a modernity/postmodernity optic and suggest some connections between migration on the one hand, and governance and international relations on the other.

MIGRATION, GOVERNANCE, AND INTERNATIONAL RELATIONS

Current forms and meanings of migration emerge from the intersections of modernity and postmodernity at the local, societal, and international levels. By modernity I have in mind the combination of specific characteristics of modern states, economies, and societies with the effects of the technological transformations of time and space that began more than one hundred years ago. The maturation of the Westphalian state set on course a series of life-altering institutional and normative changes, first in Europe, then elsewhere (Benko and Strohmayer 1997). This was perhaps most evident in England (not Great Britain or the United Kingdom as a whole), France, and some Central European countries in the mid–eighteenth century (Hall 1999; Corrigan and Sayer 1985; Tilly 1975, 1992, chaps. 4–6; cf. Ertman 1997). A major culture shift in the meanings of time and space occurred in much of the world in the decades following 1880 (Kern 1983). It was triggered by innovations in long-distance communication and travel. Time and space were compressed through progressively faster travel and eventually instantaneous electronic communication (Harvey 1989, 1996).

These developments made migration easier and a much less "lumpy decision." In earlier times, and in some settings even fairly recently, the decision to migrate—particularly across great distances, with or away from family—entailed huge risks (Hatton and Williamson 1998). Until these innovations in transportation and communication—and, equally important, the secularization of the state and depersonalization of the economy—were achieved, transnational migration was a life-altering decision. It was seen as leaving behind one way of life and building another, the details and risks of which were hardly knowable in advance. They were venturing into a more or less alien setting, with different customs, social and public institutions, and often language.

In the decades after World War I, developments in transportation and changes in the way migration came to be conceived made migration seem less of an irreversible act. For many, maintaining contact with their places of origin became relatively easy, and sometimes public and private organizations in the sending countries, ranging from political parties and local governments to churches and family associations, cultivated ties with émigrés (B. Heisler 1985). "Returning home" became a widely held aspiration.[11]

In the second half of the twentieth century, swift long-distance travel and communication were brought within the reach even of people whose economic means and educational resources were below the global medians. Travel, keeping in touch with the people in the places of origin, and the portability of cultural media became democratized in ways and degrees that would have astonished an observer two or three generations earlier. For many or most who moved from one country to another, these developments transformed the nature and meaning of migration. In many parts of the world—especially those that have served as the referents for the conceptual and theoretical work on migration of late—these developments have challenged the Westphalian state's sovereignty and the Westphalian international order of which it has long been a cornerstone.

The ability to change countries of residence with relative ease and the possibility of reversing the move can vitiate the need to make lasting identitive commitments.[12] Identities can thus be partial, intermittent, and reversible in the modern Western democratic state (M. Heisler 1990). Order no longer depends on unalloyed loyalty stemming from immutable national identity—identity for which there is no plausible or legitimate alternative. Countries' borders are not seen as coextensive with a comprehensive political community. In the language of international political economy some decades ago, the compromises in state sovereignty exacted by international interdependence may also lower the threshold for acceptable levels of "positive sovereignty," i.e., the ability to define and sustain internal order.

But most countries today are not at this postnational stage of social and political development. Like Western democracies in the (not-too-distant) past, their elites are committed to safeguard the prerogatives of sovereignty lest economically, culturally, or otherwise more powerful states and other actors interfere with their autonomy. And their ability to maintain order internally ("positive sovereignty" in Jackson's terms [1990]) depends in large measure on fostering and guarding the solidarity, identitive coherence, and loyalty of their populations.

Two configurations of identities/borders/orders, as seen through the optic of migration, are apparent: the "here and now" and the "there and then." In the former, migration tends to attenuate territorial sovereignty, monolithic order, and identitive solidarity. In the latter, "developmental angst" or uncertainty about the solidness of identities, order, and perhaps even borders points to the need to defend (negative) sovereignty. It also militates in favor of either the assimilation or exclusion of aliens (and cultural minorities) from the dominant population groups on which the regime's order rests.

Intersections of Migration and Identities, Borders, and Orders

The pattern of semisettlement by migrants, discussed above, was stimulated by technological innovations and lower costs for long-distance travel and communication, but particular changes in host societies were necessary to make it a stable, sustainable pattern. A new politics of identity has helped to condition the expectations of migrants, their families, and communities in their countries of origin, and important segments of the host societies (e.g., seasonal and informal labor market employers) in this regard. The new politics of identity or, in Charles Taylor's terms, "politics of recognition" (Gutmann 1994) dates from the mid-1970s (Elshtain 1995). It militates in favor of bounding populations that can be distinguished in cultural or ethnic or other ascriptive terms (e.g., gender).

It is in this intellectual, and subsequently political, context that attention came to be paid anew to *citizenship* as a bordering mechanism (M. Heisler and B. Heisler 1991). Postmodernity, multiculturalism, and demands for group-based recognition undermined the modern enterprise that was characterized by broadly encompassing secular and impersonal institutions and unity through abstract symbols. Citizenship became a common denominator. It could be used to bound the population for which authoritative decisions were made in politics, and, concomitantly, authority would flow from citizens.

But immigrants, especially semisettled migrants, may not be citizens. It is, therefore, plausible that the exclusion of migrants is as much or more a quality of postmodern political and social life as of timeless xenophobia or insecurities in the host society (M. Heisler and B. Heisler 1991). Thus, the presence of migrants—indeed, the processes and facts of migration—may have bounding and ordering functions for postmodern societies.

The proximity of the Other may be an indispensable element in the social (re)construction of citizenship in such emerging postmodern societies as those of North America and Western and Central Europe (cf. Patterson 1995). If identity is increasingly subsocietal in content, the formal marker of citizenship takes on greater importance for governance. It bounds the population for which the polity acts and from which it derives its authority. But, as already noted, at least or especially in these societies there are nontrivial external influences on the shape and content of domestic order, through internalized elements of international human rights, migration-related bilateral agreements, and international organizations. Consequently, while the reconstituted notions of citizenship may exclude (noncitizen) migrants, citizenship as a bordering device does not determine, by itself, domestic order.

This reflexive process embodies the triad of identity, borders, and orders at the core of this volume, at least for Western host societies. It operates in a parallel fashion in non-Western receiving countries, but there the construction is that of national identity; the borders of the sovereign state and the forms and contents of order are modern or premodern (or, at any rate, pre-postmodern). Pressure is applied to relate identity and citizenship in the fashion of what used to be discussed as nation building (M. Heisler 1990). Borders are Westphalian, as are the foundations for delineating and applying order. This is one of two significant sources of linkage between the domestic and international levels that emanate from transnational migration. The other is the development of such coherent identity without transgressing the normative parameters sketched by Western liberal democracies regarding human rights, compelling assimilation and denial of the cultural integrity of indigenous as well as migrant minorities.

Modernity is embodied in symbols, abstractions, and impersonal formal institutions. In Marshall Berman's title phrase, in modernity "all that is solid melts into air" (Berman 1982). Those abstractions are fleeting and presume the capacity of large numbers of people to understand them in at least superficially, if not essentially, similar ways. Viable institutions, whether social or formal, and effective governance require high levels of cognitive proximity in modern settings (Douglas 1986). Thus, cultural integration is required for the successful operation of the modern nation-state, especially if it is to have realistic aspirations to evolving a democratic regime.

The task confronting both receiving countries and many sending countries is to govern effectively with relatively low levels of cognitive proximity. In the past, countries that are now mature democracies approached the challenge of building cognitive proximity through homogenization, including loyalty tests, disregard for subsocietal identities and cultures, and, in not a few instances, practices we now term ethnic cleansing. But what was justifiable, indeed, "recommended" then is now deemed at least politically incorrect and increasingly subject to externally imposed sanctions by external state and intergovernmental actors—and the "international community."[13] In sum, what was acceptable "here" at an earlier developmental stage is no longer acceptable "there now."

The democratic West proscribes the use by less integrated, often new countries of means such as those it once used to achieve identitive coherence and order within its borders. This is not the place to speculate about the origins of the injunctions against ethnic cleansing, compulsory assimilation, and more drastic means of integration by the successors of those who climbed their high moral platforms on similar steps. It may suffice to venture that in countries in which votes count it may be popular to intimate that societies that have lived down often shameful pasts in the treatment of the less privileged have accumulated moral capital that can now be used to instruct those who may commit similar transgressions. There is profound silence regarding the means that may be permissible for the latecomers to achieve the levels of solidarity and identitive coherence needed for establishing and maintaining order. Current international relations discourses about conflicts between human rights and state sovereignty may stem, in some measure, from the West's self-exculpatory reconstructions of its own history.

Since migration both reflects and refracts the current waves of change in societies and in the international system, it could be expected to figure prominently in discussions of international relations theory. It does not. As has often been remarked, migration vitiates state boundaries and established (Westphalian) notions of sovereignty in a variety of ways. It is a catalyst for limiting the sovereignty of many receiving countries through the human rights discourse and practices to which it gives rise (see, e.g., M. Heisler 1986; Jacobson 1996; Sassen 1996). Some spokespersons for sending countries also claim that, in particular circumstances, having large numbers of nationals living and working abroad may impinge on the sovereignty of the countries of origin. Such claims suggest that migration may cut across the debate between state-centric and transnational—or realist and liberal—perspectives.

Normative Perspectives and the Nexus of Migration, Identities, Borders, and Orders

For more than forty years, the Cold War made for "abnormal" international relations (Jackson 1995). Restrictions on movement included barriers to exit as well as to enter. Freedom to move across state borders became an ideologically charged litmus test: "bad" countries locked their people in; "good" countries allowed, indeed, encouraged, free movement. During the Cold War most migration was driven by economic forces, dictated by labor needs in the wealthier countries and poverty and surplus populations in the poorer ones. But the international political economy of large-scale transnational migration was undergirded by Cold War ideological rhetoric.

The moral tone of Western demands to "let your people go" directed toward the Soviet Union, its allies, and other countries that denied or severely restricted their citizens' exit implied that migration is "natural" and perhaps even a right to be enjoyed by all (see, e.g., Barry and Goodin 1992). But just as the achievement of the right of exit seemed imminent, at the end of the 1980s, the countries that had championed it tightened their restrictions on entrance. The prospect of large-scale migration by formerly "captive peoples" coincided with very substantial increases in the flow of refugees from conflicts in imploding Yugoslavia, civil strife in several African and Asian countries, and the failure of a growing number of states to maintain even the rudiments of domestic order.

The international human rights versus state sovereignty argument correlates highly with other value differences within societies. Thus, the views and values of those who tend to support the incorporation of international human rights into domestic practice differ markedly on a number of issues from the values of those who expound the primacy of core cultural values (see, e.g., Hoskin 1991, especially chapter 6). The former tend also toward multiculturalist positions in social relations, while the latter defend what they see as integral national or "native" values (*Eurobarometer,* Nov. 1989). The international human rights versus sovereignty and the multicultural- ist versus culture defense stances reflect multidimensional, if not comprehensive, cleavages between cosmopolitan and parochial world- views. They affect not only attitudes toward migrants and migration or international relations but often also stances in domestic politics. Attitudes toward immigration are likely to be weakly, if at all, cor- related with such "objective" factors as the actual loss of jobs to mi- grants (Hoskin 1991; but cf. Schor 1985, part 4).

While these changes have contributed to the "debordering" of some states, they have not had similar consequences for others. In fact, in some states classic notions of sovereignty seem more rele- vant than ever before. The "shrinkage of the world" through inno- vations in transportation and communication, the advent of eco- nomic interdependence, and other forces of globalization have not affected all states in similar ways (cf. Albert and Brock 1996, espe- cially 71ff.). These differences are also evident in the ways the dy- namics of migration play out, in the meanings of migration, and in the fates or circumstances of migrants. In sum, the effects have not been monotonic for the system of states. Postmodernity may be erod- ing some states' claims to exclusive control of territory and jurisdic- tion within their borders but not the claims of others. Migration serves to bridge the two types of states.

MIGRATION AND THE CONSTRUCTION OF COLLECTIVE POLITICAL AND PSYCHOLOGICAL SPACES

Transnational migration today also confronts a mixture of modern and postmodern aspects of reality as regards space (cf. Benko and Strohmayer 1997). The Westphalian state and system of states marked an important watershed in the spatialization of politics. It made for substantial uniformity across states through normative and diplo- matic suasion. By the late nineteenth or early twentieth centuries, structural similarities developed in most parts of the world in re- sponse to external and internal challenges. The best way to survive in a world of powerful Westphalian states was to become more like a Westphalian state. Uniformity increased through diffusion aided by power. But, as already noted, the Westphalian state and system also made possible the rise of profound differences and asymmetries.

Before Westphalia, space was controlled by a multitude of authority claimants. In fact, a common and important feature of the pre-Westphalian arrangements of space was the coexistence of multiple and overlapping claims to jurisdiction—functionally, structurally, and temporally competing claims to authority, based on different principles. These included feudal nobility and landed aristocracy; the (Roman Catholic) church, at least in Europe and its colonial territories; and even brigands and pirates in some "no-go" areas.[14] Ordinary people had little or no control over space. Social and economic relationships spilled over boundaries created by formal authorities, but they could not supplant them (Wroe 1995). While those boundaries sometimes fostered the development of loyalties and identitive attachments, it was the subsequent Westphalian order that made possible the integration, homogenization, and, in some sense, rationalization of the relationship between space and identity through the melding of authority claims and territory (cf. Walker 1993, 116–17). It did not transmit control over space to ordinary folk, but, through the extension and diversification of property rights, it opened the door to private and social control and the imposition of order designed to serve the interests of those with such control.

Multiple, often shifting claims to authority over territory in the pre-Westphalian world precluded a fusion of identity and space on any but the smallest scale or in a lasting and legitimate way (cf. Wroe 1995). Between the beginning of the Westphalian era, in the mid–sixteenth century, with the Treaty of Augsburg (Krasner 1993), and the mid–eighteenth century—by which time the ancien régimes were consolidated in most of Europe—such linkages became normal, perhaps even essential. The Westphalian nexus of space and identity was predicated on the formal authority of central government, or, more precisely, it was driven by claims asserted by the government. But loyalty to and identification with those small places/units persisted long after the establishment of absolutist Westphalian states. Identification with and cardinal loyalty to such authority was not to become grounded in social consciousness and institutions until much later, when national societies and states coincided in appreciable degree. That, of course, did not happen in most of the world.

The advent of constitutional governments and democratic regimes in some places further fostered that relationship. Such developments did not vitiate the central authorities' claims to jurisdiction over the entire territory of the state, but they did loosen their hold on the identity structure they and their feudal and ecclesiastic predecessors had monopolized. One of the hallmarks of mature democracy in the last decades of the twentieth century is the ability, and presumed right, of people to mediate important elements of the space-identity nexus through various sorts of social institutions. Thus, the identities of residents of the social institution that is a neighborhood or of the somewhat formalized social institution that is the condominium or cooperative apartment house influence and are influenced by the spaces that are their containers. Those inside tend to exercise considerable influence over entry and have myriad ways to restrict or deny entry to newcomers. This is true even where formal laws and rules seek to regulate entry, and even where the social institution associated with the space is poorly or not at all organized.

A second, less commonly considered set of effects on time and space derives from the central (state and societal) versus local distinctions that indwell the issue-area of migration. The state is expected to manage migration-related policies centrally, but the most important impacts of migration are local. Immigrants reside and work in towns and cities, not in a country as a whole. They live, shop, and send their children to school in neighborhoods, not in integral societies. To the extent they serve as markers of change, they do so at the local level. It is there that they are perceived as threats to employment or familiar ways of life or, alternately, as valued workers and the sources of welcome cultural enrichment of the local community.

Neighborhoods, schools, factories, shops, buses, sidewalks, parks, and other public spaces have attributes as social institutions, not only as formal state or economic entities. The people who live and work there—more precisely, the people who lived there when newcomers arrived—have history with each other. They may have formed various kinds and degrees of solidarity; invariably, the patterns of their relationships have produced structures of accommodation. Local cultures have greater concreteness than the broad lines of language, religion, shared myths, and other components of societal or national identity. The small gestures, tones, body language, and recollected common experiences—a flood six years ago, the championship the local team almost won, the deference to be accorded to the veterans of the last war—embodied by and embedded in social institutions often matter more than the wider but more distant abstractions of societal culture or state institutions and laws (cf. Harvey 1996).

Local social spaces are constructed over time. In the past, newcomers were expected to adjust gradually. Immigrants, the first generation, were also often expected to accept less than full social rights and inferior status. Over time, they, but more likely only their children and grandchildren, the second and third generations, were expected to assimilate. That is, they were expected to integrate into and internalize the norms and values of the dominant cultural core of the society in which they settled. In postmodern settings, the rise of subsocietal multiculturalism has made that problematic, and, in a number of Western democracies, such policies as bilingual education and the subsidization of migrant cultural activity makes it even more difficult (cf. Rath 1991).

Finally, the increasing significance of transnational communities contributes a further instance of the inside/outside Möbius strip quality of migration. Viewed as social institutions, transnational communities perform preserving, ontogenetic, and transforming functions for identities and for orders. They help to preserve local identity and, of course, ties to the place of origin, in local rather than general or societal terms. They are ontogenetic in that they create new communities of migrants in which the "from/in/back" dynamics and raisons d'être of the transnational enterprise differentiate their members from both the surrounding host populations and those who stay at home. At the same time, they provide a distinctive basis for integration for the members. Their enterprise is not about staying in the place of origin, nor is it about settling and integrating into the host society. Their lives differ principally in that they are about living in two places (Massey et al. 1987; Pries 1999).

CONCLUSIONS

Migration has reinforced or accelerated the construction of communitarian spaces. Immigrant enclaves have always constituted such spaces, but individuals or small groups could step out of the enclaves and into the larger society. This was the promise of modernization (Walzer 1997). Now the larger society in the West is increasingly attenuated, and its most apparent and enduring aspects are formal institutions, in both the state and the economy. It is there that migrants and their hosts meet.

That terrain is a vast and often only partially visible mesh of socially mediated spaces. When migrants cross borders, they enter not only the territory of a (more or less) sovereign state, with predominant legal powers within its boundaries, but also that maze of social relationships and institutions. Skill, luck, and often support from other migrants are needed to negotiate those relationships and informal institutions successfully. But regardless of their effectiveness in managing those tasks, migrants must also cope with the formal institutions. It is at the intersection of the formal and social institutions that most of the action takes place, and that nexus remains largely opaque.

The expectations of people in host societies are largely reflections of the content and texture of their constructions of the past and the present. These are emphatically not monolithic or homogeneous—or, in some cases, even compatible. The variegated experiences and expectations of those populations need to be studied for an understanding of the kinds and distributions of those dispositions toward immigration and immigrants. The attitudes involved are dynamic, and it is not only customary economic or migratory or cultural variables that need to be taken into account in studying them but the politics of migration as well.

We also need to gain better understanding of a wider range of transnational communities. In most instances their functioning is refracted through the state system (Pries 1999; Faist 1997; Kearney 1995). They consist largely of informal or social institutions, and these need to be studied on their own terms. One arena in which work on the transnational dimensions of migration has begun to integrate the social and formal (state and international) dimensions is that of human rights, in legal terms and, more broadly, in discourses in the language of rights (Jacobson 1996; Juss 1998/99).

Much complexity and confusion stem from attempts to treat the ramifications of migration in positivistic terms. Post-positivist analyses are necessary (Lapid 1989; and Lapid in this volume), but these will not suffice alone, either. While norms are clearly important, they need to be considered as both the foundations and products of constructions. In the present usage, norms are at once key elements of a cognitive and constructivist perspective, but they are also data. As it goes with the politics of ethnic relations, so too with migration; things are much more what they are made out to be than how "objective reality" would have them.

NOTES

I am grateful for constructive suggestions made by Friedrich Kratochwil and the editors of this volume on earlier drafts. Were I wiser, perhaps I would have followed all rather than merely most of those suggestions.

1. For a stimulating discussion of this theme, with applications closer to my concerns here, see Kearney (1995) and several of the chapters in Cox (1997).

2. Since the early 1980s, James Rosenau has referred to the simultaneous manifestation and interplay of globalization and localization as "fragmegration" (see Rosenau 1983, 1997).

3. See the discussions of multiculturalism and the politics of recognition by Charles Taylor and others in Gutmann (1994), as well as Glazer (1997) and Elshtain (1995).

4. This is often the case with regard to statistical relationships between "immigrants" and crime, for instance. See Tonry (1997).

5. In the mid-1950s, David Easton defined politics as "authoritative allocation of values [and, presumably, valued things] *for a society*" (Easton 1971, 129–41; emphasis added). While several aspects of this formulation gave rise to lively discussions in the literature of political science in the ensuing years, the phrase "for a society" was ignored or assumed to be commonly understood and subject to being treated as an uninvestigated constant.

6. Societal security can be conceptualized in several ways. Here I intend both the defensive cultural posture discussed in Wæver et al. (1993) and the organic and functional cultural conservatism reflected in the contents and title phrase of Robert Nisbet's *The Quest for Community* (1953).

7. These two categories are neither exhaustive of all contemporary states nor, strictly speaking, mutually exclusive. Some states do not closely resemble either type, and some exhibit a mixture of traits. From a heuristic standpoint, however, these are the two preeminent and politically, as well as analytically and theoretically, most interesting types.

8. The proportion of such extrasocietal populations ranges from nearly one-third in such countries as Luxembourg to approximately 5 percent in larger Western host societies. As I note below, the criteria for determining

who is a member of the core society and who is not are complex, controverted, and in flux (see Dauenhauer 1996; Wiener 1997).

9. The international system militated in favor of maintaining the zones of colonial administration transmuted into state boundaries, regardless of the social, political, or economic diversity they encompassed. That external juridical buttress of statehood therefore tacitly justified "nation-building" practices no longer deemed acceptable or politically correct in Western states—including the former European colonial powers (see Jackson and Rosberg 1982).

10. Europe here should be viewed as an expanding arena for fostering democracy, human rights, free movement, and establishment of persons and transnationally delineated migration regimes (see M. Heisler and Van-Deveer 1997).

11. There is an assumption in the literature on migration that the "myth of return" harbored by many migrants was no more than a myth for most. Large enough numbers do return to the countries of origin, however, to sustain and even reinforce the myth. See Miller (1986, 72f.); B. S. Heisler (1986, especially note 11).

12. This is not to say that many migrants today do not make such commitments to either their new country of residence or that of their origin.

13. This is vividly illustrated by NATO's intervention in Kosovo in 1999.

14. No-go areas are places within the borders of states where states do not make serious, practical efforts to enforce law and order. An example of a no-go area is a "bad part of town," where even police do not go. My notion of no-go areas comes from Dahrendorf (1985).

11

The Political Nature of Identities, Borders, and Orders: Discourse and Strategy in the Zapatista Rebellion

NEIL HARVEY

> The men and women of the EZLN, the faceless ones, the ones who walk in the night and who belong to the mountains, have sought words that other men and women could understand. And so they say: First. We demand that there be free and democratic elections.... (Comité Clandestino Revolucionario Indígena-Comandancia General [CCRI-CG], Ejército Zapatista de Liberación Nacional [EZLN], Chiapas, February 1994)

> [We call for the formation of] a political force that does not aim to take power, a force that is not a political party.... A political force that can organize the demands and proposals of the citizens so that those who govern, govern by obeying. (EZLN, 4th. Declaration of the Lacandon Forest, Chiapas, January 1996)

The armed uprising on January 1, 1994, by over three thousand Mayan Indians in the southern Mexican state of Chiapas took most observers by surprise. The Zapatista Army of National Liberation (EZLN) briefly occupied six towns in the central highlands of the state before retreating to bases in the Lacandon forest in the face of the federal army's military offensive. The Zapatistas, who take their name from the peasant revolutionary Emiliano Zapata (1879–1919), issued a broad list of demands for "jobs, land, food, housing, health care, education, independence, liberty, democracy, justice, and peace." Despite the Mexican government's attempt to crush the rebellion through military force, the EZLN succeeded in gaining widespread support from sectors within Mexican and international civil society, obliging the government to call off its military offensive and accept the need for negotiations. However, peace talks failed to produce any solutions, leading to a worsening of local conditions and an escalation of violent attacks against Zapatista supporters by government-backed paramilitary groups. At stake in Chiapas is the transformation of political relations between the Mexican state and indigenous peoples, a process that can be understood in terms of the struggle for effective citizenship.

Although the rebellion has many implications for Mexico, it also raises more general questions regarding our understanding of citizenship and the state. The value of the identities, borders, and orders (IBO) triad is that it allows us to conceptualize citizenship and the state in new ways. This period of uncertainty and flux demands concepts that are open to multiple combinations rather than closed by any overriding imperative of a single identity, single border, or single order. This reconceptualization should therefore be open to perspectives that have traditionally been seen as marginal to the experience of modernity, such as indigenous peoples, women, migrants, refugees, and the underclass. As Franke Wilmer has argued, we need to pay attention to "marginal sites" of world politics, rather than continue to privilege the military or economic power of the "center" (1996). It is from such sites that we can gain new perspectives on the creation of identities, borders, and orders in an increasingly decentered world.

Although identities, borders, and orders constitute "ever-interesting and indispensable" key concepts, we still need to show how they can be used in a methodology that would support comparative, multiarea, and multidisciplinary research. If the fluidity of identities, borders, and orders is a marker of our current global reality, then the political assumes a renewed urgency, since there are fewer and fewer "givens" and more and more "negotiables." This state of affairs can lead to permanent conflict or to the recognition of limits, potentially opening the way to greater pluralism and democratic negotiation among multiple actors.

The chapter is divided into five parts. The first explains how the conceptualization of IBO can be furthered by poststructuralist discourse analysis and the affirmation of the "primacy of the political." In terms of bordering, this approach requires attention to discursive strategies of inclusion and exclusion. The second part discusses the ways in which regional conditions in Chiapas limited the impact of the national government's inclusionary populist discourse in the decades following the 1910–1917 Revolution. These limitations were compounded in the 1980s by a series of dislocations that undermined the coherence of a new productivist discourse geared toward integrating indigenous farmers into commodity markets. How these dislocations were interpreted by the EZLN is the subject of the third part, noting the hybridization of mestizo and indigenous identities in the new Zapatista discourse. The fourth section discusses the evolution of the strategies, tactics, and alliances of the EZLN and the Mexican government between 1994 and 1999. It shows how the Zapatistas' initial successes were the result of the strategic articulation of a broad range of popular demands in a democratic network for which citizenship was the articulating principle. It continues with an analysis of the government's attempt to gradually dismantle this network and force the EZLN back into a defensive position. This section also discusses how the EZLN has sought to regain the political initiative by renewing its connections with new civic and social movements in Mexican civil society. The conclusions discuss the historical distinctiveness of the Zapatista rebellion and highlight the value of a poststructuralist discourse analysis for developing new comparative studies on the political nature of identities, borders, and orders.

IBO AND THE PRIMACY OF THE POLITICAL

Until now, the utility of IBO has been explored within the context of distinct disciplinary or subdisciplinary debates. The field of international relations is clearly the most active in this regard, but, as demonstrated by this book, IBO is finding an echo in political geography, sociology, comparative politics, and anthropology. However, if it is agreed that IBO does not "belong" to any one discipline, this is because its roots are deeper than any one of our respective fields. The fact that various disciplines are simultaneously searching for new conceptual tools is not so surprising given the dramatic changes in social theory and global politics in recent years. What is remarkable is that a productive intersection has been created through the IBO framework. However, we still need to answer why IBO is so appealing to such a variety of scholars. My answer to this question is that the goal of IBO is not to name, in empiricist fashion, already constituted identities, borders, and orders. It is not simply a way of describing what exists, but rather a means of interrogating the processes of identification, bordering, and ordering.

One of the main claims of poststructuralism is that there is no immediately available area of certainty, that nothing exists independently of discourse and signification. For example, a rock at the bottom of a mine exists, but it only has meaning when it is placed within discourse. The discourses of geology or economics "create" the rock through classification (as granite or bauxite) or valorization (as commodities that enter a system of production and exchange) (Laclau and Mouffe 1987, 82). The same could be said of a political border separating two nation-states. The boundary line has no meaning on its own. It only "exists" within an infinite number of discourses or "language games" (on security, trade, immigration, drugs, the environment, etc.). What this initial step does is to remove the traditional faith of Western philosophy in some preexisting presence that can be represented in a pure, ideal, or unmediated fashion. For Derrida it was precisely this "metaphysics of presence" (or "essence") that had to be challenged. In doing so, he criticized any method in which "everything not intelligible in the light of a 'preestablished' teleological framework...is reducible to the inconsequentiality of accident and dross" (Derrida 1978a, 25).

A second, related effect of poststructuralism is that it questions the notion that societies or structures have "centers" that somehow transcend the particular elements that they are believed to coordinate. Derrida noted how any center or logos is constituted through acts of exclusion, rather than existing in an a priori privileged position (Derrida 1978b). His point was not to deny the historical existence of various centers, but to show how such a center is constituted on the terrain of contingency, rather than the terrain of necessity (Smith 1994, 173).

This movement away from essence and center leads to the recognition of the discursively constructed nature of identities, borders, and orders. Discourse is no longer seen as a set of ideas that attempt to reflect reality, since there is no independent reality "out there" against which discourse can be measured. Our attention is instead directed toward the political processes through which discourses are able to provide a sense of meaning to the social field. This is particularly evident at times of crisis and severe dislocation. Since dislocations lack any inherent principle of explanation (given that there is no pure essence), their interpretation is of vital political importance. Whereas traditional approaches seek to explain dislocation in terms of some ultimate rationality or logic, poststructuralism asserts the decentered nature of competing representations of dislocation.

It should be stressed that rationalism is not replaced by pure contingency, since this would only invert the structure-agency opposition while leaving its essential premise intact. The method of deconstruction instead dissolves the opposition itself and forces us to think of agency as already structured, but not in any ultimately decidable way. Moreover, if this undecidability blocks the achievement of full self-consciousness, it is also what opens up the field of social interaction to multiple forms of identification (Laclau 1996). Identity exists as an incomplete process of identification rather than as a culturally given trait or structurally determined consciousness. The place of identities in IBO should therefore be conceptualized in terms of decisions taken on an undecidable terrain.

Now, if the metaphysics of presence is undermined by the undecidability of the social, and if meaning is contingent on competing discourses, we must replace the search for origins or truth with a genealogy of political interventions that attempt to create new discourses that "sediment" identities, borders, and orders. For the student of politics, what is important here is the interrogation of these interventions, to reveal their contingency rather than their necessity, their political nature rather than their structural determination. Any political act is also therefore an act of bordering, since a decision to do one thing must mean that alternatives are excluded. In this way, by naturalizing the decisions of inclusion and exclusion, the creation of political frontiers conceals the fault lines of social order.

Order can therefore be seen as the result of the always partial configuration of power relations through acts of bordering. Order is already contaminated by disorder and ambiguity. The function of borders is to reduce or eliminate this ambiguity, expelling it to the margins or periphery of a coherent system. Order requires that societies forget that their political institution originated in acts of bordering, that is, acts of power. This "sedimentation" of borders is a precondition for the stability of any order. However, the fact that borders must conceal the traces of their ignoble beginnings also means that they remain permanently threatened by that which has been excluded. This is what Derrida called the "constitutive outside" of any identity or order.

If all identities, borders, and orders are always incomplete, they remain open to new possibilities. In this account, the political retains a constitutive rather than merely reflective role. This is evidenced by the fact that the maintenance of hegemony cannot rely on a simple reproduction of the original act of political bordering. As societies change, new points of antagonism emerge, requiring the construction of newer and newer political frontiers, a process that can have no final point of rest (a fully unified order in which the political would disappear), nor that can guarantee the reproduction of the same lines of social division. As a result, the "rationality" of individuals, cultures, or structures dissolves in the face of an always already decentered field of undecidability, upon which social agents, nevertheless, decide. This is in fact a condition of our freedom, for if there were no "undecidables," we would be restricted to giving programmed responses to pregiven conditions. Seen in this light, political analysis finds itself privileging antagonism, rather than the essence of already constituted actors, identities, and institutions. The negativity of the social displaces the positivity of the structure, necessitating a far more meticulous methodology that emphasizes the strategic deployment of political frontiers in a continuous "war of position" (Laclau 1990; Laclau and Mouffe 1985).

THE LIMITS OF POPULISM AND PRODUCTIVISM IN CHIAPAS

In the decades following the 1910–1917 revolution, Mexican governments had varying degrees of success in establishing a new populist discourse of national integration. Regional factors played a significant role in that the centralization of political authority was contingent on the support of local elites. This was particularly evident in Chiapas, where counterrevolutionary landowners successfully mobilized to keep autonomous control of native society during the armed phase of the Mexican Revolution. Their order was based on the racist exclusion of the state's large indigenous Maya population. Indians had challenged this order on several occasions, including armed rebellions in 1712, 1867, and 1911. However, the various factions of the landed elite repeatedly put down the rebels with force and reestablished strong ethnic borders that allowed for the continued exploitation of Indian land, labor, and production. In this context, Indians were unable to establish any significant alliances with outside actors. In those cases where alliances were constructed, the consequences were usually negative as local elites reacted quickly and violently to punish such transgressions. Consequently, Indian rebellions tended to suffer from political isolation, military weakness, and the absence of effective allies.[1]

Postrevolutionary state governments in Chiapas were therefore able to maintain a measure of autonomy from a new central government that was happy to settle for accommodation in exchange for loyalty. By the 1940s, loyalty meant votes for the ruling Institutional Revolutionary Party (PRI) and the president of the Republic. Traditional forms of patron-client relations were gradually institutionalized, bringing local communities under the centralized authority of new agencies designed to provide land, jobs, and resources, thereby assimilating Indians into the nation. Ironically, it was the local elites who presented the greatest resistance to these policies, not out of respect for indigenous cultures, but out of fear that they would lose their privileged access to Indian land and labor. As a result, the local branches of government agencies were controlled by local bosses who effectively limited the impact of one of the key elements of populist discourse, land reform.

Despite some redistribution of generally unproductive plots in the 1930s, land reform in Chiapas tended to avoid affecting private landowners. Instead, the federal and state governments encouraged Indians to migrate to unused lands in the Lacandon rainforest in the eastern portion of the state. During the 1960s and 1970s, over ten thousand migrant colonists built new communities along the valleys, or *Cañadas*, of the forest. However, they were often threatened with eviction because of competing claims from loggers, ranchers, and other colonists. Many of the villagers formed local organizations to petition for land titles, but were usually met with bureaucratic delays, corruption, or repression. Indians were often violently evicted from their land, arrested, and tortured. During the 1980s and early

1990s, human rights abuses increased as state governors sought to repress a proliferation of popular movements in Chiapas. Electoral fraud and corruption of municipal authorities created further resentment. This resentment would eventually find expression in the 1994 rebellion.

In the Lacandon forest, most of the indigenous communities became politically organized in the 1970s through the efforts of the Catholic Diocese of San Cristóbal de Las Casas. As such they gained experience in dealing with government agencies and local officials. During the 1980s they also sought to improve economic conditions by joining together in the Rural Collective Interest Association (ARIC)—"Unión de Uniones." The ARIC was created in response to the shifting nature of rural development policies in which a new discourse of productivism attempted to integrate small farmers into national and global commodity markets. However, the crisis of this strategy in Chiapas would lead over half the ARIC membership to join the EZLN in the early 1990s.

The decision to take up arms came in response to three main dislocations. First, the promise of gaining access to land was one of the means by which indigenous peasants continued to work within the legal channels of agrarian reform. However, during the 1980s the state and federal government accelerated a shift in policy away from land redistribution and toward greater productivity. In Chiapas state governors moved to protect large landowners from expropriation by using force in the eviction of peasants who were classified as "land invaders." At the same time, large ranchers were protected by new documents that put their holdings beyond the legal reach of agrarian reform.

Second, the promise of integration into new markets (a central goal of the new productivist discourse) tended to have a short and precarious life. During the early 1980s the federal government encouraged small farmers to plant coffee and even helped some cooperatives build their own processing and marketing capacity. In the Lacandon forest, the largest and most successful of these cooperatives formed the ARIC. By 1988 over 12,000 households were members of ARIC, many of whom pinned their expectations on the continuing profitability of the coffee market. In June 1989 their hopes were dashed when the world price fell by over 50 percent. Thousands of small growers went out of business as they were unable to cover production costs or to retain their access to credit. This crisis was exacerbated by the simultaneous withdrawal of the state from the provision of subsidies, crop insurance, credit, and technical assistance. Finally, the new productivist policies had encouraged the formation of grassroots organizations. This was a way of co-opting elements of the indigenous communities into a new alliance with government agencies and coffee traders. It also was meant to isolate those organizations that continued to demand the redistribution of private landholdings. However, these alliances were not enough to protect the new organizations from the repressive actions of municipal and state authorities. The discourse of associational autonomy had insufficient support from the federal government, and by the end of the 1980s, repression had become so commonplace that the Catholic diocese of San Cristóbal de Las Casas was prompted into establishing a center for the protection of human rights.

The end of land reform, the failure of the productivist alternative and the absence of guarantees for associational autonomy led to the radicalization of young indigenous peasants and their eventual support for the armed uprising. This process was also accelerated by the federal government's decision in 1992 to amend Article 27 of the Mexican Constitution, effectively bringing land reform to an official close. These reforms were designed to give greater protection to private landowners by removing the threat of redistribution. They also provided for the legal purchase and sale of communal lands, raising the fear of a massive reconcentration of private landholdings. In Chiapas the implications of these reforms were perceived as particularly threatening, given that, at the time of their announcement, there was still a backlog of over three thousand unresolved land petitions.

THE EMERGENCE OF ZAPATISTA DISCOURSE

Although these various dislocations undermined the coherence of the government's populist and, later, productivist discourses, their eventual appropriation by the EZLN was a contingent rather than pregiven outcome. Our attention should therefore focus on discourse and strategy in explaining indigenous support for the EZLN.[2] Marcos recounts that the EZLN was born on November 17, 1983, out of the meeting of three indigenous people and three mestizos, including himself (EZLN 1995, 131). The previous year had seen the violent evictions of peasants from three communities in the Lacandon forest. The impunity with which these actions occurred, and their increasing frequency during the administration of governor Absalón Castellanos Domínguez (1982–1988), did not go uncontested. The EZLN had to respond to the need for self-defense in the face of unrelenting repression. In fact, this appears to have been the initial rationale for the formation of the EZLN. In Chiapas, at least, it was born not as a guerrilla movement with a clear revolutionary strategy for taking power, but as a regional network of armed self-defense units (García de León 1994, 26–28). In interviews, Marcos recounted how the EZLN was born:[3]

> I went to teach what the people wanted: literacy and Mexican history. In 1984, I joined the first group of indigenous *guerrilleros* in the mountains. They had a lot of political experience already, having participated in mass movements and they knew all about the problems of the left political parties. They had also been in prison, suffered torture, all of that. But they also demanded what they called *la palabra política* (the "political word"): history. The history of this country and of the struggle. So that was the task I arrived with.

Marcos won people's trust by integrating fully into the armed group that lived in the forest's harsh mountainous terrain, *la montaña*. He participated with this first group in making the area habitable. It was here that the ideological discourse of Marxism ran up against the distinctive cultural beliefs of the indigenous communities. To live in *la montaña* was to inhabit a respected and feared place of stories, myths, and ghosts. Marcos began to appreciate how indigenous notions of time and history were radically different from those of Westernized mestizos: "You didn't know what period they were telling you about, they could be recounting a story which might have occurred a week ago just as easily as five hundred years ago or at the time when the world began."

The source of historical knowledge was the culture itself, not the scientific reasoning and laws of causality that are familiar tools of Western philosophy. This history was passed on by the elders, not in written form, but in the manner of stories. Communities chose certain members who would be responsible for memorizing their history. They would become important figures since they represented a kind of "talking book." Marcos noted that they told history very precisely, describing the conditions during the nineteenth century or before the Spaniards arrived as accurately as any modern textbook. In adjusting to this culture, Marcos discovered the need to listen. He commented that the Latin American Left knew how to talk, but not always how to listen. Learning the indigenous languages and understanding their own interpretations of their history and culture led to an appreciation of the political importance of patience. Learning how to wait was, for Marcos, the most difficult exercise, but one that was now imposed by the indigenous leaders and their method of organization.

By 1986 the group had twelve members, eleven indigenous and Marcos, who was later joined by two more mestizos. Support began to spread as the word was passed on through kinship lines that stretched throughout the *Cañadas*. Activities such as the provision of food and the gathering of weapons were carried out at night, which caused some suspicion that people were engaged in witchcraft. The Zapatistas had to become more open, at least within the *ejidos,* in order to avoid such accusations. By the end of 1986, however, support had grown to an extent whereby the armed group could freely enter their first village, at the invitation of one of the indigenous founders of the EZLN, *el viejo Antonio.* In explaining the popular support for the Zapatistas at this stage, it is important to emphasize the cultural basis of their struggle. Instead of arriving directly from the city or the university, the EZLN emerged out of *la montaña,* that magical world inhabited by the whole of Mayan history, by the spirits of ancestors, and by Zapata himself.

One of the distinctive features of the Zapatista rebellion was that the above-mentioned dislocations were interpreted through a hybrid of indigenous and mestizo discourses. The Marxist political discourse within which Marcos had been formed was not readily understandable. "Your word is very hard, we don't understand it," he was told. The political message required a new language and it was found in the convergence of a Marxist critique of Mexican history and the indigenous people's own stories of humiliation, exploitation, and racism. Crucially, this convergence allowed the latter to gain political direction over the movement. Marcos recognized that a process of "cultural contamination" of Marxist ideas was occurring. "It obliged us (the mestizos) to adapt our politics and way of viewing our own historical process as well as the national political process."

This point is important in establishing not only the novelty of the EZLN in the history of the Mexican Left, but also in challenging our understanding of the history of political ideas. Rather than assume a single point of origin that can be uncovered by good detective work (the methodology that, in 1995, allowed police investigators to reveal the mestizo and Marxist identity of Marcos), the EZLN invites a more complex, culturally sensitive genealogy. In fact, the political origins of Marcos lose their significance as they give way to the histories and spirits of the Lacandon forest. Marcos recognized this fact very clearly:

> We had a very fixed notion of reality, but when we ran up against it, our ideas were turned over. It is like that wheel over there, which rolls over the ground and becomes smoother as it goes, as it comes into contact with the people in the villages. It no longer has any connection to its origins. So, when they ask me: "What are you people? Marxists, Leninists, Castroites, Maoists, or what?" I answer that I don't know. I really do not know. We are the product of a hybrid, of a confrontation, of a collision in which, luckily I believe, we lost.

This "defeat" proved to be decisive and the EZLN grew rapidly as a result. Fathers recruited sons, sons recruited brothers, cousins, and uncles. During the year 1988–89, the number of armed combatants grew from 80 to 1,300. Many *ejidos* that had participated in the ARIC saw their members join the Zapatistas, who began to organize their own committees of clandestine government and purchase guns. Money that had previously been used for religious fiestas was redirected to purchasing arms on the black market. There was no massive or sudden sale of arms to the EZLN. Instead, they gradually and clandestinely built up their own collection of weapons and munitions. By 1992 support for the Zapatistas had spread throughout the *Cañadas* of Ocosingo, Altamirano, and Las Margaritas. The armed group was subordinated to the political leadership of the clandestine committees and entrusted with organizing armed self-defense units. Political decisions remained under the control of the indigenous communities. The EZLN was their secret, the secret that would reveal its new word on January 1, 1994.

DEMOCRATIC IDENTITY AND POLITICAL BORDERING

Historically, the suppression of Indian rebellions in Chiapas has been followed by the renewal of exclusionary borders that attempted to fix identities in mutually exclusive categories. These categories would become articulated in modern political discourse as "elite" versus "popular" subject positions. However, the eventual stabilization of ethnic and class relations required the partial incorporation of the excluded Other ("the popular") in an inclusionary discourse that, in time, undermined the political efficacy of earlier forms of exclusion, leading once more to the reimposition of strong borders and the expulsion of political demands to the margins of social order (see Table 1). What was different about 1994 is that political demands could no longer be expelled so easily, especially given their articulation in terms of citizenship and justice, since these are sufficiently broad to include the entire national population. However, if political demands are limited to particular goals, they can be quickly forced back into a defensive position. This is the strategic dilemma that has confronted the Zapatistas since the January 1994 uprising.

For the first eight months of 1994 the EZLN held the political initiative, not by asserting the goal of indigenous autonomy, but by calling on all sectors of Mexican society to demand democratic elections, an end to corruption, accountable government, and new economic and social policies to meet the needs of all citizens. In these months, many groups joined in this new movement for democratic change, one that was not reducible to the program of any political party. Students and civic and church groups mobilized support in the cities and hauled caravans of aid to Zapatista communities in the heart of the Lacandon forest. When negotiations with the government began in February, the EZLN representatives were protected by "peace cordons" comprised of indigenous and nonindigenous citizens, members of local and national nongovernmental organizations, human rights groups, and women's movements. Buoyed by the outpouring of popular support, the Zapatistas decided to reject as insufficient the package of reforms that government negotiators had offered in the February talks. Then, prior to the national elections in August, the EZLN organized a three-day-long National Democratic Convention (CND), inviting all citizens who wanted to participate in a national movement for democracy and justice in Mexico. The Zapatistas considered these goals to be far more inclusive than

Table 1. Cycles of power and resistance in Chiapas

	Years and Stages of Each Cycle			
	Polarization	Stabilization	Destabilization	Rupture
Cycle 1	1523	1570	1700	1712
Cycle 2	1713	1720	1861	1867
Cycle 3	1870	1880	1900	1911
Cycle 4	1915	1920	1989	1994–99
Cycle 5	1994–99			
	Characteristics of Each Stage			
	Polarization	Stabilization	Destabilization	Rupture
Decisions	Violence from above	Eventual renegotiation of rule	Attempts to shore up or renew unstable political frontiers	Rebellion from below
Strategies	Assertion of a strategy of exclusion	Partial absorption of the Other through a strategy of inclusion	Instability of contradictory strategies of inclusion and exclusion	Tension between assertion of difference and search for alliances
Identities	Denial or demonization of the Other	Less rigid identities, but constant surveillance and enforced separation	Reemergence of rigid identities	Invoking cultural, religious, and political practices of autonomy
Borders	Imposition of borders in an attempt to assert complete control	Recognized borders, but insecure	Pressures that undermine coherence of political borders	Attempt from below to set new borders by asserting autonomy
Orders	Collapse of old order/ imposition of new order	Relative order through hegemony	Dislocations that reveal the political contingency of unstable orders	Revealing need for reordering social, political, and economic relationships

the agendas of any political party and stressed the role of ordinary citizens without partisan affiliation.

The August 1994 elections marked a turning point for the Zapatistas. The presidential elections were seen by most observers as the cleanest in recent Mexican history. Charges of fraud existed but the PRI candidate, Ernesto Zedillo, was able to claim victory over his two main rivals who, significantly, accepted the result. The PRD's Cárdenas made a very poor showing, losing many of the votes that he had won in the 1988 election. In Chiapas, where fraud was much more prevalent, voters also elected a new state governor. The PRI candidate, Eduardo Robledo, claimed victory, despite the strong support for Amado Avendaño, who led a civil pro-Zapatista movement and ran with a PRD ticket. The EZLN, which had naturally hoped for a different outcome in both elections, suddenly saw the political initiative slip away from its control. It threw its weight behind Avendaño and his struggle to claim the governorship. Zedillo, on the other hand, threw his weight behind Robledo and, despite threats from the EZLN of a renewal of hostilities if Robledo were imposed, the president went ahead and inaugurated the new PRI governor on the scheduled date in early December. The Zapatistas responded by briefly occupying the town halls of 38 (of a total of 110) municipalities, revealing that the extent of Zapatista support spread far further than the Lacandon forest. At this time Zedillo, with less than a month in office, appeared weak and vacillating, especially in the face of a dramatic decline in foreign exchange reserves that alarmed foreign investors and creditors. His new government was forced to devalue the peso by over 50 percent in the final week of December, bringing 1994 to a disastrous end.

The government regained the political initiative at the start of 1995 in a series of maneuvers that sought to disarticulate the Zapatistas' democratic alliances, which had already been weakened by the electoral outcomes of 1994 and leadership rivalries within the CND. The most effective action was the joint military and propaganda offensive unleashed on February 9. On this day, Zedillo announced on national media that the Attorney General's Office had discovered the true identity of Marcos, claiming that he was really Rafael Sebastián Guillén Vicente, a former philosophy professor at a Mexico City university and member of the leadership of the FLN Marxist guerrilla movement. Zedillo declared that arrest warrants had been issued against over a dozen EZLN leaders, including Marcos, and that judicial police (backed by federal troops) had been dispatched to search Zapatista communities and carry out the arrest. Marcos escaped capture, fleeing with Zapatista soldiers prior to the army's arrival in Guadalupe Tepeyac, one of the main EZLN bases. The military offensive clearly placed the EZLN in a weak bargaining position. Troops destroyed farming equipment, food and water supplies, and ransacked houses and stores, making it impossible for Zapatistas to return to their communities. Instead, over the next several months, the army gave selective help to pro-government communities, which included everything from new roofing materials to free dental treatment and haircuts. Those villages abandoned by Zapatistas were repopulated by anti-Zapatista groups who received similar benefits. Observers correctly described the government's strategy as one of "low-intensity conflict" and noted the similarities with U.S. strategy in Vietnam and Central America (López Astrain 1996).

In these conditions, the EZLN was unable to maintain its democratic alliances of the previous year. Many groups continued to protest human rights abuses and demand the release of political prisoners accused of being Zapatistas. However, the government worked quickly to dismantle the linkages between the EZLN and other popular movements. In Chiapas, the federal government implemented an agrarian reform program that consisted of purchasing some private landholdings from their owners (many of whom had preferred to leave Chiapas altogether) and redistribute them to more than a dozen peasant and indigenous organizations (Harvey 1998b). By the end of 1995 the government could declare that it had met the demand for land reform in Chiapas, thereby stealing another of the Zapatistas' banners. Although land disputes continued, peasants were now more likely to be evicted by the state police than invited to negotiations. This strategy had the effect of driving a wedge between the EZLN and the peasant movements in Chiapas, leading Marcos to denounce the leaders of these movements as traitors.

When substantive peace talks finally resumed in October 1995, the item for discussion concerned indigenous rights and culture. A minimal accord was signed in February 1996, raising hopes that the rebellion would at least have had a positive impact in overcoming the marginalization of the country's indigenous peoples (Hernández 1997). However, here again the government sought to limit the impact of any new legislation. It failed to send the accords to Congress for the purpose of enacting constitutional reforms in favor of indigenous rights. During the rest of 1996 and all of 1997 the government instead decided to carry out its own consultations with lawyers, declaring that the February 1996 accord needed to be revised in order to comply with constitutional norms. In particular, the government argued that the accord potentially threatened the unity of the nation by allowing for separate authorities in indigenous regions. As it happened, this was a bogus claim, since the accord never included any mention of territorial autonomy, but the effect was nevertheless as intended. It cast the Zapatistas as intransigent radicals who were ready to undermine national unity, while raising questions about the status of individual human rights in autonomously governed indigenous communities or regions.

The EZLN continued to wage political and ideological battle, calling for the formation of a civil Zapatista Front of National Liberation (FZLN) in early 1996 and organizing several meetings on indigenous rights, political reform, and international solidarity against neoliberalism. Faced with the lack of movement on constitutional reforms, the Zapatistas also attempted to give their own interpretation of the content of the accord on indigenous rights. Between 1995 and 1998 the EZLN established thirty-eight autonomous rebel municipalities in the Lacandon forest and highland regions. However, by the start of 1997, the Zapatistas were hemmed in militarily by over 40,000 federal troops and, back in the cities, public attention had shifted to day-to-day problems of economic survival and personal security amid a wave of violent crime.

One final factor that must be stressed is the growth of paramilitary groups that have attacked indigenous Zapatista supporters (Centro de Derechos Humanos Fray Bartolomé de Las Casas 1996, 1998). Over three hundred people have been killed in such attacks since 1995, and thousands of others have been forced to leave their homes. The paramilitaries are backed by local and possibly higher state officials who have provided police protection, arms, and supplies. Their actions culminated in the massacre in December 1997 of forty-five unarmed Zapatista sympathizers (mostly women and children) in the highland village of Acteal. Despite a new outcry from many sectors of Mexican and international society, the Zedillo government continued to adopt a hard-line position against the

Zapatistas during 1998. It presented its own proposal on indigenous rights for debate in the national Congress, effectively bypassing the EZLN and its supporters (as well as the government's own peace commission and an independent mediation commission) (Harvey 1999). The government also launched a campaign against the Zapatistas' rebel governments, sending police to destroy buildings and offices and, in the process, deporting dozens of foreign human rights observers.

Following several months of silence in the face of these actions, in July 1998 the Zapatistas issued a new call for a peaceful solution to their demands. Denouncing the government's repressive strategy, the EZLN retook the political initiative by announcing that it would organize a national referendum on indigenous rights and culture with the goal of reaffirming the accords signed in February 1996. In carrying out this referendum, the EZLN aimed to mobilize broad support within Mexican civil society with the goal of forcing the government to accept the original accords as the basis for a renewal of peace negotiations.

As we have noted, the various actions of the government have sought to dismantle the system of alliances that had allowed the EZLN to overcome its political isolation. These measures can be seen as part of a strategic deployment of three political frontiers. The first demarcates a distinction between the government's commitment to upholding "the rule of law" (*un estado de derecho)* and the lawlessness of the Zapatistas. The second delimits "legitimate" and "illegitimate" forms of political action, counterposing the institutional sphere of parties and elections to that of armed struggle. Finally, the government has invoked the defense of national sovereignty against the attempts to involve foreigners in support of the Zapatista movement. A new discourse is thereby created, casting the EZLN as an intransigent opponent that operates according to the "law of the jungle," promotes an illegitimate form of politics, and conspires against the nation. The government, on the other hand, portrays its own position as the defender of the rule of law, institutionality, and sovereignty.

These frontiers, although predictable responses to the Zapatista rebellion, have the potential to rebound against the Mexican government. By resting its legitimacy purely on constitutional grounds, it leaves itself vulnerable to the disbelief of the majority of Mexicans for whom the rule of law can only seem like a bad joke. The infiltration of the judicial system by drug cartels, the proliferation of politically connected gangs of kidnappers (by 1998 over one hundred operated in Mexico City alone), high-level political assassinations, government protection of corrupt banking practices, and the daily abuse of civil rights make the rule of law argument a particularly tenuous one. When electoral fraud continues, especially in rural areas such as Chiapas, Guerrero, and Oaxaca, and when elected officials are implicated in corruption and drug trafficking, the distinction between legitimate and illegitimate means of political struggle also loses much of its force. Similarly, when economic policies and financial mismanagement lead the country to even greater dependency on the IMF and the United States, the defense of national sovereignty sounds increasingly hollow. Instead of these political frontiers defining the regime's identity, they appear more as ad hoc measures in an effort to divert attention from the ongoing crisis in Chiapas, revealing a lack of democratic imagination in responding to that crisis. Just as urban Mexicans should continue to support and learn from the Zapatistas' struggles for grassroots democracy, the EZLN should look to build alliances with all those aggrieved by official impunity, the lack of public accountability and economic mismanagement, particularly in the financial sector where revelations of narco-related money laundering add to the crisis of credibility.

Social movements that address these issues already exist. For example, in the spring of 1998, the Movimiento Cívico Morelense (MCM), a multiclass alliance of civic groups in the state of Morelos, protested vehemently against the police protection given to a notorious band of kidnappers, eventually forcing the resignation of the PRI governor. We can also point to the debtors' organization *El Barzón,* which groups together not only the rural poor, but also owners of small- and medium-sized businesses facing bankruptcy in the new era of free trade. This group has strongly protested the government's decision to transfer the cost of bailing out private banks to the public debt, especially in light of the allegations of money laundering.

During late 1998 and early 1999, the Zapatistas appealed again to groups such as these to support the referendum on indigenous rights, scheduled for March 21, 1999. The referendum was deemed a success in terms of the number of people who cast their vote of support, estimated at 2.5 million Mexicans, or over 1 million more than had participated in a similar referendum in August 1995. After a period of seeming isolation from broader struggles for democracy in Mexico, the Zapatistas could again claim their place amid a broad and shifting network of social movements. If it is the case that the Zapatistas are not the only ones facing an erosion of civil rights and public accountability, the possibility of reverting the rule of law discourse against the government becomes more feasible. Whereas the latter has attempted to associate rising levels of public disorder in Mexico City with the lawlessness of groups such as the Zapatistas, necessitating a stronger hand for the forces of order, the Zapatistas and their urban allies could argue the opposite by pointing to the corruption of those same forces as the very source of social disorder, fear, and daily stress. A national dialogue on the deteriorating quality of citizenship in Mexico is not only necessary, but may also provide a new political opportunity to address the effects of militarization on indigenous communities in Chiapas and other states.

The ability of the Zapatistas to retake the political initiative was also affected by the national elections in 2000. Just as the government was deploying its strategy of low intensity warfare in Chiapas, national attention shifted to the presidential race and the campaigns of the political parties. On July 2, 2000, the PRI lost the presidency for the first time since its founding in 1929 as the center-right PAN candidate, Vicente Fox Quesada, capitalized on the electorate's desire for change and gained 43 percent of the vote, against 35 percent for the PRI candidate, Francisco Labastida Ochoa. During and after his successful campaign, Fox declared that he would seek to reopen peace talks with the Zapatistas by pulling back federal army troops and by requesting congressional approval for the accords on indigenous rights, which had been signed in February 1996. The Zapatistas did not make any public statement regarding Fox's victory and his promises regarding the peace process in Chiapas. Nor did they respond to the follow-up victory of opposition candidate for governor of Chiapas, Pablo Salazar Mendiguchía, on August 20. With the PRI having finally lost executive power at both national and state levels, many awaited some sign from the Zapatistas that they were ready to return to peace negotiations and even contemplate handing over their arms. The fact that they stayed silent led some observers to conclude that the EZLN was facing its final moments as a political force, especially since the transition to democracy had now been effectively accomplished through the ballot box rather than through armed rebellion. However, given the history described in this chapter, it is more likely that the Zapatistas were waiting for actions rather than simply campaign promises before declaring their position regarding the new conjuncture. Violent attacks against their supporters continued unabated during the summer and fall of 2000, despite the optimism in Mexico City and foreign capitals over the electoral triumph of Vicente Fox. In short, it remains to be seen what actions the new government will take in meeting the demands of the Zapatistas.

In this regard, the analysis offered in this chapter should direct our attention to the following question. Referring to the cycles of power and resistance noted in Table 1, will the new governments of Fox and Salazar be able to move from "polarization" to "stabilization"? It appears that their promises to withdraw federal troops and gain approval for the indigenous rights accords are meant to move in such a direction. However, there are problems with each of these measures, and, as always, the devil is in the detail. For example, what percentage of the federal troops will be removed from the conflict area? Will they be relocated to their positions prior to January 1, 1994, or only to those occupied prior to the offensive taken on February 9, 1995? Will the government also take effective steps to dismantle the eighteen or so paramilitary groups operating in Chiapas? Will the national Congress try to amend the indigenous rights accords in ways that the Zapatistas may find unacceptable?

None of these questions will be easy to answer, but they do form the core issues facing the new government in Chiapas. Beyond the immediate conjuncture, however, it is also necessary to recognize a different challenge than the admittedly complicated one of moving from polarization to stabilization. By this I mean the possibility of stopping the whole cycle of power and resistance once and for all. As we have noted, stabilization may last for relatively short or long periods of time. Eventually, however, the coherence of "stabilized" political borders breaks down, leading to rupture and, in turn, polarization. Is it possible to break this cycle? If the main goal of politics is to gain power and exercise hegemony, then it is indeed unlikely that the cycle can be overcome. For example, if President Fox's policies in Chiapas are simply meant to stabilize the sociopolitical and ethnic divisions in the state, without effectively reducing or dissolving their conflictive nature, we can expect that "destabilization" will reemerge before too long. In fact, given the depth and breadth of violent confrontation in Chiapas, it is questionable whether stabilization can be achieved without some radical changes in how power is exercised in the state. For this reason, it may be necessary to develop a different type of politics, one that is not reducible to strategic calculation, power, hegemony, and violence. Although the latter have informed the dominant understanding of politics in the West (including Mexico), there may be alternative means of dealing with conflicts that rely more on dialogue and respect for the Other, not in an instrumental fashion whereby different actors attempt to convince or coerce each other into accepting their worldview, but in terms of a recognition of the radical otherness of the Other. Such a possibility has been raised in Derrida's recent work on democracy, ethics, and friendship (1996, 83; 1997).

In such a scenario, competing forces would have to accept the limits of their hegemonic pretensions and, instead, learn to live with difference as an irreducible part of building more open and democratic institutions. This can be termed a new "politics of disarmament," which in Chiapas (and perhaps in other conflictive areas of the world) would go beyond the "stabilization" of a polarized society. It would open up new ways of ordering political life that may reduce the propensity of the cycle of power and resistance to repeat itself, without implying that political conflict would disappear. In practical terms, this new "politics of disarmament" would require new approaches to such key areas of international concern as conflict resolution, peace negotiations, human rights, collective rights, ethnic and religious identities, citizenship, nationalism, sovereignty, and globalization. In the case of Chiapas, a "politics of disarmament" would need to rebuild trust and solidarity within and between communities by crossing cultural and political divides, while simultaneously reforming the broader economic and political structures that continue to propagate poverty and violence. This is certainly a more difficult and ambitious task than repositioning federal troops, but if the cycle is to be broken rather than simply stabilized, it is a task worthy of support and the necessary resources.

CONCLUSIONS

This chapter has addressed a theoretical and practical problem that by no means is limited to Chiapas. This problem concerns the status of citizenship today as a meaningful concept and practice. It was noted that several authors have drawn attention to the limits of citizenship when referring to the marginalization of ethnic minorities, such as the indigenous peoples of Chiapas. In this case, citizenship is defined not in terms of a set of universal traits but as the point around which a plurality of social groups challenge different forms of domination by adhering to the ethical and political ideals of equality and liberty (Mouffe 1993, 84). The Zapatistas' search for "words that others might understand" is an example of this articulation. This search has been conceptualized here as the attempt to construct a new discourse that links particular identities together in a relative universalization (Laclau 1995). Such linkages do not precede the political practice of articulation itself. Instead they are attempts to establish or contest hegemonic understandings of what it means to be indigenous, Mexican, and a citizen. The goal of this strategy is not to seize power but to democratize power, to ensure that "those who govern, govern by obeying."

This political and discursive construction of citizenship can lead in many directions, including its absorption by an authoritarian discourse of law and order. Another possibility, the one suggested by the EZLN since 1994, is the creation of a radical democratic discourse. It is democratic because the discourse remains open to the expression of difference in determining the content of citizenship, rather than imposing a universal definition that would negate particularity. It is radical in the sense that there can never be a final point of closure, but recognizes the need to democratize all social relations now and always. Although the government has been successful in averting such a possibility, there is no theoretical reason why it cannot be pursued in the future. The referendum on indigenous rights appeared to rekindle enthusiasm for such a strategy, renewing the energy of a national civic and social movement in support of democratization beyond the electoral system.

Given the above, what does this analysis tell us about identities, borders, and orders? The "primacy of the political" directs our attention to the discourses that create and contest identities, borders, and orders. In the case of Chiapas, we do not find an essential indigenous identity, but rather the reworking of multiple identities within the context of political organization. In the 1990s, identity was recreated through broader inclusionary discourses that transcend difference but do not necessarily negate particularity. Analysis should therefore focus on processes of identification rather than the manifestation of pre-given identities. This approach differs from the rationalist, culturalist, and structuralist paradigms of comparative politics, each of which have tended to assume the presence of unified actors prior to political engagement. In this regard, the combination of discourse analysis and IBO provides a particularly useful framework for the comparative analysis of political struggle.

This type of analysis also stresses the political nature of bordering and how the three concepts of identities, borders, and orders are related through acts of power. This is brought out clearly in the case of Chiapas, where ethnic and class identities have historically resulted from the political outcomes of violent imposition and/or rebellion. However, since the 1990s, it is politically impossible to reestablish order upon such a strategy of exclusion. Bordering has become much more complex and contested. Bordering is not solely a matter of exclusion of the indigenous Other. Political frontiers, if they are to have any chance of sedimentation, must use a mix of inclusionary and exclusionary strategies. The selective inclusion of some elements of the Other helps legitimize a political frontier, although it entails an inevitable contradiction. On the one hand, bordering requires the homogenization of the Other if it is to separate radically distinctive identities. In Chiapas, this means that, at certain moments, the various indigenous peoples have been bordered by the signifier "Indian." At other times local and national elites have sought to assert their rule by attempting to convert "Indians" to Westernized culture through processes of evangelization or assimilation. Throughout history we can observe attempts to selectively co-opt elements of indigenous communities into the various discourses of modernization (including populism and productivism). In Chiapas, the limits of these discourses have been revealed by regional politics and indigenous rebellions. However, the limits of rebellion also suggest that the social field is never divided into two antagonistic camps, but displays a more complex pattern of partial inclusions and exclusions, where the boundary lines are never finally fixed.

This approach is also useful for understanding the indeterminacy of political orders. In particular, it can trace important contradictions that would pass unnoticed in other analyses that assume the existence of fully constituted entities. In the case of Chiapas, this type of analysis, rather than predicting the structurally determined demise of the Zapatistas, has revealed the strategic reappropriation of citizenship in ways that may be undermining the political efficacy of the government's law and order discourse, thereby allowing for a renewal of democratic alliances. The conditions of possibility here include the activism of civic organizations and the type of linkages which the EZLN have been able to maintain with democratic movements since 1994.

The Zapatista rebellion has been discussed here not as a case study to add to the existing wealth of information on popular protest in developing countries. Nor has the aim been to discover the ultimate causes of rebellion. Rather, the intention has been to stress the political nature of IBO through the lens of a poststructuralist analysis. This approach may be useful in developing new comparative research agendas, particularly with regard to the struggles to transform power relations between dominant political actors and indigenous peoples and minorities in many parts of the world today. For example, within history and anthropology, the recovery of perspectives from colonized or marginalized groups under the rubric of "subaltern studies" has already done much to provide alternative accounts of ethnic relations. Although some of these accounts tend to reify the presence of a pure indigenous Other (Prakash 1994), they are an example of the kind of multiarea, comparative research agendas that are sought by an IBO reconfiguration of international, comparative, and area studies. Such a research agenda can help create new networks for dialogue between disciplinary and area studies specialists. It could also help the protagonists of these struggles learn from each others' experiences and collectively develop new political strategies. IBO offers a theoretical and practical framework for furthering each of these goals.

NOTES

I would like to thank Maria Harvey and Chris Halverson for their critical reading of earlier versions of this chapter. I am also grateful to the participants of the Las Cruces Group for the intellectual stimulation created by the collaborative project on identities, borders, and orders. I also acknowledge the Ford Foundation for supporting this project under its Crossing Borders: Revitalizing Area Studies initiative.

1. On the 1712 rebellion, see Gosner (1992). On the Chamula rebellion of 1867, see Rus (1983). For a general discussion of the history of ethnic relations in Chiapas, see Benjamin (1996).

2. Material for this section is taken from Harvey (1998a).

3. Information in this section is taken from the interview conducted with Subcomandante Marcos by Carmen Castillo and Tessa Brisac, Aguascalientes, Chiapas, November 24, 1994, and published in Gilly, Subcomandante Marcos, and Ginzburg (1995, 129–42).

Conclusion

MATHIAS ALBERT AND FRIEDRICH KRATOCHWIL

The post–Cold War world continues in refusing to succumb to many of the theoretical designs that are on offer in the IR marketplace. The only factor that remains certain seems to be a continuing uncertainty as the prime defining characteristic of the present *conditio orbis*. Such a situation provides fertile ground for arguments seeking refuge in concepts and solutions that promise at least some degree of certainty. These certainties need not take the form of simplistic concepts. They may be sought after in the form of complex research programs and designs. The ascendancy of a chronically ill-defined "constructivism" within the heartlands of IR theorizing may serve as the best example to underscore this point. There may hardly be an agreement on the appropriate connotations of the term, but no doubt a substantial degree of complacency about having found a new main route along which to explore world politics can be detected in the scholarly field of international relations. The present volume provides a counterpoint to such tendencies of prematurely fixing and "nouning" the new. With its conceptual setting as well as in the various thematic cuts represented by the individual chapters, it creates more of an unsettling experience than a point of crystallization for a new and coherent theoretical approach. The refusal to provide students of IR with certainties in times of flux is perhaps nowhere better exemplified than by choosing a triad of seemingly all-encompassing concepts as the analytic point of departure. Nonetheless, in this case this refusal does not pose a problem, but constitutes a program. As aptly pointed out in Lapid's introduction, it does not replace certainty with fuzziness, but rather explores the possibilities of a conceptual as well as a disciplinary pluralization that is made possible by choosing a combination of (meta)concepts that are, to paraphrase Lapid, endlessly interesting, endlessly relevant, and endlessly problematic in and for *all* of the social sciences.

To draw a conclusion on a project that is explicitly conceived as a point of many departures in the voyage of IR theory may seem to constitute a rather futile exercise. It is in this sense that this concluding chapter must be seen not as an attempt to instantly recap what has been just opened, but rather as an attempt to take up and combine some of the ideas and arguments of our fellow IBO travelers and provide them with some suggestions as to where they may be heading to, within, and beyond the IR academic field.

Without doubt, a number of intricacies are entailed in the concept of an IBO triad. We feel that we share with many readers a certain discomfort regarding IBO as a concept that on the one hand seems to be amorphous and elusive if an attempt is made to pin it down in abstract terms, yet on the other hand is analytically rich if it is put to analytical uses in a variety of realms. We will try to trace the sources of this discomfort by relating IBO to other modes of theorizing, in IR in particular and the social sciences in general. An underlying question here is whether the perceived uneasiness is due to IBO not succeeding in its effort to walk the (pluralist) fine line between a theoretical substantialism on the one hand and a theoretical fuzzyism on the other hand, or if it is rather the case that IBO indeed strikes the right theoretical chord and that our unease is more the result of ourselves not yet being accustomed to the new tune. In that context, we will again emphasize that this new tune is but a representation of a broader movement of social theory and the philosophy of the social sciences, namely the increasing emphasis on process as opposed to structure.

Neither the IBO triad nor the majority of the preceding individual chapters fit squarely into a nicely defined and well-bounded disciplinary realm of international studies or, for that matter, political science. Rather, as is aptly expressed in the volume's structuring, "the international," "the political" and "the disciplinary" themselves are being contested, with special emphasis on the "nouning" "the" in each case. As already elaborated by Lapid at the outset of this volume, IBO is about rethinking and disaggregating these terms, about opening up new routes of inquiry by utilizing techniques of cross-disciplinary hybridization. This observation and our argument about the emphasis of process over substance notwithstanding, we would like to hint at some possible substantial overlaps in the ways in which the contributions to this volume seek to reconceptualize fundamental problems as well as individual facets of world order. While we fully accept and applaud the attempt to utilize IBO as a heuristic device to move beyond what appears to constitute an increasingly arbitrary and only institutionally legitimized set of disciplinary boundaries, this volume in its own subtitle acknowledges that individually and taken together its contributions also carry subtexts that can be situated within the closer confines of IR theory. While we find the new directions within IR theory to be anticipated and reflected in quite a number of scholarly undertakings in the field, the IBO triad seems to have been particularly helpful in explicitly distilling them.

WHAT IS "IBO" AND WHERE DOES IT FIT?

Contemporary IR theorizing still seems to be marked by a dividing line between those employing the gesture of anchoring knowledge about world affairs in grounds they take to be solid (without this necessarily precluding a theoretically rich reflection on these grounds) and those who prioritize the gesture of critically examining and unsettling these grounds and the ways they affect even the microlevel analysis of specific issues. This dividing line is, of course, not very clear-cut and not concomitant with many familiar ordering devices that are applied to the theoretical field of IR (e.g., "great debates"). Additionally, as witnessed in the rise of "constructivist" thought in the field, it is increasingly difficult to unequivocally associate a certain epistemological stance with a given theoretical label.

Be that as it may, it is clear where IBO and most contributions to this volume stand. They partake in the enterprise of critically examining and questioning the units and levels of analysis that are still taken as more or less given in many approaches to IR theory. They do so, moreover, without claiming to do it from the standpoint of a firm—or even privileged—method or epistemology. Although at first sight the IBO triad *could* be regarded as a new self-proclaimed candidate for yet another "grand theory," this impression certainly should have vanished at the end of the current volume. The IBO triad does not predetermine substantive theorizing. This, for one thing, has to do with the basically processual character of the triad (which more correctly would have to be read as the interplay between processes of identification, bordering, and ordering). This impression is, however, reinforced by the fact that although all authors of the present volume in some way touch upon issues that are localized within the triad, they do so from substantially different points of theoretical departure. If IBO does not present a grand theoretical design of its own, or one that is anchored in solid epistemological ground, then what constitutes its "plurality" that is supposed to distinguish it from "fuzziness"? What is the distinguishing feature between the plural and the fuzzy (which seems to imply a naive form of relativism) in this case? We propose to get a clearer understanding of the possibilities for localizing IBO in that respect by relating it to the broader issue of the possibility of drawing up cross-disciplinary research designs. Does an increasing proliferation of knowledge and meaning in information society leave room for such an ambitious undertaking at all?

Famously coined by Jean-François Lyotard (1984), the *Postmodern Condition* denotes a state of knowledge in Western advanced industrial societies in which the "metanarratives" of romanticism and emancipation have lost their integrating force for legitimizing knowledge. The point of interest here is not whether the term "postmodern" is the most appropriate to describe the evolutionary state of modern society. It is rather to point out and reiterate that Lyotard's observation is not logical (Habermasian universal pragmatics would indeed claim it is paradoxical since it assumes a meta-metanarrative that allows judging on metanarratives), but historical-sociological. What Lyotard observes is the simple fact of a proliferation of legitimizing narratives that cease to be integrated by a metanarrative, and thus in many cases pose the only standard of validity to themselves (an argument that is structurally similar to that of autopoiesis). However, such a proliferation of narratives—standards of validity and knowledge—does in no way preclude some form of communication between those mininarratives; it only precludes—again, not logically, but historically-sociologically—the reassertion of a dominance of a metanarrative. It is important to be clear about these issues in order not to commit the error of taking Lyotard's dictum to mean that it is no longer possible to develop far-reaching (long-range, grand) theories and conceptual designs. The only thing that follows from the "end of metanarratives" is that theories, no matter how far-reaching, cannot seek recourse in the solid epistemological foundations of a metanarrative. It does not follow from it that theorizing in "grand style" per se would cease to be legitimate.

That grand-style theorizing is not in abundance in contemporary IR should be plainly visible to students in the field. As such, the "grand old texts" from Morgenthau to Bull and Waltz stand unassailed. The great debates have not provided conclusive results, and currently it does not seem to be at all clear whether there is such a thing as a great debate going on. Given Lyotard's observation, such a situation should hardly come as a surprise. Even within a tiny academic (sub)discipline, the standards and legitimizing (meta)narratives have proliferated and disseminated to a degree where very often representatives from various corners of the field are unable to communicate with each other. However, it is exactly against this background that the IBO triad opens up some new possibilities and a fresh perspective. The IBO triad does not provide or attempt to provide a new big theory for the academic field of international relations. What it does do is deliver fully on the demand of (re)constituting international relations, including its numerous facets, as a social science—a demand that has been aired frequently in recent years. IBO tries to achieve this by placing IR at the intersection of a number of grand theorizings, within but also across disciplines, opening routes of communication between them, yet fully acknowledging the impossibility of coming up with an integrated grand theory under the postmodern condition in the end.

But what would such a theorizing look like when all the familiar givens are gone, when the familiar terms of neither nations nor states represent the foundations for our analysis? Rather than terms, conceptual relationships or practices (bordering!) provide the foci now. We believe that the IBO approach suggests a possible way for theorizing without submitting to the essentialist categories of the "state" or an unproblematic notion of an actor created for the sake of analytical convenience (such as the *homo oeconomicus*) or the speculations of a philosophy of history popularized by certain versions of globalization and the emergence of a world (civil) society. Instead, we suggest that in focusing on three sets of problems we can give new impulses to theory building that is more appropriate to the rapid changes we observe in (inter)national politics and in the social order problematique in general. These problems are (1) the primacy of process over structures; (2) the problem of bordering, i.e., of drawing boundaries and delimiting systems; and (3) issues of political order in an unevenly integrated but nevertheless globalized world.

PROCESS OVER SUBSTANCE AND STRUCTURE

The choice of words of IBO (identities, borders, orders) could be taken as an argument about the primordial importance of these concepts and the realities they stand for. To that extent the argument made against essentialism and the primacy of the given, be it actors, structure, or whatever, seems strange indeed. But, as the various contributions in this book suggest and Lapid's introduction emphasizes again and again, what we are looking at are not distinct concepts standing for some immutable parts of reality, but rather relations between concepts and their changing patterns of meaning. Furthermore, precisely because we want to capture the changing nature of these interactions, we have to focus less on the stabilizations that these relationships sometimes achieve, i.e., their content, than on the *activities* that account for the changes and for which the temporary stabilizations are just limiting cases. To that extent the meaning of the terms is not given by the world "out there," but rather by the mutual references these terms make to each other, by the processes of including or excluding something from the concepts, and by the resulting implications of these changing semantic fields. To that extent understanding these terms means not so much to clarify the referents as it implies to be able to go on with the social and political practices and, through reflection, make sense out of them.

This turn from things or objects to activity as the basic focus of investigation is deeply against the grain of traditional analysis that is beholden since the beginning of Western philosophy to notions and conceptual dichotomies such as matter and form, objects and properties, and to a conceptualization of change that consists in some alteration of an ideally fixed object. After all, "true being" is identified in classical ontology as changelessness, which, in turn, is often conceived as nonsusceptibility to corruption, since change could only be conceptualized as decay if being was conceived as a state of unchanging identity. Plato's ontology with all its reverberations throughout the Middle Ages and the Renaissance most clearly exemplifies this model. But even the more dynamic Aristotelian formulations concerning development and change still are beholden to an ontology in which forms and matter are distinguished and where changes can be analyzed in terms of the sequence of forms observable in or on a substance. How important this hold is becomes visible even nowadays in analytical philosophy. Thus, the contemporary philosopher Strawson has objected to a process (re)orientation in metaphysics because, given the space-time commitment of our conceptual schemes and given the character of the major categories we employ, changes can only be observed on material bodies that have to be, epistemologically speaking, "basic particulars" (Strawson 1959, 30).

Of course, we cannot provide here an explicit justification for a radical reformulation of the traditional ontological problem by emphasizing the fluid character of things, by giving primacy to processes and activities over structures and matter, by conceiving definite objects as limiting cases of successful, even though always only temporary, stabilizations. Two justifications should, however, be mentioned in passing, one from the social sciences and one, more principled challenge, provided, for example, by the process metaphysics advocated by Whitehead and Rescher.

As to the social sciences there are several notable attempts to conceive of systems not in terms of givens or stable structures, but rather in terms of objects, be they states, structures, or actors, as the result of activities whereby changes can be minimized and stabilizations can occur. Thus Michael Mann's (1986) monumental study *The Sources of Social Power* views the emergence of the state as a successful attempt of certain "caging" processes that give more definite shape to otherwise rather amorphous social interactions. Similarly, Ferguson and Mansbach's (1996a) study of transformative change in international politics uses process and patterns of integration and disintegration as the basic analytical organizing device. Mansbach and Wilmer's contribution on the changing patterns of community construction and the regulation of violence can similarly be understood as being part of this historically oriented approach focusing on process. Finally, Susan Strange (1988), concerned with the interaction of state and market as organizational forms, found

the essentialist interpretations of these terms of little help in understanding the changing nature of both market and political forces.
Instead, she proposed to consider four streams or processes (production, innovation, credit creation, and security procurement) in order
to derive from their interaction some insights into the basic changes
that are usually lumped together under the rubric "globalization" or
"changes in the international system."

But while these recent attempts at theorizing international relations might lend a certain plausibility to our efforts here, they certainly do not demonstrate the superiority or even feasibility of turning traditional ontology on its head. After all, one could object that
looking at the interaction of several systems à la Strange puts the
decisive theoretical question only one step further back. Systems
themselves, one could argue, have then again to be conceived as
stable patterns among certain objects, precisely in the fashion Strawson argued above, quite aside from the equally hoary question of
how many systems there are that have to be considered. These are
certainly difficult questions to raise, and while we do not pretend to
have a ready-made answer to them, there are solutions to some of
the above puzzles raised by process philosophy. In order to refute
Strawson's objections we would need not only a different conception of "system," we also would have to show that his criticisms can
be met. To that extent at least a prima facie case for the feasibility of
a process ontology could be made. Since we deal with the problem
of social systems and their conceptualization more explicitly below,
only a few remarks concerning the first problem are in order here.

Nicholas Rescher, an advocate of process philosophy, has pointed
out that Strawson's objections are invalid, since all the features that
his analysis requires (spatiotemporal stability and endurance, diversity, richness, interpersonal accountability, and the like) are possessed
every bit as much by physical processes as by the things that are or
possess material bodies. It is not material substances (things) alone
that can be distinguished and reidentified within nature's spatiotemporal framework, but occurrence-complexes (processes) as well. Processes are physically realized without being literally embodied.

Although this approach seems to dissolve all solid things into a
flux, we had better remember that even physical objects are dissolved
by modern physics. The notion of solid material objects consisting
of indivisible material particles has been discarded by modern quan-

tum theory. A gravitational or electromagnetic field is not a thing whose existence and functioning can be described in terms of some underlying substance; we can only talk about it in terms of certain processes it engenders. To that extent substances have been reconceptualized as manifolds of identifiable processes that satisfy certain conditions of identifiability over time. In other words, "A process is a coordinated group of changes..., an organized family of occurrences that are systematically linked to one another, either causally or functionally" (Rescher 1995, 62). We only want to note that classical substance metaphysics must—somehow strangely—conceive of substance origination as instantaneous after which the substance persists throughout until expiration. But here again a sudden turn toward nonexistence needs to be adduced. As Whitehead has pointed out, concrete physical particulars always arise through processes and thus inevitably owe them their existence. Conversely, "death" has to be conceived as an abrupt instantaneous occurrence, even though common sense allows for a process of dying, a mystery already to St. Augustine's ontological reflections. Conceptually, process philosophy has given rise to many puzzling problems including Schrödinger's cat problem and the need for fuzzy logic (imprecisely bounded intervals) as well as truth value gaps (statements that something exists or not at certain times are neither true nor false but simply indeterminate).

BORDERING AND SOCIAL SYSTEMS

Determining and classifying the processes that make up the social world is therefore of paramount importance and well in tune with the standards of modern science. True, such an approach still seems at odds with the standard structuralist forms of analysis and the prevalent (and hardly justifiable) understanding of "the" scientific method among social scientists. Nevertheless, although the agent-structure debate has created an opening for more process-oriented thinking in the social sciences, the implications that arise from the special features of recursivity characteristic of social and self-reproducing systems are only slowly being realized. Not only are social systems not things, and much of the traditional vocabulary for analyzing the phenomena, therefore, gets in the way, there are also several problems that make adherence to the canons of a traditionally conceived social science highly problematic. Thus, equifinality, the emergence of functional equivalences, and the path dependence of historical developments in the reproduction of the social system make the simple conceptual instruments of a historical, mechanical, causal imputation simply inapt. Causes have then more to do with following certain paths and with counterfactual reasoning than with observations à la Hume or with reliance on universal and immutable laws.

More particularly, given the recursivity problem in the genesis of social systems, two important caveats need to be mentioned. One concerns the issue that the terms we use in describing the system are neither neutral nor can they be depicted as concepts that somehow stand more or less adequately for the real world out there. The second has to do with drawing the appropriate conclusion from this realization. A brief discussion is in order.

As to the first problem, let us ask whether the state of war described by Hobbes is actually a statement about reality, as is the description of the observations in an experiment. Two things come to mind. First, although Hobbes used some form of *Gedankenexperiment* (thought experiment) and counterfactual reasoning in order to justify his deductions, he was quite clear that "there was never such a time, nor condition as this; and I believe it was never generally so, over all the world" (Hobbes 1968, 187). So much for the alleged universality of the reality described. Second, if Hobbes's analysis of the state of nature is not a simple description of some facts, independent of the actions and ideas of the actors about the game they are involved in, then this recursive loop has to be part of our theoretical interest. Thus language, as the way we conceive of something, matters. For example, changing the vocabulary from the metaphor of the body politic or from the image of an architecture—in which certain segments of society are seen as serving as buttresses and checks on certain other elements—to that of a contract cannot be interpreted as hitting somehow on a more accurate description of the world out there. Instead, as Rorty suggests, finding this new vocabulary, redescribing the familiar elements of social reality in new terms, means seeing them in a new light and creating new opportunities for practices and experiences that sidestep the problems of the old way of referring to political things that have now gotten in the way. Thus the creation of new vocabularies is not like fitting together the pieces of a puzzle or approaching the truth ever more closely through our conceptual apparatus by a process of trial and error. Actually something entirely different is at stake here. Rather than seeing our concepts as mirrors of the things or the world out there, they are intrinsically bound up with constituting the world they allegedly only describe. Rorty suggests that we conceive of vocabularies as instruments, even though his form of instrumentalism has little to do with the instrumentalist position of Milton Friedmann or the type of as-if theorizing that is in vogue again. They are not discoveries of a reality behind the appearances of an undistorted view of the whole picture with which to replace myopic views of its parts. The proper analogy is with the invention of new tools to take the place of old tools. To come up with such a vocabulary is more like discarding the lever and the fulcrum because one has envisioned the pulley (Rorty 1989, 12).

PROBLEMS OF WORLD ORDER

Given these characteristics of social systems and vocabularies, it is not surprising that all of the contributions in this volume have to wrestle with this problem to some extent. Since the old vocabulary of the state, of the system, of power, even of society is increasingly getting in the way, we have to reinvent how we make understandable to ourselves the practices and processes that seem to have lost their referent. For example, Albert and Brock's chapter examines this phenomenon on the level of the traditional distinctions drawn between the concepts of *Gesellschaft* (society) and *Gemeinschaft* (community). By showing the insufficiency of the traditional categories for the analysis of the ongoing processes that these concepts try to capture, the notion of *Vergesellschaftung* (society-formation) itself becomes problematic in an era in which the traditional boundaries provided by the territorial state, serving as the secure container for society, have become permeable.

Similarly, Heisler's warning that our traditional vocabulary for describing migrations is woefully inadequate is situated perhaps closer to the ground and inspired more by the worry of a practicing social scientist than by concerns of grand social theory. But he makes essentially the same point of how, in this case, some notion about migrants and foreigners, inspired by liberal thought, has not only skewed the analysis of modern migrations but is more likely to result in faulty policy advice. Antje Wiener's and David Jacobson's chapters voice a similar concern. Dealing with issues of legitimization, they both find that the traditional notion of the popular will as the legitimizing source of law is difficult to square with both the emergence of human rights law and the increasing role of the judiciary in creating norms and adjusting existing practices of inclusion and exclusion in the U.S. and EU contexts. Such observations point also to the new, more discursively oriented approaches that bestow legitimacy on decisions, relying increasingly on procedures and fluid movements rather than on a constituted people (citizens) deciding in single clear acts of will on their destiny.

That these new developments are not simply part of a trend from lesser to more inclusive forms of democracy or from the traditional citizenship of bounded polities, based on membership and a certain cultural identity, to a cosmopolitan notion of politics is aptly argued by Chris Brown, Rey Koslowski, and Ronnie Lipschutz. Brown shows the problematic nature of the conceptual distinctions in the liberal and communitarian debate by pointing to some usually unacknowledged "bordering exercises" by cosmopolitans when practical questions arise. Not only are such fallbacks to largely unarticulated criteria considerably weakening the coherence and persuasiveness of the cosmopolitan position, there is, in addition, the question of whether some of the advocated remedies, such as the bestowal of multiple citizenships, are really addressing the right problems. As Koslowski nicely demonstrates, multiple ambivalent and apolitical identities are as much a part of our present reality as are strong ties to former homelands or, even more so, specific groups in other states. To that extent one could ask whether the advocacy of the bestowal of dual nationality as an answer to migrations is not based again upon the increasingly problematic notion of an all-purpose political organization, territorially bound and clearly demarcated by membership criteria. Can we have degrees of participation and various levels of rights? It seems that present practices are more in tune with this interpretation than with conceptual debates that add heat but little enlightenment to many of the contemporary political debates.

While extending citizenship to people who have made their new home in another country and are willing to bear the burdens as well as the rights of full citizenship makes sense when compared to the notion of *jus sanguinis,* which automatically favors people with practically no connection to the country (aside from some historical fact), things are a bit more complicated in the case of ambivalence toward, or even the rejection of, many of the cultural features characteristic of the new home. What does this mean for politics and for the community that has to establish a public sphere in which the "thing common to all" (res publica) has to be institutionalized as an ongoing and transgenerational concern? To reduce the admittedly rather confused debates in this area to the simple dichotomies between outmoded communitarians and progressive cosmopolitans is obviously not very helpful as it leads to poor analysis of the respective problems.

Lipschutz's analysis should also provide much food for thought, especially for those who too willingly submit to the universalist rhetoric about the victory of democracy and free markets as victories of universalist thinking. His rather caustic remarks about consumer sovereignty and its advantages are well taken and deserve further critical reflection. But aside from interpreting this rhetorical ploy as an attempted imposition of a peculiar American form of morality on an increasingly ungovernable international reality, Lipschutz points to the fundamental change that occurs when traditional deterrence that presupposed functioning states is substituted by disciplinary deterrence against rogue states and radical dissenters.

Even if we do not share this particular assessment, Lipschutz's analysis raises a more fundamental issue that is also broached in Bigo's essay on surveillance. Both focus on the new possibilities and techniques of rapid and comprehensive information retrieval that can virtually instantly identify perpetrators. The denial of access rather than reliance on traditional sanctions that threaten some deprivation but cannot prevent transgressions has become the main mode of disciplining. Both Foucault and Luhmann have called attention to this fact of modernity: instead of threats, surveillance is substituted; instead of social integration through common values, increasingly information provided through "codes" takes over the task of stabilizing the actors' expectations. Indeed, this observation not only analyzes a fundamental change in the way of social control, it also fundamentally challenges our implicit model of society. One nearly trivial example drives home this point.

Traditional societies needed either to rely on personal trust or on the strong arm of the state in order to facilitate exchanges. While trust developed through personal ties and rigid distinctions between insiders and outsiders, the Hobbesian solution to social order already replaced personal trust through *the trust in a system of expectations* based on the threat of the sovereign to punish any potential transgressor. Therefore, the increasing anonymity of social transactions, their complexities, and the unavailability of a strong value consensus in increasingly differentiated societies make it more and more problematic to rely on threats and values as a means for stabilizing expectations and facilitating exchanges. At least partly, modern information technology fills this void. Rather than relying on increasingly ineffective criminal sanctions, the American middle class and businesses are kept in line by reporting systems and the virtually instantaneous denial of access to all types of transactions. Anyone who has had the misfortune of having his credit report tampered with will understand this new disciplining effect, which exercises control without relying on official sanctions.

This trivial example has, however, larger implications for our theory building. It shows us at least indirectly why our thinking concerning global society can no longer be that of a normal national society written large. To that extent perhaps both communitarianism and the universalist aspirations of the cosmopolitans are beholden to an outmoded model of society. Both see society as integrated by threats and values, rather than the assembly of various processes going not only right through the concrete societies (states) but through the very actors themselves. World society then needs an entirely new model for the processes characterizing the interactions and their necessary stabilizations that does not solely rely on the actors and their normatively secured conformity (either through threats or socialization), but rather takes account of the ways in which systems of meaning can evolve, stabilize, and develop independently of a generalized normative-integrative mode of expectation. This would also open up the possibility of subjecting world society to the *theory of society,* the classic realm of social theory from which it has been shielded under the unquestioned reign of the territorial-integrative model of society. Thus inspired, a whole world of codes and evolutionary-communicative dynamics of world society, which work behind the intentions of the actors, can be discovered. Luhmann's theory of society (1997) and systems theory (1994) only provide the most shining and fully developed examples of an ambitious social theorizing that becomes possible on such grounds.

In other words, social systems can no longer be understood simply in terms of actor-oriented systems of action but need to take impersonal forces and codes into account that go beyond the intentional actions of the actors. To that extent not only the unintended consequences of yesteryear, which was grist for the structuralist mill, but also the agent-structure debate and constructivists' attempts to revive a social systems theory in terms of actor orientations share important conceptual shortcomings. It also becomes clear why realism is no longer a normatively viable prescriptive theory nor a descriptively appropriate theory of international politics. While the criticism against realists was largely directed at their neglect of forces emerging from complex interdependencies, the realist response usually consisted in denying the importance of such phenomena. Implicit in such a dismissal was the classical notion of social order as a result of individual actions that are directed largely by threats (or habituation backed by threats). But even this fallback position is no longer available as soon as we realize that this model of society might get in the way. To that extent the insistence on strong identity-based forms of governance through an all-purpose organization claiming and effectively wielding the monopoly of legitimate force might indeed be a prescription that has greater relevance for societies that emerge from the breakdown of archaic social stratifications and that hope to create a new unity through homogenization and by centralization, particularly of the means of violence. It will be of lesser importance for societies that are being transformed by new forms of organization and power that we usually identify as part of the globalization process.

This certainly does not mean that the world can now be nicely divided into zones of peace (postmodern regions) and of turmoil (emerging and modernizing regions), as the sources of disorder can clearly be seen in the postmodern world, too (e.g., when yuppies are left to their own devices to speculate on currency and commodity markets). Besides, dividing up the world again in spatial categories demarcated by clear (or even fuzzy) boundaries shows only once more the powerful hold of the traditional vocabulary when it is used unreflectively. We can no longer be satisfied with such conceptual distinctions even if they have a certain plausibility and empirical validity (as has the observation that the sun circles the earth). Instead of assuming on the basis of certain observations that "here" is peace and "there" is war, we have to investigate more diligently, as the sources of conflict have shifted every- and elsewhere. This is an issue that is very well illustrated by the references to the Israel-Palestine conflict in the context of Newman's argument in this volume.

Furthermore, we have to realize that the old prescriptions of creating political order are unlikely to work when people not only act and speak differently about the practices they are involved in than we were accustomed to, but when many of the processes have taken on a life of their own that can no longer be steered by the traditional means of control. While in the contemporary discussion this problem is sometimes discussed in terms of the ascendancy of the market over the state, our analysis suggests that such a conceptualization misses important dimensions of the transformational changes brought about by globalization. Rather than thinking about a zero-sum situation in which the gain in importance of one organizational form necessarily implies the decrease of importance of the other, the change we are witnessing is of a different kind. The state—far from presiding over its own demise through the emergence of international regimes, organizations, and nonstate actors who have become important participants in the setting of agendas and of decisions—has fundamentally changed its concerns (this change, for example, is sometimes described as a change from the welfare state to the competition state). Thus, the state is not disappearing, as political economists of all colors have often told us, not least since it remains the best guarantor and protector of property rights around.

Nonetheless, to argue this way implies a fundamental change in our conception of politics. Political orders have traditionally been based on membership criteria, even though membership was often defined by territory (all members were, after all, subjects). But how is politics possible when networks, rather than publics of the traditional kinds, are charged with making collectively binding decisions? On whose behalf are these decisions now made when the image of the body politic or even of the social contract no longer inspires our understanding, and when arm-length trisections of the market appear to become the decisive root metaphor? How are responsibilities assigned? How can possible externalities be abated if they can be displaced onto those who are not even part of the transaction or the networks? Who can or will represent those who are not able to participate in these newly created transnational links?

These are indeed troubling questions—and Harvey's chapter in particular drives home the point that they matter as much in local (or "glocal") contexts as they do in global ones. Although the process of judicialization analyzed above by Jacobson might provide a partial answer, it is questionable whether such an expansion of judicial powers will be sustainable in the absence of other elements of political and social solidarity. To that extent, the growth of judicial and administrative structures, even if paternalistically oriented, is hardly an inspiring vision. It may also not be a viable one considering the fragility of legal orders and administrative structures when they are not buttressed by other social forces of identification and solidarity. The focus on identities, borders, and orders should at least have made this clear and should have set an agenda for future inquiries that are neither beholden to the projects of progress and modernity or to that of immutably given organizations like states or communities. The future global order will be of a different kind than either the cosmopolitan visions or the traditional communities that have usually served as our guides for imagining and constructing the cities of man.

Bibliography

Abbott, Andrew. 1995. "Things of Boundaries." *Social Research* 62 (4): 857–67.

Abromeit, Heidrun. 1995. "Volkssouveränität, Parlamentssouveränität, Verfassungssouveränität: Drei Realmodelle der Legitimation staatlichen Handelns." *Politische Vierteljahresschrift* 36 (1): 49–66.

Agnew, John. 1994. "The Territorial Trap: The Geographical Assumptions of International Relations Theory." *Review of International Political Economy* 1 (1): 53–80.

——. 1998. *Geopolitics: Re-Visioning World Politics.* New York: Routledge.

Agnew, John, and Stuart Corbridge. 1995. *Mastering Space: Hegemony, Territory, and International Political Economy.* London: Routledge.

Albert, Mathias. 1997. "Security as Boundary Function: Changing Identities and 'Securitization' in World Politics." *International Journal of Peace Studies* 3 (1): 23–46.

——. 1999a. "On Boundaries, Territory, and Postmodernity: An International Relations Perspective." In Newman 1999c, 53–68.

——. 1999b. "Complex Governance, Morality, and the Evolution of World Society." *Global Society* 13 (1): 77–93.

——. 1999c. "Observing World Politics: Luhmann's Systems Theory of Society and International Relations." *Millennium* 29 (2): 239–65.

Albert, Mathias, and Lothar Brock. 1996. "Debordering the World of States: New Spaces in International Relations." *New Political Science* 35: 69–106.

Alker, Hayward. 1996. Preface and acknowledgment to *Challenging Boundaries*, ed. Michael Shapiro and Hayward Alker, ix–xiii. Minneapolis: University of Minnesota Press.

Anaya, S. James. 1996. *Indigenous Peoples in International Law.* New York: Oxford University Press.

Anderson, Benedict. 1991. *Imagined Communities.* Rev. ed. London: Verso.

———. 1996. Introduction to *Mapping the Nation,* ed. Gopal Balakrishnan, 8–9. London: Verso.

———. 1998. "Nationalism, Identity, and the World-in-Motion: On the Logics of Seriality." In *Cosmopolitics: Thinking and Feeling beyond the Nation,* ed. Pheng Cheah and Bruce Robbins, 117–33. Minneapolis: University of Minnesota Press.

Anderson, Malcolm. 1996. *Frontiers: Territory and State Formation in the Modern World.* Cambridge: Polity Press.

Anderson, Malcolm, et al. 1996. *Policing the European Union.* Oxford: Clarendon.

Anderson, Svein S., and Kjell A. Eliassen, eds. 1996. "Introduction: Dilemmas, Contradictions, and the Future of European Democracy." In *The European Union: How Democratic Is It? London: Sage.*

Apel, Karl-Otto. 1988. *Diskurs und Verantwortung.* Frankfurt: Suhrkamp.

Appadurai, Arjun. 1990. "Disjuncture and Difference in the Global Cultural Economy." *Public Culture* 2 (1): 1–23.

———. 1997. *Modernity at Large.* Minneapolis: University of Minnesota Press.

Arend, Anthony Clark, and Robert J. Beck. 1994. *International Law and the Use of Force.* New York: Routledge.

Armstrong, Kenneth, and Simon Bulmer. 1998. *The Governance of the Single European Market.* Manchester: Manchester University Press.

Aron, Raymond. 1974. "Is Multinational Citizenship Possible?" *Social Research* 41 (4): 638–56.

Assmann, Aleida. 1993. "Zum Problem der Identität aus kulturwissenschaftlicher Sicht." *Leviathan* 21 (2): 238–53.

Bach, Jonathan. 1999. *Between Sovereignty and Integration.* New York: St. Martin's Press.

Badie, Bertrand. 1995. *La fin des territoires: Essai sur le désordre international et l'utilité sociale du respect.* Paris: Fayard.

Badie, Bertrand, and M. C. Smouts. 1996. "L'international sans territoire." *Cultures et Conflits,* no. 21–22 (spring/summer). Paris: L. Harmattan.

Balibar, Etienne. 1998. "The Borders of Europe." In *Cosmopolitics: Thinking and Feeling beyond the Nation,* ed. Pheng Cheah and Bruce Robbins, 216–32. Minneapolis: University of Minnesota Press.

Bancroft, George. 1849. "Letter to Lord Palmerson, Jan. 26, 1849." Reprinted in Sen. Ex. Docs. 38, 36th Congress, 1st Session, 160 (1850).

Barber, Benjamin. 1996. *Jihad vs. McWorld*. New York: Ballantine.

Barkan, E., and M-D. Shelton, eds. 1998. *Borders, Exiles, Diasporas*. Stanford: Stanford University Press.

Barnaby, Frank. 1988. *The Gaia Peace Atlas: Survival into the Third Millennium*. New York: Doubleday.

Barnett, Michael. 1996/97: "Regional Security after the Gulf War." *Political Science Quarterly* 111 (4): 597–618.

Barry, Brian. 1992. "The Quest for Consistency: A Skeptical View." In Barry and Goodin 1992, 279–89.

———. 1995. *Justice as Impartiality*. Oxford: Oxford University Press.

Barry, Brian, and Robert E. Goodin, eds. 1992. *Free Movement*. Hemel Hempstead, England: Harvester Wheatsheaf.

Barth, Fredrik, ed. 1969. *Ethnic Groups and Boundaries*. London: Allen & Unwin.

Bar Yaacov, Nissim. 1961. *Dual Nationality*. New York: Praeger.

Bauman, Zygmunt. 1996. "From Pilgrim to Tourist; or, A Short History of Identity." In *Questions of Cultural Identity*, ed. Stuart Hall and Paul du Gay. London: Sage.

———. 1998. *Globalization: The Human Consequences*. New York: Columbia University Press.

Beck, Ulrich. 1996. *The Reinvention of Politics*. Cambridge: Polity Press.

Bellamy, Richard, and Dario Castiglione, eds. 1996. *Constitutionalism in Transformation: European and Theoretical Perspectives*. Oxford: Blackwell.

Bendix, Reinhard. 1978. *Kings or People*. Berkeley: University of California Press.

Benhabib, Seyla. 1996. *Democracy and Difference: Contesting the Boundaries of the Political*. Princeton: Princeton University Press.

Benjamin, Thomas. 1996. *A Rich Land, A Poor People: Politics and Society in Modern Chiapas*. Albuquerque: University of New Mexico Press.

Benko, G., and U. Strohmayer, eds. 1997. *Space and Social Theory: Interpreting Modernity and Postmodernity*. Oxford: Blackwell.

Berger, Peter L., and Thomas Luckmann. 1967. *The Social Construction of Reality: A Treatise in the Sociology of Knowledge*. New York: Anchor Books.

Berman, Harold J. 1988: "The Law of International Commercial Transactions (Lex Mercatoria)." *Journal of International Dispute Resolution* 2: 235–310.

Berman, M. 1982. *All That Is Solid Melts into Air: The Experience of Modernity*. New York: Simon and Schuster.

Bertrand, Maurice. 1996. *La fin de l'ordre militaire*. Paris: Presses de Sciences Po.

Biersteker, Thomas. 1999. "Eroding Boundaries, Contested Terrain." *International Studies Review* 1 (1): 3–10.

Biersteker, Thomas, and Cynthia Weber, eds. 1996. *State Sovereignty as Social Construct*. Cambridge: Cambridge University Press.

Bigo, Didier. 1995. "Grands débats dans un petit monde." *Cultures et Conflits*, no. 19–20 (fall/winter).

———. 1997. "When Two Become One: Internal and External Securitisations in Europe." In *Institutions of Europe*, ed. Morten Kelstrup and Michael Williams. Copenhagen: University of Copenhagen.

———. 1998a. "L'europe de la sécurité intérieure: penser autrement la sécurité." In *Entre Union et Nations: l'Etat en Europe*, ed. Anne Marie Le Gloannec. Paris: Presses de Sciences Po.

———. 1998b. "Nouveaux regards sur les conflits." In *Perpectives critiques internationales*, ed. M. C. Smouts. Paris: Presses de Sciences Po.

Bigo, Didier, and J-Y. Haine, eds. 1996. *Troubler et inquieter: Les discours du désordre international*. Special issue of *Cultures et Conflits*. Paris: L'Harmattan.

Birkhoff, Juliana, Christopher Mitchell, and Lisa Schirch. 1995. *Annotated Bibliography of Conflict Resolution*. Fairfax, Va.: George Mason University Institute for Conflict Analysis and Resolution.

Blacklock, Cathy, and Laura Macdonald. 1998. "Human Rights and Citizenship in Guatemala and Mexico: From 'Strategic' to 'New' Universalism?" *Social Politics* (summer): 132–57.

Blejwas, Stanislaus A. 1995. "Polonia and Politics." In *Polish Americans and their History*, ed. John J. Bukowczyk. Pittsburgh: University of Pittsburgh Press.

Boggs, S. 1940. *International Boundaries: A Study of Boundary Functions and Problems*. New York: Columbia University Press.

Bohm, David. 1980. *Wholeness and the Implicate Order*. London: Routledge and Kegan Paul.

Boli, John. 1987. "Human Rights or State Expansion?" In *Institutional Structure*, ed. George Thomas et al., 133–49. Beverly Hills: Sage.

Boli, John, and Thomas, George M. 1997. "World Culture and the World Polity: A Century of International Non-Governmental Organization." *American Sociological Review* 62: 171–90.

Bourdieu, Pierre. 1982. *Ce que parler veut dire*. Paris: Fayard.

———. 1986. "Social Space and Symbolic Power." Translation of an article in *Choses dites*. Paris: Edition de Minuit.

———. 1994. *Raisons pratiques: sur la théorie de l'action*. Paris: Seuil.

Boutros-Ghali, Boutros. "Democracy: A Newly Recognized Imperative." *Global Governance* 1 (1995): 3–11.

Bowman, M. J., and David John Harris. 1993. *Multilateral Treaties: Index and Current Status Cumulative Supplement*. London: University of Nottingham Treaty Centre.

Bozeman, Adda B. 1960. *Politics and Culture in International History.* Princeton: Princeton University Press.

Brenner, Neil. 1999. "Beyond State-Centrism? Space, Territoriality, and Geographical Scale in Globalization Studies." *Theory and Society* 28: 47–48.

Brierly, J. L. 1963. *The Law of Nations.* 5th ed. New York: Oxford University Press.

Brock, Lothar. 1994. "Brüche im Umbruch der Weltpolitik." In *Frieden und Konflikt in den Internationalen Beziehungen,* ed. Gert Krell and Harald Müller, 19–37. Frankfurt: Campus Verlag.

Broeder, John M. 1996. "Clinton Seeks $1.1 Billion to Fight Terror." *Los Angeles Times,* 10 September, A1.

Bromberg, Elisabeth. 1996. "European Union Decisionmaking: The Role of Sub-National Authorities." Paper presented at the Political Studies Association Conference, Glasgow, 10–12 April 1996.

Brown, Chris. 1992. *International Relations Theory: New Normative Approaches.* Hemel Hempstead, England: Harvester Wheatsheaf.

———. 1994. "Turtles All the Way Down." *Millenium* 23 (2): 213–36.

Brown Scott, James. 1930. "Nationality: *Jus Soli* or *Jus Sanguinis.*" *American Journal of International Law* 24 (1): 58–64.

———. 1931. *Observations on Nationality.* New York: Oxford University Press.

Brubaker, Rogers. 1992. *Citizenship and Nationhood in France and Germany.* Cambridge: Harvard University Press.

———. 1996. *Nationalism Reframed: Nationhood and the National Question in the New Europe.* Cambridge: Cambridge University Press.

Brunn, Stanley D. 1999. "A Treaty of Silicon for a Treaty of Westphalia? Territorial Dimensions of Modern Statehood." In Newman 1999b, 106–31.

Brunn, Stanley D., et al. 1994. "Ethnic Communities in the Evolving 'Electronic State': Cyberplaces in Cyberspace." In *Political Boundaries and Coexistence,* ed. Werner A. Gallusser, 415–24. Bern: Peter Lang.

Bull, Hedley. 1977. *The Anarchical Society.* London: Macmillan.

Bull, Hedley, and Adam Watson, eds. 1984. *The Expansion of International Society.* Oxford: Clarendon Press.

Bundesverfassungsgericht. 1974. Judgment of 21 May, 1974, 37 (BVerGE 217).

Burton, John W. 1968. *Systems, States, Diplomacy and Rules.* Cambridge: Cambridge University Press.

———. 1972. *World Society.* Cambridge: Cambridge University Press.

———. 1984. *Global Conflict.* Brighton, England: Wheatsheaf Books.

Buzan, Barry. 1991. *People, States, and Fear: An Agenda for International Security Studies in the Post–Cold War Era.* 2d ed. Boulder, Colo.: L. Rienner.

Buzan, Barry, David Held, and Anthony McGrew. 1998. "Realism vs. Cosmopolitanism: A Debate." *Review of International Relations* 24: 387–98.

Campbell, David. 1992. *Writing Security: United States' Foreign Policy and the Politics of Identity.* Minneapolis: University of Minnesota Press.

———. 1998. *Writing Security: United States' Foreign Policy and the Politics of Identity.* Rev. ed. Minneapolis: University of Minnesota Press.

Carens, Joseph. 1992. "Migration and Morality: A Liberal Egalitarian Perspective." In Barry and Goodin 1992, 25–47.

Carville, Earle, Kent Mathewson, and Martin Kenzer, eds. 1996. *Concepts in Human Geography.* Lanham: Rowman & Littlefield.

Castles, Stephen. 1998. "Globalization and Migration: Some Pressing Contradictions." *International Social Science Journal* 156: 179–86.

Catanzaro, Raimondo. 1993. "La régulation sociale par la violence: Le rôle de la criminalité organisée dans l'Italie méridionale." *Cultures et Conflits,* no. 9–10.

Centro de Derechos Humanos Fray Bartolomé de Las Casas. 1996. *Ni Paz ni Justicia, ó Informe general y amplio acerca de la guerra civil que sufren los Choles en la Zona Norte de Chiapas, diciembre de 1994 a octubre de 1996.* San Cristóbal de Las Casas, Chiapas: Centro de Derechos Humanos Fray Bartolomé de Las Casas.

———. 1998. *Camino a La Masacre. Informe Especial Sobre Chenalhó.* San Cristóbal de Las Casas, Chiapas: Centro de Derechos Humanos Fray Bartolomé de Las Casas.

Cerny, Philip. 1999. "Globalizing the Political and Politicizing the Global: Concluding Reflections on International Political Economy as a Vocation." *New Political Economy* 4 (1): 147–63.

Cesari, Jocelyne. 1997. *Faut-il avoir peur de l'islam?* Paris: Presses de Sciences Po.

Ceyhan, Ayse. 1997. "Migrants as a Threat: A Comparative Analysis of Securitarian Rhetoric in France and in the U.S." Paper presented at the Annual Convention of the International Studies Association, Toronto.

Chay, Jongsuk, ed. 1990. *Culture and International Relations.* New York: Praeger.

Cheah, Pheng. 1998. "The Cosmopolitical: Today." In *Cosmopolitics: Thinking and Feeling beyond the Nation,* ed. Pheng Cheah and Bruce Robbins, 20–44. Minneapolis: University of Minnesota Press.

Checkel, Jeffrey T. 1998. "The Constructivist Turn in International Relations Theory." *World Politics* 50: 324–48.

Chia, Robert. 1997. "From Organizational Structures to the Organization of Thought." *Organization Studies* 18 (4): 685–707.

Clarke, Ann Marie, Elisabeth J. Friedman, and Kathryn Hochstetler. 1998. "The Sovereign Limits of Global Civil Society: A Comparison of NGO

Participation at UN World Conferences on the Environment, Human Rights, and Women." *World Politics* 51: 1–35.

Closa, Carlos. 1995. "Citizenship of the Union and Nationality of Member States." *Common Market Law Review* 32: 487–518.

Cohen, Joshua. 1996. "Procedure and Substance in Deliberative Democracy." In *Democracy and Difference,* ed. S. Benhabib, 95–119. Princeton: Princeton University Press.

———. 1997. "Deliberation and Democratic Legitimacy." In *Deliberative Democracy: Essays on Reason and Politics,* ed. James Bohman and William Rehg, 67–91. Cambridge: MIT Press.

Cohen, Joshua, and Charles Sabel. 1997. "Directly-Deliberative Polyarchy." *Law and European Integration* 3 (4): 313–42.

Cohen, Youssef, Brian R. Brown, and A. F. K. Organski. 1981. "The Paradoxical Nature of State Making: The Violent Creation of Order." *American Political Science Review* 75 (4): 901–10.

Conversi, Daniele. 1995. "Reassessing Current Theories of Nationalism: Nationalism as Boundary Maintenance and Creation." *Nationalism and Ethnic Politics* 1 (1): 73–85.

Corrigan, P., and D. Sayer. 1985. *The Great Arch: English State Formation as Cultural Revolution.* Oxford: Basil Blackwell.

Council of Europe. 1963. "Convention on the Reduction of Cases of Multiple Nationality." European Treaty Series, no. 43. Strasbourg: Council of Europe.

———. 1993. "Second Protocol Amending the Convention on the Reduction of Cases of Multiple Nationality and Military Obligations in Cases of Multiple Nationality." European Treaty Series, no. 149. Strasbourg: Council of Europe.

———. 1995. *European Bulletin on Nationality* (DIR/JUR [95]; January). Strasbourg: Council of Europe.

———. 1996. "A Review of the Implementation of Community Relations Policies," by the Migration Policy Group, presented to the 6th Conference of European Ministers Responsible for Migration Affairs, MMG-6 [96] 1E. Brussels: Migration Policy Group.

———. 1997a. "European Convention on Nationality and Explanatory Report (Provisional)" (DIR/JIR [97]; May). Strasbourg: Council of Europe.

———. 1997b. "European Convention on Nationality." European Treaty Series, no. 166. Strasbourg: Council of Europe.

———. 1997c. *European Bulletin on Nationality* (DIR/JIR [97] 4; March). Strasbourg: Council of Europe.

Cowhey, Peter F., and Jonathan D. Aronson. 1993. *Managing the World Economy: The Consequences of Corporate Alliances.* New York: Council on Foreign Relations Press.

Cox, K. R., ed. 1997. *Spaces of Globalization: Reasserting the Power of the Local.* New York: Guilford Press.

Crawford, Neta C. 1994. "A Security Regime among Democracies: Cooperation among Iroquois Nations." *International Organization* 48 (3): 345–85.

Cronin, Bruce, and Samuel Barkin. 1994. "The State and the Nation: Changing Norms and Rules of Sovereignty in International Relations." *International Organization* 48 (1): 107–30.

Dahl, Robert A. 1994. "A Democratic Dilemma: System Effectiveness versus Citizen Participation." *Political Science Quarterly* 109: 23–34.

Dahrendorf, Ralf. 1985. *Law and Order.* Boulder, Colo.: Westview Press.

Dalby, Simon. 1990. *Creating the Second Cold War.* London/New York: Pinter Guilford.

D'Amato, Gianni. 1997. "Gelebte Nation und Einwanderung: Zur Trans-Nationalisierung von Nationalstaaten durch Immigrantenpolitik am Beispiel der Schweiz." In *Transnationale Staatsbuergerschaft,* ed. Heinz Kleger, 132–59. Frankfurt: Campus Verlag.

Dauenhauer, B. P. 1996. *Citizenship in a Fragile World.* Lanham, Md.: Rowman & Littlefield.

Dehousse, Renaud. 1995. "Constitutional Reform in the European Community: Are There Alternatives to the Majoritarian Avenue?" *West European Politics* 18: 118–36.

Della Sala, Vincent. 1999. "Governance of Politics without a Centre." In unpublished manuscript, Carleton University.

Der Derian, James. 1992. *Antidiplomacy: Spies, Speed, Terror, and War.* Oxford: Blackwell.

———. 1997. "Virtual Violence: Mimesis in Theory, Politics and War." Copenhagen. Manuscript.

Derrida, Jacques. 1978a. "Force and Signification." In *Writing and Difference,* trans. Alan Bass, 3–30. Chicago: University of Chicago Press.

———. 1978b. "Structure, Sign, and Play in the Discourse of the Human Sciences." In *Writing and Difference,* trans. Alan Bass, 278–93. Chicago: University of Chicago Press.

———. 1996. "Remarks on Deconstruction and Pragmatism." In *Deconstruction and Pragmatism,* ed. Chantal Mouffe, 77–88. London and New York: Routledge.

———. 1997. *Politics of Friendship.* Trans. George Collins. London: Verso.

Dervin, Brenda. 1993. "Verbing Communication: Mandate for Disciplinary Invention." *Journal of Communication* 43: 45–54.

Dervin, Brenda, and Robert Huesca. 1997. "Reaching for the Communicating in Participatory Communication: A Meta-Theoretical Analysis." *Journal of International Communication* 4 (2): 46–74.

Deudney, Daniel. 1996. "Ground Identity, Nature, Place, and Space in Nationalism." In Lapid and Kratochwil 1996, 129–45.

Deudney, Daniel, and John Ikenberry. 1999. "The Nature and Sources of Liberal International Order." *Review of International Studies* 25: 179–96.

Deutsch, Karl W. 1969. *Nationalism and Its Alternatives*. New York: Random House.

Deutsch, Karl W., et al. 1957. *Political Community and the North Atlantic Area*. Princeton: Princeton University Press.

de Vattel, Emmerich. 1970. "Preface to the Law of Nations." In *The Theory of International Relations*, ed. M. G. Forsyth, H. M. A. Keens-Soper, and P. Savigear, 89–112. New York: Atherton Press.

Devetak, Richard. 1995. "Incomplete States." In *Boundaries in Question: New Directions in International Relations*, ed. J. MacMillan and A. Linklater, 19–31. London: Pinter.

Dezalay, Yves, and Bryant G. Garth. 1996. *Dealing in Virtue: International Commercial Arbitration and the Construction of the Transnational Legal Order*. Chicago: University of Chicago Press.

Dicken, Peter. 1992. *Global Shift: The Internationalization of Economic Activity*. London: Chapman and Hall.

Diez, Thomas. 1996. "Postmoderne und europäische Integration: Die Dominanz des Staatsmodells, die Verantwortung gegenüber dem Anderen und die Konstruktion eines alternativen Horizonts." *Zeitschrift für Internationale Beziehungen* 3: 255–81.

Dillon, Michael. 1997. *Politics of Security: Towards a Political Philosophy of Continental Thought*. London: Routledge.

———. 1999. "Another Justice." *Political Theory* 27 (2): 155–75.

Dillon, Michael, and Julian Reid. 1999. "Metis and the Problematic of Hypersecurity." Paper presented at the ISA meeting, Washington, D.C., February.

Dillon, Sam. 1996. "Mexico Is Near to Granting Expatriates Voting Rights." *New York Times,* 16 June.

do Amaral, Ilidio. 1994. "New Reflections on the Theme of International Boundaries." In *Global Boundaries*, ed. Clive H. Schofield, 16–22. World Boundaries, vol. 1. London: Routledge.

Dogan, Mattei. 1996. "Political Science and Other Social Sciences." In *A New Handbook of Political Science*, ed. Robert Goodin and Hans-Dieter Klingemann, 97–132. New York: Oxford University Press.

Doty, Roxanne Lynn. 1996. "The Logic of Difference in International Relations: U.S. Colonization of the Philippines." In *Post-Realism*, ed. Francis A. Beer and Robert Hariman, 331–46. East Lansing: Michigan State University Press.

Douglas, M. 1986. *How Institutions Think*. Syracuse, N.Y.: Syracuse University Press.

Douglas, Mary. 1993. "Governability: A Question of Culture." *Millennium* 22 (3): 463–81.

Drainville, André. 1995. "Of Social Spaces, Citizenship, and the Nature of Power in the World Economy." *Alternatives* 20 (1): 51–79.

Driver, Felix. 1991. "Political Geography and State Formation: Disputed Territory." *Progress in Human Geography* 15 (3): 268–80.

Duchacek, Ivo D., et al., eds. 1988. *Perforated Sovereignties and International Relations: Trans-Sovereign Contacts of Subnational Governments.* New York: Greenwood Press.

Dummett, Ann. 1992. "The Transnational Migration of People Seen from within a Natural Law Tradition." In Barry and Goodin 1992, 169–80.

Dunn, John. 1979. *Western Political Theory in the Face of the Future.* Cambridge: Cambridge University Press.

Durkheim, Emile. 1984. *The Division of Labor in Society,* trans. W. D. Halls. New York: Free Press.

Dyer, Hugh. 1993. "Eco-Cultures: Global Culture in the Age of Ecology." *Millennium* 22 (3): 483–504.

Easton, D. 1971. *The Political System: An Inquiry into the State of Political Science.* 2d ed. New York: Alfred A. Knopf.

Edelman, Murray Jacob. 1991. *Pièces et règles du jeu politique.* Paris: Seuil.

Eisenstadt, Shmuel. 1998. "Modernity and the Construction of Collective Identities." *International Journal of Comparative Studies* 39 (1): 138–58.

Elfstrom, G. 1990. *Ethics for a Shrinking World.* New York: St. Martin's Press.

Eliot, N., and D. Newman, eds. 2000. *Geopolitics at the End of the Twentieth Century: The Changing World Political Map.* London: Frank Cass.

Elkins, David J. 1995. *Beyond Sovereignty: Territory and Political Economy in the Twenty-First Century.* Toronto: University of Toronto Press.

Elshtain, J. B. 1995. *Democracy on Trial.* New York: Basic Books.

Emirbayer, Mustafa. 1997. "Manifesto for a Relational Sociology." *American Journal of Sociology* 103 (2): 281–317.

Ertman, Thomas. 1997. *Birth of the Leviathan: Building States and Regimes in Medieval and Early Modern Europe.* Cambridge: Cambridge University Press.

Estel, Bernd, and Tilman Mayer, eds. 1994. *Das Prinzip Nation in modernen Gesellschaften.* Opladen: Westdeutscher Verlag.

Etzioni, Amitai. 1993. *The Spirit of Community.* New York: Touchstone.

Eurobarometer. 1989. Special Issue on Racism and Xenophobia. Brussels: Commission of the European Communities.

Everson, Michelle. 1998. "Administering Europe?" *Journal of Common Market Studies* 36: 195–74.

Ewald, François. 1996. *Histoire de l'État providence.* Paris: Livre de poche.

Ewing, Katherine Pratt. 1998. "Crossing Borders and Transgressing Boundaries: Metaphors for Negotiating Multiple Identities." *Ethos* 26: 262–67.

EZLN (Ejército Zapatista de Liberación Nacional). 1995. *Documentos y comunicados.* Vol. 2. Mexico City: Era.

Fairbank, John K., ed. 1968. *The Chinese World Order.* Cambridge: Harvard University Press.

Faist, T. 1997. "International Migration and Transnational Social Spaces: The Bridging Functions of Social Capital." Unpublished, Universität Bremen.

Falah, Ghazi, and David Newman. 1995. "The Spatial Manifestation of Threat: Israelis and Palestinians Seek a 'Good' Border." *Political Geography* 14 (8): 189–206.

Falk, Richard. 1990. "Culture, Modernism, Postmodernism: A Challenge to International Relations." In *Culture and International Relations,* ed. Jongsuk Chay. New York: Praeger.

Feldblum, Miriam. 1998. "Reconfiguring Citizenship in Western Europe." In *Challenge to the Nation-State: Immigration in Western Europe and the United States,* ed. Christian Joppke, 231–70. Oxford: Oxford University Press.

Ferguson, Yale H., and Richard W. Mansbach. 1989. *The State, Conceptual Chaos, and the Future of International Relations Theory.* Boulder, Colo.: Lynne Rienner.

————. 1996a. *Polities: Authority, Identities and Change.* Columbia: University of South Carolina Press.

————. 1996b. "Political Space and Westphalian States in a World of Polities." *Global Governance* 2: 261–87.

————. 1996c. "The Past as Prelude to the Future? Identities and Loyalties in Global Politics." In Lapid and Kratochwil 1996, 21–46.

Fialkowski, Jürgen, Hans Merkens, and Folker Schmidt, eds. 1991. *Dominant National Cultures and Ethnic Identities.* 2 vol. Berlin: Free University of Berlin.

Fijnaut, C. J., and R. H. Hermans. 1987. *Police Co-operation in Europe.* Lochem: Van Den Brick.

Fineman, Mark. 1997. "West Indies Islands put Citizenship up for Sale." *Los Angeles Times,* November 28.

Flournoy, Jr., Richard W., and Manley O. Hudson, eds. 1929. *A Collection of Nationality Laws of Various Countries as Contained in Constitutions, Statutes, and Treaties.* New York: Oxford University Press.

Forsberg, Tuomas, ed. 1995. *Contested Territory: Border Disputes at the Edge of the Former Soviet Empire.* Aldershot: Edward Elgar.

Forsyth, M. G., H. M. A. Keens-Soper, and P. Savigear, eds. 1970. *The Theory of International Relations: Selected Texts from Gentili to Treitachke.* New York: Atherton.

Foucault, Michel. 1989. "Sécurité, territoire, et population." In *Résumé des cours, 1970–1982.* Paris: Julliard.

———. 1994. *Dits et écrits.* Paris: Gallimard.

———. 1997. *Il faut défendre la société.* Paris: Seuil Gallimard.

Franck, Thomas M. 1996. "Clan and Superclan: Loyalty, Identity, and Community in Law and Practice." *American Journal of International Law* 90 (3): 359–83.

Frankfurter, Felix. 1958. Majority opinion. *Perez v. Brownell,* 356 U.S. at 50.

Friedman, Lawrence. 1994. *Total Justice.* New York: Russell Sage.

Fukuyama, Francis. 1992. *The End of History and the Last Man.* New York: Free Press.

———. 1999. "The Great Disruption: Human Nature and the Reconstitution of Social Orders." *Atlantic Monthly* (May): 55–80.

Fuller, Graham. 1997. "Redrawing the World's Borders." *World Policy Journal* (spring): 11–21.

Galtung, Johan. 1994. "Coexistence in Spite of Borders: On the Borders in the Mind." In *Political Boundaries and Coexistence,* ed. Werner A. Gallusser, 5–14. Bern: Peter Lang.

García de León, Antonio. 1994. "Prológo." In *EZLN: Documentos y Comunicados,* 11–29. Vol. I. Mexico City: Era.

Geertz, Clifford. 1973. *The Interpretation of Cultures.* New York: Basic Books.

Gerring, John. 1999. "What Makes a Good Concept?" *Polity* 31 (3): 357–93.

Giddens, Anthony. 1985. *The Nation State and Violence.* Cambridge: Polity Press.

Gill, Stephen. 1995. "The Global Panopticon? The Neoliberal State, Economic Life, and Democratic Surveillance." *Alternatives* 20 (2): 1–49.

Gilly, Adolfo, Subcomandante Marcos, and Carlo Ginzburg. 1995. *Discusión Sobre La Historia.* Mexico City: Taurus.

Glazer, N. 1997. *We Are All Multiculturalists Now.* Cambridge: Harvard University Press.

Goertz, Gary, and Paul F. Diehl. 1992. *Territorial Changes and International Conflict.* London: Routledge.

Goffman, Erving. 1971. *Relations in Public: Microstudies of the Public Order.* New York: Basic Books.

Goldstein, Eugene, and Victoria Piazza. 1996. "Naturalization, Dual Citizenship, and the Retention of Foreign Citizenship: A Survey." *Interpreter Releases* 73 (16): 517–21.

Goodin, Robert. 1996. "Inclusion and Exclusion." *Archives of European Sociology* 37 (2): 334–371.

Goodwin-White, Jamie. 1998. "Where the Maps Are Not Yet Finished." In *The Immigration Reader,* ed. David Jacobson. Oxford: Blackwell.

Gosner, Kevin. 1992. *Soldiers of the Virgin: The Moral Economy of a Colonial Maya Rebellion*. Tucson and London: University of Arizona Press.

Gottlieb, Gidon. 1993. *Nation against State: A New Approach to Ethnic Conflicts and the Decline of Sovereignty*. New York: Council on Foreign Relations Press.

Grande, Edgar. 1996. "Demokratische Legitimation und europäische Integration." *Leviathan* 3: 339–59.

Green, Philip, ed. 1993. "'Democracy' as a Tested Idea." In *Democracy*, 2–18. Atlantic Highlands, N.J.: Humanities Press.

Grimm, Dieter. 1995. "Does Europe Need a Constitution?" *European Law Journal*, 1 (3): 282–302.

Grotius, Hugo. 1957. *Prolegomena to the Law of War and Peace*. New York: Bobbs-Merrill.

Guéhenno, Jean-Marie. 1995. *The End of the Nation-State*. Minneapolis: University of Minnesota Press.

Guetzkow, Harold. 1955. *Multiple Loyalties: Theoretical Approach to a Problem in International Organization*. Princeton, N.J.: Center for Research on World Political Institutions.

Gusterson, Hugh. 1993. "Realism and the International Order." *Social Research* 60 (2): 279–300.

Gutmann, A., ed. 1994. *Multiculturalism*. 2d ed. Princeton: Princeton University Press.

Haas, Ernst B. 1993. "Nationalism: An Instrumental Social Construction." *Millennium* 22 (3): 505–45.

Habermas, Jürgen. 1992a. "Citizenship and National Identity." *Praxis International* 12 (1).

———. 1992b. *Faktizität und Geltung*. Frankfurt: Suhrkamp.

———. 1992c. "Staatsbürgerschaft und nationale Identität." In *Faktizität und Geltung*, 632–660. Frankfurt: Suhrkamp.

Hall, Rodney B. 1999. *National Collective Identity: Social Constructs and International Systems*. New York: Columbia University Press.

Halliday, Fred. 1995. "International Relations and Its Discontents," *International Affairs* 71 (4): 733–46.

Hammar, Tomas. 1985. "Dual Citizenship and Political Integration." *International Migration Review* 19 (3): 438–50.

———. 1990. *Democracy and the Nation-State: Aliens, Denizens, and Citizens in a World of International Migration*. Aldershot, England: Avebury.

Handlin, Lilian. 1984. *George Bancroft: The Intellectual as Democrat*. New York: Harper & Row.

Hartshorne, Richard. 1936. "Suggestions on the Terminology of Political Boundaries." *Annals of the Association of American Geographers* 26 (1): 56–57.

Harvard Law School. 1929. "Nationality, Responsibility of States, and Territorial Waters, Drafts of Conventions Prepared in Anticipation of the First Conference on Codification of International Law, The Hague, 1930," *American Journal of International Law* 23 (supplement).

Harvey, David. 1989. *The Condition of Postmodernity: An Enquiry into the Origins of Cultural Change.* Oxford and Cambridge, Mass.: Blackwell.

———. 1996. *Justice, Nature, and the Geography of Difference.* Oxford and Cambridge, Mass.: Blackwell.

Harvey, Neil. 1998a. *The Chiapas Rebellion: The Struggle for Land and Democracy.* Durham, N.C.: Duke University Press.

———. 1998b. "Rural Reforms and the Question of Autonomy in Chiapas." In *The Transformation of Rural Mexico: Reforming the Ejido Sector,* ed. Wayne A. Cornelius and David Myhre, 69–89. San Diego: Center for U.S.-Mexican Studies, University of California.

———. 1999. "Between Hope and Frustration: The Peace Process in Chiapas." In *Comparative Peace Processes in Latin America,* ed. Cynthia Arnson, 129–52. Stanford: Stanford University Press and Woodrow Wilson Center Press.

Hatton, T. J., and J. G. Williamson. 1998. *The Age of Mass Migration: Causes and Economic Impact.* New York: Oxford University Press.

Haushofer, Karl. 1939. *Grenzen in ihrer geographischen und politischen Bedeutung.* Berlin: K. Vowinckel.

Hegel, G. W. F. 1956. *The Philosophy of History.* New York: Dover Press.

———. 1991. *Elements of the Philosophy of Right.* Cambridge: Cambridge University Press.

Heilbronner, Kai. 1992. *Einbürgerung von Wanderarbeitnehmern und doppelte Staatsangehörigkeit.* Baden-Baden: Nomos.

Heisler, B. S. 1985. "Sending Countries and the Politics of Emigration and Destination." *International Migration Review* 19 (3): 469–84.

———. 1986. "Immigrant Settlement and the Structure of Emergent Immigrant Communities in Western Europe." *Annals of the American Academy of Political and Social Science* 485 (May): 76–86.

———. 1992. "The Future of Immigrant Incorporation: Which Models? Which Concepts?" *International Migration Review* 26 (2): 623–45.

Heisler, B. S., and M. O. Heisler. 1986. "Transnational Migration and the Modern Democratic State: Familiar Problems in New Form or a New Problem?" *Annals of the American Academy of Political and Social Science* 485 (May): 12–22.

Heisler, M. O. 1986. "Transnational Migration as a Small Window on the Diminished Autonomy of the Modern Democratic State." *Annals of the American Academy of Political and Social Science* 485 (May): 153–66.

———. 1990. "Ethnicity and Ethnic Relations in the Modern West." In *Conflict and Peacemaking in Multiethnic Societies,* ed. J. V. Montville, 21–52. Lexington, Mass.: Lexington Books/D. C. Heath.

———. 1992. "Migration, International Relations, and the New Europe: Theoretical Perspectives from Institutional Political Sociology," *International Migration Review* 26 (2): 596–622.

———. 1994. "Some Normative Caveats in the Pursuit of the Rights of Ethnic Minorities," *Journal of Ethno-Development* 4 (1): 79–82.

———. 1996. "The Transnational Nexus of Security and Migration." Paper presented at the International Political Science Association.

———. 1998: "Cross-Boundary Population Movements and Security in Korea: Gradual Rapprochement and Other Scenarios." In *Environmental Security in Northeast Asia,* ed. M. Schreurs and D. Pirages. Seoul: Yonsei University Press.

———. 1998/99. "Contextualizing Global Migration: Sketching the Socio-Political Landscape in Europe." *UCLA Journal of International Law and Foreign Affairs* 3 (2): 557–593.

Heisler, M. O., and B. S. Heisler. 1991. "Citizenship—Old, New, and Changing: Inclusion, Exclusion, and Limbo for Ethnic Groups and Migrants in the Modern Democratic State." In *Dominant National Cultures and Ethnic Identities,* ed. J. Fijalkowski et al. Berlin: Free University of Berlin.

Heisler, M. O., and Z. Layton-Henry. 1993. "Migration and the Link between Social and Societal Security." In *Identity, Migration, and the New Security Agenda in Europe,* ed. Ole Wæver et al., chap. 8. London: Frances Pinter.

Heisler, M. O., and B. G. Peters. 1977. "Toward a Multidimensional Framework for the Analysis of Social Policy." *Annals of the American Academy of Political and Social Science* 434 (November): 58–70.

Heisler, M. O., and S. D. VanDeveer. 1997. "The Diffusion of Virtue? International Institutions as Agents of Domestic Regime Change." Paper presented at the annual meeting of the Northeast Political Science Association, Philadelphia, November.

Held, David. 1992. "Democracy: From City-States to a Cosmopolitan Order?" *Political Studies* 40: 10–39.

———. 1997. "Democracy and Globalization." *Global Governance* 3: 251–67.

Hernández, Luis. 1997. "Entre la memoria y el olvido: guerrillas, movimiento indígena y reformas legales en la hora del EZLN." *Chiapas* 4: 69–92.

Herzog, Lawrence A., ed. 1992. "Changing Boundaries in the Americas. An Overview." In *Changing Boundaries in the Americas,* 3–24. San Diego: University of California, San Diego, Center for U.S.-Mexican Studies.

Hey, Colin, and David Marsh. 1999. "Introduction: Toward a New (International) Political Economy?" *New Political Economy* 4 (1): 5–23.

Hinsley, F. H. 1986. *Sovereignty*. 2d ed. New York: Cambridge University Press.

Hirst, Paul, and Grahame Thompson. 1992. "The Problem of 'Globalization': International Economic Relations, National Economic Management, and the Formation of Trading Blocs." *Economy and Society* 21 (4): 357–96.

———. 1999. *Globalization in Question: The International Economy and the Possibilities of Governance*. 2d ed. Malden, Mass.: Polity Press.

Hix, Simon. 2000. "Executive Selection in the EU: Does the Commission President Investiture Procedure Reduce the Democratic Deficit?" In *European Integration after Amsterdam: Institutional Dynamics and Prospects for Democracy*, ed. Karlheinz Neunreiter and Antje Wiener, 95–111. Oxford: Oxford University Press.

Hobbes, Thomas. 1962. *Leviathan*. New York: Collier.

———. 1968. *Leviathan*, ed. C. B. McPherson. Harmondsworth, England: Penguin.

Hobsbawm, Eric J. 1990. *Nations and Nationalism since 1780: Programme, Myth, Reality*. Cambridge: Cambridge University Press.

Hoffmann, Stanley. 1992. "Delusions of World Order." *New York Review of Books* (9 April): 37.

Holm, Hans-Henrik, and George Sørensen, eds. 1995a. *Whose World Order: Uneven Globalization and the End of the Cold War*. Boulder, Colo.: Westview.

Holm, Hans-Henrik, and George Sørensen. 1995b. "Introduction: What Has Changed?" In Holm and Sørensen 1995a, 1–18.

Hopf, Ted. 1998. "The Promise of Constructivism in International Relations Theory." *International Security* 23 (1): 171–200.

Hoskin, M. 1991. *New Immigrants and Democratic Society: Minority Integration in Western Democracies*. New York: Praeger.

House, John W. 1980. "The Frontier Zone: A Conceptual Problem for Policy Makers." *International Political Science Review* 1 (4): 456–77.

———. 1981. "Frontier Studies: An Applied Approach." In *Political Studies from Spatial Perspectives*, ed. Alan D. Burnett and Peter J. Taylor, 291–312. New York: John Wiley.

Huntington, Samuel P. 1996. *The Clash of Civilizations and the Remaking of World Order*. New York: Simon and Schuster.

Hurrell, Andrew, and Ngaire Woods. 1995. "Globalisation and Inequality." *Millennium* 24 (3): 447–70.

Huth, Paul. 1997. *Standing Your Ground: Territorial Disputes and International Conflict*. East Lansing: Michigan State University Press.

Huysmans, Jeff. 1996. *Making Unmaking the European Disorder.* Master's thesis, University of Leuven.

Ikenberry, John. 1998. "Constitutional Politics in International Relations." *European Journal of International Relations* 4 (2): 147–77.

Inayatullah, Naeem. 1996. "Beyond the Sovereignty Dilemma: Quasi-States as Social Construct." In *State Sovereignty as Social Construct,* ed. Thomas J. Biersteker and Cynthia Weber, 50–80. Cambridge: Cambridge University Press.

Inglehart, R. 1997. *Modernization and Postmodernization: Cultural, Economic, and Political Change in 43 Societies.* Princeton, N.J.: Princeton University Press.

International Law Commission. 1954. *International Law Commission Yearbook 1954* II, sec. 42, 48.

Jachtenfuchs, Markus. 1995. "Theoretical Perspectives on European Governance." *European Law Journal* 1 (2): 115–33.

Jackson, Patrick. 1999. " 'Civilization' on Trial." *Millenium* 28 (1): 141–54.

Jackson, Patrick, and Daniel H. Nexon. 1999. "Relations before States: Substance, Process, and the Study of World Politics." *European Journal of International Relations* 5 (3): 291–332.

Jackson, Robert H. 1990. *Quasi-States: Sovereignty, International Relations, and the Third World.* Cambridge: Cambridge University Press.

———. 1995. "International Community beyond the Cold War." In *Beyond Westphalia? State Sovereignty and International Intervention,* ed. G. M. Lyons and M. Mastanduno. Baltimore: Johns Hopkins University Press.

Jackson, Robert H., and Carl G. Rosberg. 1982. "Why Africa's Weak States Persist: The Empirical and the Juridical in Statehood." *World Politics* (October): 1–24.

Jacobson, David. 1996. *Rights across Borders: Immigration and the Decline of Citizenship.* Baltimore: Johns Hopkins University Press.

———. 1997. "New Frontiers: Territory, Social Spaces, and the State." *Sociological Forum* 12: 121–34.

Jacquin, Dominique, et al. 1993. "Culture in International Relations: An Introduction to the Special Issue." *Millennium* 22 (3): 375–77.

Jepperson, Ron, et al. 1996. "Norms, Identity, and Culture in National Security." In *The Culture of National Security,* ed. Peter Katzenstein, 32–75. New York: Columbia University Press.

Joerges, Christian, and Juergen Neyer. 1997. "From Intergovernmental Bargaining to Deliberative Political Processes: The Constitutionalisation of Comitology." *European Law Journal* 3: 273–99.

Johnston, Ronald J. 1995. "Territoriality and the State." In *Geography, History, and Social Sciences,* ed. George B. Benko and Ulf Strohmayer, 213–25. Dordrecht: Kluwer.

Jones, Steven B. 1943. "The Description of International Boundaries." *Annals of the Association of American Geographers* 33: 99–117.

———. 1959. "Boundary Concepts in Setting Time and Space." *Annals of the Association of American Geographers* 49 (3): 241–55.

Jordan, Amos A., and Jane Khanna. 1995. "Economic Emergence of Natural Economic Territories in the Asia-Pacific." *Journal of International Affairs* 48 (2): 433–62.

Juss, S. 1998/99. "Sovereignty, Culture, and Community: Refugee Policy and Human Rights in Europe." *UCLA Journal of International Law and Foreign Affairs* 3 (2): 463–95.

Kaldor, Mary, and Ivan Vejvoda. 1997. "Democratization in Central and East European Countries." *International Affairs* 73: 59–82.

Kane, Hal. 1995. "Wars Reach a Plateau." In *Vital Signs,* ed. Linda Starke, 110–65. New York: Norton.

Kaplan, Robert D. 1994. "The Coming Anarchy." *Atlantic Monthly* 275: 44–76.

Kapstein, Ethan B. 1993. "Territoriality and Who Is 'US'?" *International Organization* 47 (3): 501–3.

Katzenstein, Peter J. 1989. "International Relations Theory and the Analysis of Change." In *Global Changes and Theoretical Challenges,* ed. Ernst-Otto Czempiel and James Rosenau, 291–304. Lexington, Mass.: Lexington Books.

———. 1994. *Coping with Terrorism: Norms and Internal Security in Germany and Japan.* Ithaca, N.Y.: Cornell University Press.

Kaufman, Stuart. 1997. "The Fragmentation and Consolidation of International Systems." *International Organization* 51 (2): 173–208.

Kearney, M. 1995. "The Local and the Global: The Anthropology of Globalization and Transnationalism." *Annual Review of Anthropology* 24: 547–65.

Kelsen, Hans. 1945. *General Theory of Law and State.* Cambridge: Harvard University Press.

Kennan, George F. 1985/86. "Morality and Foreign Policy." *Foreign Affairs* (winter): 205–18.

Keohane, Robert O. 1995. "Hobbes' Dilemma and Institutional Change in World Politics, Sovereignty, and International Society." In Holm and Sørensen 1995a, 165–86.

Keohane, Robert O., and Joseph S. Nye. 1977. *Power and Interdependence.* Boston: Little & Brown.

Kern, S. 1983. *The Culture of Time and Space, 1880–1918.* Cambridge: Harvard University Press.

Kifner, John. 1995. "Bombing Suspect: Portrait of a Man's Frayed Life." *San Francisco Examiner* (31 December), A4.

Klare, Michael T., and Peter Kornbluh, eds. 1988. *Low Intensity Warfare: Counterinsurgency, Proinsurgency, and Antiterrorism in the Eighties.* New York: Pantheon.

Klotz, Audie. 1995. "Norms Reconstituting Interests: Global Racial Equality and U.S. Sanctions against South Africa." *International Organization* 49: 451–78.

Knight, David. 1982. "Identity and Territory: Geographic Perspectives on Nationalism and Regionalism." *Annals of the Association of American Geographers* 72 (4): 514–31.

———. 1994. "People Together, Yet Apart: Rethinking Territory, Sovereignty, and Identity." In *Reordering the World: Geopolitical Perspectives on the Twenty-First Century,* ed. George J. Demko and William B. Wood, 71–86. Boulder, Colo.: Westview Press.

Kolossov, Vladimir A. 1992. "Ethno-Territorial Conflicts and Boundaries in the Former Soviet Union." Boundary and Territory Briefing, no. 2. Durham, N.C.: International Boundaries Research Unit.

Koslowski, Rey. 1994. "Intra-EU Migration, Citizenship, and Political Union." *Journal of Common Market Studies* 32 (3): 369–402.

———. 1996. "Migration, the Globalization of Domestic Politics, and International Relations Theory." Paper presented at the Annual Convention of the International Studies Association, San Diego, 17–22 March 1996.

———. 1997. "Migration and the Demographic Context of European Political Institutions." In *Immigration into Western Societies: Problems and Policies,* ed. Emek Ucarer and Donald J. Puchala, 70–94. London: Pinter Press.

Koslowski, Rey, and Friedrich Kratochwil. 1994. "Understanding Change in International Politics: The Soviet Empire's Demise and the International System." *International Organization* 48: 215–47.

Krasner, Stephen. 1993. "Westphalia and All That." In *Ideas and Foreign Policy: Beliefs, Institutions, and Political Change,* ed. J. Goldstein and R. O. Keohane. Ithaca, N.Y.: Cornell University Press.

———. 1994. "International Political Economy: Abiding Discord." *Review of International Political Economy* 1 (1): 13–19.

———. 1995. "Compromising Westphalia." *International Security* 20 (3): 115–51.

Kratochwil, Friedrich. 1986. "Of Systems, Boundaries, and Territoriality: An Inquiry into the Formation of the State System." *World Politics* 39 (1): 27–52.

———. 1989. *Rules, Norms, and Decisions: On the Conditions of Practical and Legal Reasoning in International Relations and Domestic Affairs.* Cambridge: Cambridge University Press.

———. 1996a. "Citizenship: On the Border or Order." In Lapid and Kratochwil 1996, 181–200.

———. 1996b. "Is the Ship of Culture Returning or at Sea?" In Lapid and Kratochwil 1996, 201–22.

Kratochwil, Friedrich, and Edward D. Mansfield, eds. 1994. *International Organization: A Reader.* New York: Harper Collins.

Krause, Jill, and Renwick, Neil. 1996. *Identities in International Relations.* Oxford: St. Anthony's College.

Krause, K., and M. C. Williams. 1996. "Broadening the Agenda of Security Studies: Politics and Methods." *Mershon International Studies Review* 40, suppl. 2 (October): 229–54.

Kugler, Richard. 1995. *Toward a Dangerous World.* Santa Monica, Calif.: RAND.

Kymlicka, Will. 1995. *Multicultural Citizenship.* Oxford: Oxford University Press.

Laclau, Ernesto. 1990. *New Reflections on the Revolution of Our Time.* London: Verso.

———. 1995. "Subject of Politics, Politics of the Subject." *Differences* 7 (1): 146–64.

———. 1996. "Deconstruction, Pragmatism, Hegemony." In *Deconstruction and Pragmatism,* ed. Chantal Mouffe, 47–67. London: Routledge.

Laclau, Ernesto, and Chantal Mouffe. 1985. *Hegemony and Socialist Strategy: Towards a Radical Democratic Politics.* London: Verso.

———. 1987. "Post-Marxism without Apologies." *New Left Review* 166 (November/December): 71–106.

Ladeur, Karl-Heinz. 1997. "Towards a Legal Theory of Supranationality: The Viability of the Network Concept." *European Law Journal* 3: 33–54.

Laffan, Brigid. 1996. "The Politics of Identity and Political Order in Europe." *Journal of Common Market Studies* 34 (1): 81–102.

Lapid, Y. 1989. "The Third Debate: On the Prospects of International Theory in a Post-Positivist Era." *International Studies Quarterly* 33 (3): 235–54.

Lapid, Yosef. 1996. "Culture's Ship: Returns and Departures in International Relations Theory." In Lapid and Kratochwil 1996, 3–20.

Lapid, Yosef, and Friedrich Kratochwil, eds. 1996. *The Return of Culture and Identity in IR Theory.* Boulder, Colo.: Lynne Rienner.

Lazarsfeld, P., F. B. Brelson, and H. Guadet. 1944. *The People's Choice: How the Voter Makes Up His Mind in a Presidential Campaign.* New York: Columbia University Press.

Leach, William. 1999. *Country of Exiles.* New York: Pantheon Books.

League of Nations. 1930a. "Military Obligations in Certain Cases of Double Nationality." 178 *League of Nations Treaty Series* 227.

———. 1930b. "Special Protocol Concerning Statelessness." *U.K. Treaty Series* 112.

———. 1930c. "Certain Case of Statelessness." 179 *League of Nations Treaty Series* 116.

———. 1930d. "Hague Convention on Certain Questions Relating to the Conflict of Nationality Laws." 179 *League of Nations Treaty Series* 89.

Lebow, Richard Ned. 1997. "Transitions and Transformations: Building International Cooperation." *Security Studies* 6 (3): 154–79.

Leftwich, Adrian, ed. 1984. *What is Politics?* New York: Blackwell.

Levine, Donald. 1996. "Sociology and the Nation-State in an Era of Shifting Boundaries." *Sociological Inquiry* 66: 252–66.

Linklater, Andrew. 1992. "The Question of the Next Stage: A Critical-Theoretical Point of View." *Millennium* 21: 77–98.

———. 1998. *The Transformation of Political Community.* Cambridge: Polity Press.

Lipschutz, Ronnie D. 1995. "On Security." In *On Security,* ed. Ronnie D. Lipschutz, 1–23. New York: Columbia University Press.

———. 1998. "From 'Culture Wars' to Shooting Wars: Cultural Conflict in the United States." In *The Myth of "Ethnic Conflict,"* ed. Beverly Crawford and Ronnie D. Lipschutz, 394–433. Berkeley: University of California at Berkeley, Institute of Area Studies Press.

———. 1999a. "Members Only? Citizenship in a Time of Globalization." *International Politics* 36 (2): 203–33.

———. 1999b. "Terror in the Suites: National Security and the Political Economies of Fear." *Global Society* (October).

———. 1999c. "Deep Impacts? or Metaphors and Rhetorics of Doom in Global Politics." Paper prepared for Symposium on Metaphors and Politics, 22d annual meeting of the International Society for Political Psychology, 18–21 July, Amsterdam.

———. 2000a. *After Authority: War, Peace, and Global Politics in the 21st Century.* Albany: State University of New York Press.

———. 2000b. "The State as Moral Authority in an Evolving Global Political Economy." In *The Art of the Feud: Reconceptualizing International Relations,* ed. Jose V. Ciprut. Westport, Conn.: Praeger.

Lizarraga Chavez, Pablo. 1997. "Creating a United States-Mexico Political Double Helix: The Mexican Government's Proposed Dual Nationality Amendment." *Stanford Journal of International Law* 33: 119–51.

López Astrain, Martha Patricia. 1996. *La Guerra de Baja Intensidad en México.* Mexico City: Universidad Iberoamericana and Plaza y Valdés Editores.

Luhmann, Niklas. 1972. *A Sociological Theory of Law.* Boston: Routledge and Kegan Paul.

———. 1994. *Social Systems*. Stanford, Calif.: Stanford University Press.

———. 1997. *Die Gesellschaft der Gesellschaft*. 2 vols. Frankfurt: Suhrkamp.

Lyotard, Jean-François. 1984. *The Postmodern Condition: A Report on Knowledge*. Manchester: Manchester University Press.

Macdonald, Laura. 1994. "Globalising Civil Society: Interpreting International NGOs in Central America." *Millennium* 23: 267–85.

MacMillan, J., and A. Linklater, eds. 1995. *Boundaries in Question: New Directions in International Relations*. London: Pinter.

Majone, Giandomenico. 1994. "The Rise of the Regulatory State in Europe." *West European Politics* 17: 77–101.

———. 1997. "From the Positive to the Regulatory State: Causes and Consequences of Changes in the Mode of Governance." *Journal of Public Policy* 17: 139–67.

Makinda, Samuel. 1998. "The United Nations and State Sovereignty: Mechanism for Managing International Security." *Australian Journal of Political Science* 33 (1): 101–15.

Malkki, Liisa. 1995. "Refugees and Exile: From 'Refugee Studies' to the National Order of Things." *Annual Review of Anthropology* 24: 495–523.

Mann, Michael. 1986. *The Sources of Social Power*. 2 vols. Cambridge: Cambridge University Press.

Mansbach, Richard, and Frank Wilmer. 1998. "War and the Westphalian State of Mind." Paper presented to the ISA, Minneapolis.

Mansfield, Edward, and Jack Snyder. 1995. "Democratization and War." *Foreign Affairs* 74 (4): 79–97.

March, James, and Johan Olsen. 1998. "The Institutional Dynamics of International Political Orders." *International Organization* 52 (4): 943–69.

Margolis, Joseph. 1999. *What, after All, Is a Work of Art?* University Park: Pennsylvania State University.

Marshall, T. H. 1964. "Citizenship and Social Class." In *Class, Citizenship, and Social Development: Essays by T. H. Marshall*. Chicago: University of Chicago Press, 71–134.

Martinez, Oscar J. 1994. "The Dynamics of Border Interaction: New Approaches to Border Analysis." In *Global Boundaries*, ed. Clive H. Schofield, 1–15. World Boundaries, vol. 1. London: Routledge.

Marx, Gary. 1988. "La société de sécurité maximale." *Déviance et société*, no. 2.

Massey, D., et al. 1987. *Return to Aztlan: The Social Process of International Migration from Western Mexico*. Berkeley and Los Angeles: University of California Press.

Mayall, James. 1990. *Nationalism and International Society*. Cambridge: Cambridge University Press.

Mazey, Sonia, and Jeremy J. Richardson, eds. 1993. *Lobbying in the European Community*. Oxford: Oxford University Press.

McKinley, James C., Jr. 1996. "African Firestorm." *New York Times* (28 October), A6.

McLennan, Gregor. 1995. *Pluralism*. Minneapolis: University of Minnesota Press.

McSweeney, Bill. 1996. "Identity and Security: Buzan and the Copenhagen School." *Review of International Studies* 22 (1): 81–94.

Mead, Walter Russell. 1995/96. "Trains, Planes, and Automobiles: The End of the Postmodern Moment." *World Policy Journal* 12 (4): 13–31.

Menschenrechte, Forschungsgruppe. 1998. "Internationale Menschenrechtsnormen, transnationale Netzwerke und politischer Wandel in den Ländern des Südens." *Zeitschrift für Internationale Beziehungen* 5: 5–42.

Meyer, David S. 1990. *A Winter of Discontent: The Nuclear Freeze and American Politics*. New York: Praeger.

Meyer, John, John Boli, and George Thomas Francisco Ramirez. 1997. "World Society and the Nation-State." *American Journal of Sociology* 103: 144–81.

Miller, David. 1995. *On Nationality*. Oxford: Oxford University Press.

Miller, M. J. 1986. "Policy Ad-Hocracy: The Paucity of Coordinated Perspectives and Policies." *Annals of the American Academy of Political and Social Science* 485 (May): 64–75.

Miller, Mark J. 1989. "Dual Citizenship: A European Norm?" *International Migration Review* 23 (4): 945–50.

Minghi, Julian V. 1963. "Boundary Studies in Political Geography." *Annals of the Association of American Geographers* 53 (3): 407–28.

———. 1991. "From Conflict to Harmony in Border Landscapes." In *The Geography of Border Landscapes,* ed. Dennis Rumley and Julian V. Minghi, 15–30. London: Routledge.

———. 1994. "European Borderlands: International Harmony, Landscape Change, and New Conflict." In *Eurasia,* ed. Carl Grundy-Warr, 89–100. World Boundaries, vol. 3. London: Routledge.

Moisi, Dominique. 1999. "Dreaming of Europe." *Foreign Policy* 115: 44–59.

Monar, Jörg. 1998. "A Dual Citizenship in the Making: The Citizenship of the European Union and Its Reform." In *European Citizenship: An Institutional Challenge,* ed. Massimo La Torre, 167–83. London: Kluwer.

Morley, David, and Kevin Robins. 1995. *Spaces of Identity: Global Media, Electronic Landscapes, and Cultural Boundaries*. London: Routledge.

Mouffe, Chantal, ed. 1993. *The Return of the Political*. London: Verso.

Murphy, Alexander B. 1996. "The Sovereign State System as Political-Territorial Ideal: Historical and Contemporary Considerations." In *State*

Sovereignty as Social Construct, ed. Thomas J. Biersteker and Cynthia Weber, 81–120. Cambridge, Cambridge University Press.

Murphy, Jeffrie, and Jules Coleman. 1984. *The Philosophy of Law.* Totowa, N.J.: Rowman and Allanheld.

Murphy, Walter F. 1995. "Creating Citizens for a Constitutional Democracy." In *Citizenship and Rights in Multicultural Societies,* ed. M. Dunne and T. Bonazzi, 235–63. Keele, England: Keele University Press.

Muus, Philip J. 1998. *Migration, Immigrants, and Policy in the Netherlands: Recent Trends and Developments.* Report for the Continuous Reporting System of Migration (SOPEMI) of the Organization for Economic Co-operation and Development. Paris: OECD.

Nagel, Joane. 1996. *American Indian Ethnic Renewal.* New York: Oxford University Press.

Nerfin, Mark. 1991. "The Future of the United Nations System: Some Questions on the Occasion of an Anniversary." In *The United Nations and a Just World Order,* ed. Richard A. Falk, Samuel S. Kim, and Saul H. Mendlovitz, 519–34. Boulder, Colo.: Westview.

Neue Zürcher Zeitung. 1993. "Over 500,000 Swiss Citizens Live Abroad Permanently," 11 August.

Neumann, Iver B. 1997. "Conclusions." In *The Future of International Relations,* ed. Iver B. Neumann and Ole Wæver, 359–70. New York: Routledge.

Newman, David. 1994. "The Functional Presence of an 'Erased' Boundary: The Re-emergence of the 'Green Line.'" In *The Middle East and North Africa,* ed. Clive H. Schofield and Richard N. Schofield, 71–98. World Boundaries, vol. 4. London: Routledge.

———. 1995. "Boundaries in Flux: The 'Green Line' Boundary between Israel and the West Bank." *Boundary and Territory Briefing,* no. 5. Durham, N.C.: International Boundaries Research Unit.

———. 1996. "Shared Spaces—Separate Spaces: The Israel-Palestine Peace Process." *Geojournal* 39 (4): 363–76.

———. 1998a. "Real Spaces—Symbolic Spaces: Interrelated Notions of Territory in the Arab-Israel Conflict." In *A Road Map to War: Territorial Dimensions of International Conflict,* ed. Paul Diehl, 3–34. Nashville, Tenn: Vanderbilt University Press.

———. 1998b. "Creating the Fences of Territorial Separation: The Discourses of Israeli Palestinian Conflict Resolution." *Geopolitics and International Boundaries* 2 (2): 1–35.

———. 1999a. "Geopolitics Renaissant: Territory, Sovereignty, and the World Political Map." In Newman 1999b, 1–16.

———. 1999b. "Into the Millenium: The Study of International Boundaries in an Era of Global and Technological Change." *Boundary and Security Bulletin* 7 (4): 63–71.

———. 1999c. *Boundaries, Territory, and Postmodernity.* London: Frank Cass.

———. 2000a. "Boundaries, Territory, and Postmodernism: Towards Shared or Separate Spaces." In *Borderlands under Stress,* ed. Martin Pratt and Janet Brown. London: Kluwer Law Academic.

———. 2000b. "Identity, Citizenship, and Location: The Changing Discourse of Israeli Geopolitics." In *Geopolitical Traditions: A Century of Geopolitical Thought,* ed. Klaus Dodds and David Atkinson. London: Routledge.

———. In press. "The Lines That Separate: Boundaries and Borders in Political Geography." In *A Companion to Political Geography,* ed. J. Agnew and Gearóid Ó Tuathail. Oxford, UK: Blackwell.

Newman, David, and Anssi Paasi. 1998. "Fences and Neighbours in a Postmodern World: Boundary Narratives in Political Geography." *Progress in Human Geography* 22 (2): 186–207.

Nijkamp, Peter. 1994. "Borders and Barriers, Bottlenecks or Potentials? A Prologue." In *New Borders and Old Barriers in Spatial Development,* ed. Nijkamp, 1–14. Brookfield, Vt.: Ashgate.

Nisbet, Robert A. 1953. *The Quest for Community.* New York: Oxford University Press.

Nolutshungu, Sam C. 1996. *Margins of Insecurity: Minorities and International Security.* Rochester: University of Rochester Press.

OECD. 1995. *SOPEMI Trends in International Migration: Annual Report 1994.* Paris: OECD, 1995.

Ohmae, Kenichi. 1990. *The Borderless World.* London: Collins.

———. 1993. "The Rise of the Region States." *Foreign Affairs* 72 (2): 78–87.

———. 1995. *The End of the Nation State: The Rise of Regional Economies.* London: Free Press.

O'Loughlin, John, and Vladimir Kolossov. 1998. "New Borders for New World Orders: Territorialities at the Fin-de-siècle." *Geojournal* 44 (3): 259–73.

O'Neill, Onora. 1994. "Justice and Boundaries." In *Political Restructuring in Europe,* ed. Chris Brown, 69–88. London: Routledge.

Ong, Aihwa. 1999. *Flexible Citizenship.* Durham, N.C.: Duke University Press.

Opotow, Susan. 1990. "Moral Exclusion and Injustice." *Journal of Social Issues* 46 (1): 1–20.

Oppenheim, L. 1955. *International Law.* 8th. ed. H. Lauterpacht. London: Longman.

Ó Tuathail, Gearóid. 1998. *Critical Geopolitics: The Politics of Writing Global Space.* Minneapolis: University of Minnesota Press.

Özdemir, Cem. 1996. Speech at the German-American Academic Council, Summer Institute on "Immigration, Incorporation, and Citizenship in

Advanced Industrial Democracies." New York: New School for Social Research, 17–27 July.

Paasi, Anssi. 1996. *Territories, Boundaries, and Consciousness: The Changing Geographies of the Finnish-Russian Border.* Chichester: John Wiley.

———. 1999a. "The Political Geography of Boundaries at the End of the Millennium: Challenges of the Deterritorializing World." In *Curtains of Iron and Gold: Reconstructing Borders and Scales of Interaction,* ed. Heikki Eskelinen et al., 9–24. Aldershot, England: Ashgate.

———. 1999b. "Boundaries as Social Processes: Territoriality in the World of Flows." In *Boundaries, Territory, and Postmodernity,* ed. David Newman, 69–88. London: Frank Cass.

Palmer, R. R. 1986. "Frederick the Great, Guibert, Bulow: From Dynastic to National War." In *Makers of Modern Strategy,* ed. Peter Paret, 91–119. Princeton: Princeton University Press.

Parekh, Bhikhu. 1999. "Theorizing Political Theory." *Political Theory* 27 (3): 398–408.

Parrineau, Mayer. 1995. *Les compartements politiques.* Paris: Armand Colin.

Parsons, Talcott. 1969. *Politics and Social Structure.* New York: Free Press.

Patterson, O. 1991. *Freedom in the Making of Western Culture.* Vol. 1. New York: Basic Books.

———. 1995. "Freedom, Slavery, and the Modern Construction of Rights." In *Historical Change and Human Rights,* ed. O. Hufton. New York: Basic Books.

Paul, Darel. 1999. "Sovereignty, Survival, and the Westphalian Blind Alley in International Relations." *Review of International Studies* 25: 217–31.

Payne, Rodger. 1998. "Wanted: Outstanding Ideas for Improving Order." *Political Science and Politics* 31 (4): 861–63.

Peterson, John. 1995. "Decision-Making in the European Union: Towards a Framework of Analysis." *Journal of European Public Policy* 2: 69–93.

Pfaff, William. 1995. "A New Colonialism?" *Foreign Affairs* 74 (1): 2–6.

Poulter, S. 1998. *Ethnicity, Law, and Human Rights: The English Experience.* Oxford: Clarendon Press.

Prakash, Gyan. 1994. "Subaltern Studies as Postcolonial Criticism." *American Historical Review* 99 (5): 1475–90.

Prescott, Victor. 1987. *Political Frontiers and Boundaries.* Chicago: Aldine Publishing Company.

Preuss, Ulrich K. 1998. "The Relevance of the Concept of Citizenship for the Political and Constitutional Development of the EU." In *European Citizenship, Multiculturalism, and the State,* ed. Ulrich K. Preuss and Ferran Requejo, 11–27. Baden-Baden: Nomos Verlagsgesellschaft.

Pries, L., ed. 1999. *Migration and Transnational Social Spaces.* Aldershot: Ashgate.

Prus, Robert. 1998. *Subcultural Mosaics and Intersubjective Realities.* Albany: State University of New York Press.

Radan, Peter. 1999. "Yugoslavia's Internal Borders as International Borders: A Question of Appropriateness." *East European Quarterly* 33 (2): 137–52.

Rath, J. 1991. *Minorisering: De sociale constructie van "ethnische minderheden."* Amsterdam: Sua.

Ratner, Steven. 1996. "Drawing a Better Line: Uti Possidetis and the Borders of New States." *American Journal of International Law* 90: 590–624.

Rawls, John. 1971. *A Theory of Justice.* Oxford: Oxford University Press.

Reich, Robert. 1991. *The Work of Nations.* New York: Knopf.

Rengger, N. J. 1997. "A Multidinous Influx of Fairy? Ethics and Community in a Neo-Medieval World Order." Copenhagen. Manuscript.

Rescher, Nicholas. 1962. "The Revolt against Process." *Journal of Philosophy* 62: 410–17.

———. 1995. *Process Metaphysics.* Albany: State University of New York Press.

Romann, Michael. 1989. "Territory and Demography: The Case of the Jewish-Arab National Struggle." *Middle Eastern Studies* 26 (3): 371–82.

Roosens, Eugeen. 1994. "The Primordial Nature of Origins in Migrant Ethnicity." In *The Anthropology of Ethnicity: Beyond 'Ethnic Groups and Boundaries,'* ed. Hans Vermeulen and Cora Govers, 81–103. Amsterdam: Het Spinhuis.

Rorty, Richard. 1989. *Contingency, Irony, and Solidarity.* Cambridge: Cambridge University Press.

Rosenau, James N. 1983. "'Fragmegrative' Challenges to National Security." In *Understanding U.S. Strategy,* ed. T. Heyns. Washington, D.C.: National Defense University Press.

———. 1984. "A Pre-Theory Revisited: World Politics in an Era of Cascading Interdependence." *International Studies Quarterly* 28 (3): 245–305.

———. 1990. *Turbulence in World Politics: A Theory of Change and Continuity.* Princeton: Princeton University Press.

———. 1997. *Along the Foreign-Domestic Frontier: Exploring Governance in a Turbulent World.* Cambridge: Cambridge University Press.

Rosenau, Pauline, and Harry Bredemeier. 1993. "Modern and Postmodern Conceptions of Social Order." *Social Research* 60 (2): 337–62.

Rosenberg, Tina. 1999. "A Bad Year for World's Border Guards." *New York Times,* 2 July, A16.

Rosenfeld, Seth. 1997. "FBI Wants S.F. Cops to Join Spy Squad." *San Francisco Examiner,* 12 January, A1.

Rowny, Edward L. 1997. "What Will Prevent a Missile Attack?" *New York Times,* 24 January (national ed.), A17.

Ruggie, John G. 1989. "International Structure and International Transformation: Space, Time, and Method." In *Global Changes and Theoretical Challenges,* ed. Ernst-Otto Czempiel and James N. Rosenau, 21–35. Lexington, Mass.: Lexington Books.

Ruggie, John Gerard. 1993. "Territoriality and Beyond: Problematizing Modernity in International Relations." *International Organization* 47 (2): 139–74.

———. 1995. "At Home Abroad, Abroad at Home: International Liberalisation and Domestic Stability in the New World Economy." *Millennium* 24 (3): 507–26.

———. 1998. *Constructing the World Polity.* New York: Routledge.

Rumley, Dennis, and Julian V. Minghi. 1991. "Introduction: The Border Landscape Concept." In *The Geography of Border Landscapes,* ed. Dennis Rumley and Julian V. Minghi, 1–14. London: Routledge.

Rus, Jan. 1983. "Whose Caste War? Indians, Ladinos, and the Chiapas 'Caste War' of 1869." In *Spaniards and Indians in Southeastern Mesoamerica: Essays on the History of Ethnic Relations,* ed. Murdo J. MacLeod and Robert Wasserstrom, 129–40. Lincoln and London: University of Nebraska Press.

Sack, Robert. 1980. *Conceptions of Space in Social Thought: A Geographical Perspective.* London: Macmillan.

———. 1986. *Human Territoriality: Its Theory and History.* Cambridge: Cambridge University Press.

Said, Edward. 1993. *Culture and Imperialism.* New York: Alfred Knopf.

Sandel, Michael J. 1996. "America's Search for a New Public Philosophy." *Atlantic Monthly* 277 (3): 57–78.

San Francisco Chronicle. 1997. "Conservative Accuses Gingrich of Cozying Up to Liberals," 6 February (wire service), A8.

Sassen, Saskia. 1991. *The Global City: New York, London, Tokyo.* Princeton: Princeton University Press.

———. 1996. *Losing Control? Sovereignty in an Age of Globalization.* New York: Columbia University Press.

———. 1998. *Globalization and Its Discontents.* New York: New Press.

Scharpf, Fritz W. 1995. "Demokratische Politik in Europa." *Staatswissenschaften und Staatspraxis* 6 (4): 565–91.

———. 1999. *Regieren in Europa. Effektiv und demokratisch?* Frankfurt and New York: Campus Verlag.

Schmitter, Philippe C. 2000. *How to Democratize the EU: And Why Bother?* Lanham, Md.: Rowman and Littlefield.

Schoch, Bruno. 1995. "Nationale Konfliktpotentiale in Westeuropa." Frankfurt: *HSFK-Report* 8.

Schor, R. 1985. *L'opinion française et les étrangers, 1919–1939.* Paris: Publications de la Sorbonne.

Shapiro, Martin. 1993. "The Globalization of Law." *Indiana Journal of Global Legal Studies* (fall): 36–64.

Shapiro, Martin, and Stone, Alec. 1994. "The New Constitutional Politics of Europe." *Comparative Political Studies* 26: 397–419.

Shapiro, Michael, and Hayward Alker, eds. 1996. *Challenging Boundaries.* Minneapolis: University of Minnesota Press.

Shaw, Martin. 1994. *Global Society and International Relations.* Oxford: Polity Press.

Sheptycki, James. 1996. *Insecurity, Risk Supression, and Segregation: Policing in the Transnational Age.* Edinburgh: University of Edinburgh.

Sibley, David. 1995. *Geographies of Exclusion: Society and Difference in the West.* London: Routledge.

Sikkink, Kathryn. 1993. "Human Rights, Principled Issue Networks, and Sovereignty in Latin America." *International Organization* 47: 411–441.

Simmel, Georg. 1950. *The Sociology of Georg Simmel,* trans. Kurt Wolff. Glencoe, Ill.: Free Press.

Sklair, Leslie. 1991. *Sociology of the Global System.* Hemel Hempstead, England: Harvester Wheatsheaf.

Smith, Anna Marie. 1994. "Rastafari as Resistance and the Ambiguities of Essentialism in the 'New Social Movements.'" In *The Making of Political Identities,* ed. Ernesto Laclau, 171–204. London: Verso.

Smith, Anthony D. 1995. *Nations and Nationalism in a Global Era.* Oxford: Oxford University Press.

Soffer, Aron. 1984. "The Changing Situation of Majority and Minority and Its Spatial Expression: The Case of the Arab Minority in Israel." In *Pluralism and Political Geography,* ed. Nurit Kliot and Stanley Waterman, 80–99. London: Croom Helm.

Soguk, Nevzat. 1999. *States and Strangers: Refugees and Displacements in Statecraft.* Minneapolis: University of Minnesota Press.

Soysal, Yasemin N. 1994. *The Limits of Citizenship: Migrants and Postnational Membership in France.* Chicago: University of Chicago Press.

———. 1996. "Changing Citizenship in Europe: Remarks on Postnational Membership and the National State." In *Citizenship, Nationality, and Migration in Europe,* ed. David Cesarani and Mary Fulbrook, 17–29. Routledge: London.

Speener, David, and Kathleen Staudt, eds. 1998. *The U.S.-Mexico Border.* Boulder, Colo.: Lynne Rienner.

Spiro, Peter J. 1997. "Dual Nationality and the Meaning of Citizenship." *Emory Law Journal* 46: 1412–85.

Steiner, Hillel. 1992. "Libertarianism and the Transnational Migration of People." In Barry and Goodin 1992, 87–94.

Stichweh, Rudolf. 1994. "Nation und Weltgesellschaft." In Estel and Mayer 1994, 83–96.

Stopford, John, et al. 1991. *Rival States, Rival Firms: Competition for World Market Shares.* Cambridge: Cambridge University Press.

Strange, Susan. 1988. *States and Markets.* London: Pinter.

Strawson, P. F. 1959. *Individuals: An Essay in Descriptive Metaphysics.* London: Methuen.

Tarrow, Sidney. 1998. "Building a Composite Polity: Popular Contention in the European Union." Working Paper 98, no. 3. Ithaca, N.Y.: Cornell University, Institute for European Studies.

Taylor, Peter J. 1994. "The State as Container: Territoriality in the Modern World-System." *Progress in Human Geography* 18 (6): 151–62.

———. 1995. "Beyond Containers: Internationality, Interstateness, Interterritoriality." *Progress in Human Geography* 19 (1): 1–15.

———. 1996. "Territorial Absolutism and its Evasions." *Geography Research Forum* 16: 1–12.

Tharoor, Shashi. 1999. "The Future of Civil Conflict." *World Policy Journal* 16 (1): 1–11.

Thomson, Janice. 1994. *Mercenaries, Pirates, and Sovereigns.* Princeton: Princeton University Press.

Tilly, Charles. 1992. *Coercion, Capital, and European States, AD 990–1992.* Rev. ed. Cambridge, Mass.: Blackwell.

Tilly, Charles, ed. 1975. *The Formation of the National States of Western Europe.* Princeton: Princeton University Press.

Tolz, Vera. 1998. "Forging the Nation: National Identity and Nation Building in Post-Communist Russia." *Europe-Asia Studies* 50 (6): 993–1015.

Tonry, M., ed. 1997. *Ethnicity, Crime, and Immigration: Comparative and Cross-National Perspectives.* Chicago: University of Chicago Press.

Torpey, John. 1998. "Coming and Going: On the State Monopolization of State Movement." *Sociological Theory* 16 (3): 239–59.

Turner, Philipp. 1991. "Capital Flows in the 1980s: A Survey of Major Trends." *Economic Paper* 30. Basel: Bank for International Settlements.

TWIG. 1995. *This Week In Germany*, 21 April.

Ulam, Adam B. 1974. *Expansion and Coexistence.* New York: Praeger.

Van Creveld, Martin. 1991. *The Transformation of War.* New York: Free Press.

Van Outrive, L., G. Renault, and J. Vanderborght. 1996. "La collaboration policière en Europe." *Déviances et sociétés* 20 (2).

Verdery, Katherine. 1994. "Ethnicity, Nationalism, and State-Making." In *The Anthropology of Ethnicity: Beyond "Ethnic Groups and Bound-*

aries," ed. Hans Vermeulen and Cora Govers, 33–58. Amsterdam: Het Spinhuis.

Veyne, Paul. 1976. *Le pain et le cirque.* Paris: Seuil

von Gentz, Friedrich. 1970. "Fragments upon the Present State of the Political Balance of Europe." In *The Theory of International Relations,* ed. M. G. Forsyth et al., 277–301. New York: Atherton Press.

von Glahn, Gerhard. 1996. *Law among Nations.* 7th ed. Boston: Allyn and Bacon.

Wæver, Ole. 1994. "Insecurity and Identity Unlimited." Working Paper no. 14/94. Copenhagen: COPRI.

———. 1995a. "Identity, Integration, and Security: Solving the Sovereignty Puzzle in E. U. Studies." *Journal of International Affairs* 48 (2): 389–431.

———. 1995b. "Securitization and Desecuritization." In *On Security,* ed. Ronnie Lipschutz. New York: Columbia University Press.

———. 1997. *Concepts of Security.* Copenhagen: University of Copenhagen, Institute of Political Science.

Wæver, Ole, et al. 1993. *Identity, Migration, and the New Security Agenda in Europe.* New York: St. Martin's Press.

Walker, R. B. J. 1990. "The Concept of Culture in the Theory of International Relations." In *Culture and International Relations,* ed. Jongsuk Chay, 3–17. New York: Praeger.

———. 1993. *Inside/Outside: International Relations as Political Theory.* New York: Cambridge University Press.

———. 1995. "International Relations and the Concept of the Political." In *International Political Theory Today,* ed. Ken Booth and Steve Smith, 306–27. Cambridge: Polity Press.

Wallace, Ernest, and Hoebl E. Adamson. 1952. *The Comanches: Lords of the South Plains.* Norman: University of Oklahoma Press.

Wallace, Helen. 1996. "Politics and Policy in the EU: The Challenge of Governance." In *Policy-Making in the European Union,* ed. Helen Wallace and William Wallace. Oxford: Oxford University Press.

Waltz, Kenneth N. 1979. *Theory of International Politics.* Reading, Mass.: Addison-Wesley.

Walzer, Michael. 1983. *Spheres of Justice.* London: Martin Robertson.

———. 1994. "Notes on the New Tribalism." In *Political Restructuring in Europe,* ed. Chris Brown, 187–200. London: Routledge.

———. 1997. *On Toleration.* New Haven and London: Yale University Press.

Wapner, Paul. 1995. "Politics beyond the State: Environmental Activism and World Civic Politics." *World Politics* 47: 311–40.

———. 1996. *Environmental Activism and World Civic Politics.* Albany: State University of New York Press.

Weber, Max. 1956. *From Max Weber: Essays in Sociology.* New York: Oxford University Press.

———. 1980. *Wirtschaft und Gesellschaft.* 5th ed. Tübingen: Mohr.

Weiler, J. H. H. 1996. "Legitimacy and Democracy of Union Governance: The 1996 Intergovernmental Agenda and Beyond." ARENA Working Paper no. 22. Blindern, Norway.

———. 1997. "The Reformation of European Constitutionalism." *Journal of Common Market Studies* 35: 97–131.

———. 1999. *The Constitution of Europe: "Do the New Clothes Have an Emperor?" and Other Essays on European Integration.* Cambridge and New York: Cambridge University Press.

Weiler, J. H. H., Ulrich Haltern, and Franz C. Mayer. 1995. "European Democracy and Its Critics: Five Uneasy Pieces." *Harvard Jean Monnet Working Paper* 1/95 (1995).

Weiner, Myron. 1996. "Nations without Borders." *Foreign Affairs* (March/April): 128–34.

Weis, Paul. 1979. *Nationality and Statelessness in International Law.* Alpen aan den Rijn: Sijthoff & Noordhoff.

Wendt, Alexander. 1996. "Identity and Structural Change in International Politics." In *The Return of Culture and Identity in IR Theory,* ed. Yosef Lapid and Friedrich Kratochwil, 47–64. Boulder, Colo.: Lynne Rienner.

Wiener, Antje. 1997. *"European" Citizenship Practice: Building Institutions of a Non-State.* Boulder, Colo.: Westview Press.

———. 1998. "The Embedded *Acquis Communautaire*: Transmission Belt and Prism of New Governance." *European Law Journal* 4: 294–315.

Wilmer, Franke. 1993. *The Indigenous Voice in World Politics.* Newbury Park, Calif.: Sage.

———. 1996. "Indigenous Peoples, Marginal Sites, and the Changing Context of World Politics." In *Realism and Rhetoric in International Relations,* ed. Francis A. Beer and Robert Hariman, 347–68. East Lansing: Michigan State University Press.

Wilson, Thomas M., and Hastings Donnan. 1998. "Nation, State, and Identity at International Borders." In *Border Identities: Nation and State at International Frontiers,* ed. Thomas M. Wilson and Hastings Donnan, 1–30. Cambridge: Cambridge University Press.

Wirls, Daniel. 1992. *Buildup: The Politics of Defense in the Reagan Era.* Ithaca, N.Y.: Cornell University Press.

World Society Research Group. 2000. "Introduction: World Society." In *Civilizing World Politics: Society and Community beyond the State,* ed. Mathias Albert et al. Lanham, Md.: Rowman and Littlefield.

Wroe, A. 1995. *A Fool and His Money: Life in a Partitioned Town in Fourteenth-Century France.* New York: Hill and Wang.

Yiftachel, Oren. 1991. "State Policies, Land Control, and an Ethnic Minority: Arabs and Jews in the Galilee Region, Israel." *Society and Space* 9 (3): 329–52.

———. 1992. *Planning a Mixed Region in Israel: The Political Geography of Arab-Jewish Relations in the Galilee.* Aldershot, England: Avebury.

Young, Iris M. 1996. "Communication and the Other: Beyond Deliberative Democracy." In *Democracy and Difference: Contesting the Boundaries of the Political,* ed. Seyla Benhabib, 120–135. Princeton: Princeton University Press.

Zerubavel, Eviatar. 1991. *The Fine Line.* New York: Free Press.

Zuleeg, Manfred. 1997. "The European Constitution under Constitutional Constraints: The German Scenario." *European Law Journal* 22: 19–34.

Zürn, Michael. 1995. "The Challenge of Globalization and Individualization: A View from Europe." In Holm and Sørensen 1995a, 137–64.

Contributors

Mathias Albert is assistant professor in the Institut für Politikwis-senschaft at Technische Universität Darmstadt. His main research interests include the sociology of the global system and new spatial articulations of politics. He is coeditor (with L. Brock and K. D. Wolf) of *Civilizing World Politics,* and he is currently working on a book titled *The Politics of World Society.*

Didier Bigo is professor of International Relations at the Institut d'Etudes Politiques de Paris. He is editor-in-chief of the journal *Cultures et Conflits* and author of *L'Europe des polices et de la sécurité intérieure.*

Lothar Brock holds a chair in International Relations at the University of Frankfurt am Main and is a research director at Peace Research Institute, Frankfurt. His research interests are focused on general IR theory, international political economy, conflict resolution, and North-South relations. He has published extensively in these contexts.

Chris Brown is professor of International Relations at the London School of Economics. He is editor of *Political Restructuring in Europe: Ethical Perspectives* and author of *International Relations Theory: New Normative Approaches* and *Understanding International Relations* and many papers in international political theory.

327

Neil Harvey is associate professor in the Department of Government at New Mexico State University. His research concerns indigenous peoples and political change in Mexico and Latin America. He is author of *The Chiapas Rebellion: The Struggle for Land and Democracy*, as well as several articles on rural social movements, land rights, and agrarian policy in Mexico.

Martin O. Heisler is professor of government and politics at the University of Maryland. His long-term theoretical interests concern relationships between formal institutions (states and international organizations) and social institutions (nationalities and ethnic and other ascriptive groups). His recent work on these subjects has been published in his *Politics in Europe* and in such journals as *Annals of the American Academy of Political and Social Science, International Migration Review, International Political Science Review,* and *UCLA Journal of International Law and Foreign Affairs,* as well as in edited volumes. He is currently working on a book on migration and refugee movements in world politics.

David Jacobson is associate professor of sociology at Arizona State University. His research area is political sociology from a legal, global, and cultural perspective. He is author of *Rights across Borders: Immigration and the Decline of Citizenship* and *Place and Belonging in America*. He is presently working on a project examining the microsociological foundations of international relations.

Rey Koslowski is assistant professor of political science at Rutgers University–Newark and a visiting fellow of the Center of International Studies at Princeton University. He is author of *Migrants and Citizens: Demographic Change in the European State System,* as well as articles published in *International Organization, Journal of Common Market Studies, Journal of Ethnic and Migration Studies, Cambridge Journal of International Studies,* and *Journal of European Public Policy.*

Friedrich Kratochwil presently holds the chair for international politics at the Ludwig Maximilians University in Munich. He is author of *Rules, Norms, and Decisions* and *International Order and Foreign Policy,* as well as coeditor (with Yosef Lapid) of *The Return of*

Culture and Identity in IR Theory. He is also coeditor of several anthologies on international law and international organization. He is currently editor of *European Journal of International Relations.*

Yosef Lapid is professor of political science at New Mexico State University. His research interests include international relations theory, nationalism, and border studies. He is coeditor (with Friedrich Kratochwil) of *The Return of Culture and Identity in IR Theory.*

Ronnie D. Lipschutz is associate professor of politics and associate director of the Center for Global, International, and Regional Studies at the University of California, Santa Cruz. His most recent book is *After Authority: War, Peace, and Global Politics in the Twenty-first Century,* and he is editor of *On Security.*

Richard W. Mansbach is professor of political science at Iowa State University. He is the author or coauthor of several books on international relations theory, including *Polities: Authority, Identities, and Change; The State, Conceptual Chaos, and the Future of International Relations; The Elusive Quest: Theory and International Politics;* and *In Search of Theory: Toward a New Paradigm for Global Politics.* He is presently coeditor of *International Studies Quarterly.*

David Newman is professor of political geography and chair of the Department of Politics and Government at Ben Gurion University of the Negev, Israel. He is currently editor of the international journal *Geopolitics.* His most recent book (coeditor with N. Kliot) is *Geopolitics at the End of the Twentieth Century.*

Antje Wiener is reader and Jean Monnet professor (politics) at the Institute of European Studies, Queen's University of Belfast. She has published widely on citizenship and polity formation in the European Union. Her current work focuses on social constructivist approaches and constitutionalism in European and global governance.

Franke Wilmer is associate professor of political science at Montana State University. Since 1995 she has traveled regularly to the former Yugoslavia, conducting research aimed at developing a social constructionist critique of war, studying the prospects for reconciliation and the reconstruction of civil society in the Yugoslav successor states.

Index

BORDERLINES